T0163093

The Reagan Imprint

John Arquilla

THE REAGAN IMPRINT

*Ideas in American Foreign Policy
from the Collapse of Communism
to the War on Terror*

Ivan R. Dee
Chicago

www.ivanrdee.com

The paperback edition of this book carries the ISBN 1-56663-726-0.

Library of Congress Cataloging-in-Publication Data:
Arquilla, John.
    The Reagan imprint : ideas in American foreign policy from the collapse of communism to the war on terror / John Arquilla.
      p. cm.
    Includes bibliographical references and index.
    ISBN 1-56663-678-7 (cloth : alk. paper)
    1. United States—Foreign relations—1981–1989. 2. United States—Foreign relations—1989–. 3. Reagan, Ronald—Influence. I. Title.

E876.A75 2006
327.73009'048—dc22   2005031778

For Wayne Hughes

Contents

Preface

OVER THE PAST TWO DECADES, something of a Reagan paradox has emerged: the more that has been written about our fortieth president, the less seems to be known. This is especially true of Ronald Reagan the person, whose affable but cool veneer continues to defy the best efforts of biographers and memoirists to penetrate it. Reagan the president has proven equally elusive, perhaps because his approach to statecraft appears to have been driven almost entirely by conflicting impulses. He was a champion of conservative free-market economics, yet he incurred staggering budget deficits that ought to earn him a place in the first rank of liberal Keynesians. He believed in cultivating a strong military, yet he used force seldom—and awkwardly, as the interventions in Grenada and Lebanon showed—during his tenure as commander-in-chief. Reagan saw the Soviet Union as the "focus of evil in the modern world" but nevertheless spent years negotiating an end to the cold war directly with the chief "evildoer," Mikhail Gorbachev, with whom he forged a remarkable working relationship and a durable peace. The list of contradictions goes on and on, and the task of understanding Reagan remains quite daunting.

Given the epochal shift in global politics since the 1980s, though, it is imperative that Reagan's ideas about foreign policy be more closely examined. Despite the inherent difficulties associated with attempts to explore his personality, it remains possible to concentrate fruitfully on the specific initiatives he crafted and pursued. Beyond the intrinsic worth of explaining the profound, enduring impact of Reagan's foreign policy, studying the record of his engagement with the world may also provide important new insights into the man and the president. My primary purpose, then, is to improve our understanding of a critical passage in diplomatic history, the secondary benefit being that this focus on policy rather than personality also indirectly reveals much about Reagan himself.

In many ways Reagan proved to be the pivot man of American foreign policy. Before him, a thirty-year-long bipartisan consensus on containing Soviet expansion and deterring nuclear war governed American national security strategy. Reagan reversed field soon after entering office, moving swiftly from containment to an emphasis on rolling back Russian influence, principally by means of arming others to fight for their own freedom. He shifted away from classical nuclear deterrence—which called for holding millions of innocent people hostage in perpetuity—to seeking direct defenses against the threat of mass destruction. In the face of a seemingly inescapable security dilemma that propelled an endless arms race, he began reducing the world's nuclear arsenals. Reagan also breathed new life into the ideological struggle that lay at the heart of the cold war, pioneering what he liked to call "information strategy" as a means of galvanizing the long-dormant power waiting to be tapped among mass publics in oppressed countries.

Reagan was thus a kind of human hurricane, sweeping away much of the old edifice of U.S. foreign policy. But here and there resistant outcroppings withstood his force and remained in his wake. The most troubling of these was the problem posed by the continued pursuit of nuclear weapons by regional states, most notably Pakistan. Because that country served as a haven for the rebels resisting Russian occupation of Afghanistan, Reagan was unwilling to pressure the ruling Pakistani military dictator to forgo his efforts to develop such deadly weapons. The consequences of this error have resonated in ever more troubling ways, as an illicit proliferation network originating in Pakistan has played a powerful role in the secret struggles of North Korea, Iran, and even the al Qaeda terror organization to acquire weapons of mass destruction of their own.

The other major policy failing of Reagan's grand strategy grew out of bitter, unresolved tensions between proponents of traditional military thought and those who attempted to introduce innovations into the policy mix. Reagan gave a blank check to the armed forces to rebuild themselves in the wake of Vietnam—which they promptly cashed for many hundreds of billions of dollars. For the most part these funds were spent preparing for a cataclysmic conventional war in the heart of Europe that was never more than a remote possibility, while at the same time terror was emerging as a form of warfare in its own right. And when some members of Reagan's team urged a re-tooling of the military to launch a commando-style preventive war on terrorism—more than twenty years ago—they were loudly shouted down by traditionalists. Even Reagan's effort to tamp down terror by engaging in a secret rapprochement with revolutionary Iran came undone and nearly unraveled his presidency in the wake of the related arms-for-hostages scandal that ensued.

In one way or another, then—though mostly for the good— Reagan's successors in office have all been profoundly influenced by the imprint of his policies. During his single term, George H. W. Bush focused on continuing nuclear arms reductions and skillfully overseeing the dissolution of the Soviet Union. As to the huge conventional military left him by Reagan, the elder Bush soon put it successfully to work in Panama and the Persian Gulf. Bill Clinton seems to have imbibed most strongly Reagan's call for "free markets and free peoples," given his fervent support for regional and global trade openness, and his emphasis on what he labeled "democratic enlargement." George W. Bush is a principal inheritor as well, pursuing several policy paths identified by Ronald Reagan. Supporting others in their freedom struggles, a central tenet of the Reagan Doctrine, has reemerged under the younger Bush as "regime change." And when it came his time to confront terror, Bush launched a preventive war, going much further than even Reagan.

These are the reasons why Reagan remains so important, why understanding his place among the presidents matters. Simply put, he charted an almost wholly new course in U.S. foreign policy, based on his core beliefs that the world could be made less nuclear, that tyranny was weak, not strong, and that the power of ideas in people's hearts and minds was as great as any armed force. These ideas illuminated Reagan's statecraft some twenty years ago and have continued to guide and to some extent govern the strategies of all three of his successors.

The best-known innovations of the Reagan era fall under the rubric of what came to be called "Reaganomics"—a set of beliefs about stimulating economic growth by means of tax cuts, "enterprise zones," and the like. All these were viewed skeptically at the time, and for the most part still are. But there is another, far more important "Reagan Revolution" that should become better known. It is the one that grew from Reagan's crafting of an idea-driven foreign policy that reshaped the world—and which still has the power to do so.

J. A.

Monterey, California
November 2005

Acknowledgments

OVER THE PAST TEN YEARS I have developed a deepening sense of unease about the general direction of American foreign policy and national security strategy. I have grown increasingly concerned that the United States is squandering the remarkable reversal of fortune in world affairs that Ronald Reagan engineered. But I felt that no useful course correction could be made until Reagan's successful grand strategy was much better understood. That is the genesis of this book. I have been exceedingly fortunate that others, including many who have played large roles in the events of the past two decades, took warmly to this notion of reexamining Reagan as the starting point of a sustained process of American strategic adjustment. I can only hope this book sparks a lively, extended discussion of U.S. policies toward the world.

Among those who played key roles in crafting a "cost-imposing" strategy against the Soviet Union that did so much to encourage Mikhail Gorbachev to negotiate with Reagan, I am especially grateful to Andrew Marshall, the longtime Pentagon "director of net assessment," for sharing his many memories and insights. RAND Corporation analyst Paul Davis, a Carter-era defense official, walked me through the various initiatives, beginning in the late 1970s, that revitalized the U.S. military after Vietnam. Brian Jenkins shared his recollections of the meeting he led in 1984, at the request of Secretary of State George Shultz, which resulted in the first serious call to launch a "war on terror." Edwin Meese III gave generously of his time to talk with me about a wide range of issues, giving particular support to the notion that it is essential to remember Reagan—beyond all the other reasons for doing so—as a strategist.

At the Claremont Institute, the late Tom Silver gave me much needed encouragement; and his successor as president there, Brian Kennedy, adroitly took up with me where Tom left off. Patrick Parker of the Aequus Institute has worn several hats: sponsor, mentor, and chief cheerleader for this project. My longtime research partner at the RAND Corporation, David Ronfeldt, has also weighed in with useful suggestions. To my other RAND colleagues I can only say that the objective, ever-searching intellectual community to which they welcomed me many years ago continues to influence my work profoundly.

Many colleagues at the Naval Postgraduate School have supported my work, especially David Tucker and Hy Rothstein, who taught my classes while I was on an extended leave of absence and carried forward a major policy initiative much more skillfully than I could have. Sherry Pennell and Ryan Stuart turned my hand-drawn figures into handsome bits and bytes; and Greta Marlatt and Jeff Rothal of the Navy School's Knox Library helped me locate much hard-to-find information with unfailing humor and grace.

Of those who have read and commented on all or parts of earlier drafts of this book, Harry Kreisler of the University of California, Berkeley, deserves special mention for toiling through the manuscript and providing trenchant observations that have greatly influenced the final product. The same can be said of my editors, Ivan Dee and Hilary Meyer, for whose support and assistance I am deeply grateful.

The Reagan Imprint

1

How to Think About Ronald Reagan

Thomas Jefferson currently holds the title of "American Sphinx," no doubt because of his complex character. A man full of contradictions, he lived and breathed liberty but owned slaves and even had children by one. He believed in a limited presidency yet used "sharp practices" to negotiate the largest territorial acquisition in American history. The list of surprises continues. Jefferson was indeed inscrutable, sphinxlike.[1] But his title may soon be wrested away by Ronald Reagan, whose apparent simplicity gave way to even deeper levels of complexity. A Democrat until he was fifty, Reagan became a true champion of conservative causes, enlivening a moribund ideology and riding it into the White House. Once there, however, a different Reagan emerged. The hawk who had worried about falling behind in the nuclear arms race became the chief dove of his own administration. The lifelong opponent of communism chose to negotiate directly with his Soviet counterpart to bring a peaceful end to the cold war.

Beyond all his surprising policies and proclivities, Reagan proved to be almost unknowable to others, even to close associates who worked with him for decades. Never was a life as public as Reagan's lived so privately. Moving constantly under the glare of media scrutiny during his several decades in show business, becoming a de facto editorial member of the broadcast news media, then finally holding high elective offices for sixteen years, Reagan nevertheless found ways to nurture his essential need for privacy.[2] He seemed to keep his deepest thoughts, feelings, and desires to himself and his wife Nancy. The former Nixon- and Ford-era national security adviser and secretary of state, Henry Kissinger, who had considerable involvement with Reagan over the course of many years—though not all of it friendly—offers perhaps the most trenchant assessment of his personality:

> Reagan's bland veneer hid an extraordinarily complex character. He was both congenial and remote, full of good cheer but, in the end, aloof. The *bonhomie* was his way of establishing distance between himself and others. If he treated everyone with equal friendliness— and regaled them all with the same stories—no one would have a special claim on him. The repository of jokes that were recycled from conversation to conversation served as protection against being blindsided. Like many actors, Reagan was the quintessential loner. . . . An individual widely perceived to have been an intimate of his said to me once that Reagan was both the friendliest and the most distant man he had ever known.[3]

All of Reagan's biographers have made this point, or one much like it. Edmund Morris, for example, recognized this distancing phenomenon and noted that it became more pronounced over the course of his presidency. Morris observed

> a growing remoteness in his manner. Now those who stayed with him began to be ever so slightly chilled by it. While never unfriendly (he remained the most outwardly genial of men) he withheld more and more of himself.[4]

Of those who served under Reagan, there is also mention of this. Peggy Noonan, one of his key speechwriters, described his inherent "emotional detachment" as Reagan's principal weakness—though she found it to be offset by an almost "Lincolnian kindness."[5] Another interesting observation from an insider comes from Larry Speakes, Reagan's press secretary from 1981 to 1987:

> On a more personal level, there is a big difference between the public Ronald Reagan, an outgoing, friendly, personable man, and the private Reagan, who is still charming and affable, but in an impersonal way. Privately, he tends to be a loner, content to spend most of his time with his wife and no one else. He almost never reveals his personal emotions to anyone but Nancy. Perhaps it's because he was an actor and his every move was closely scrutinized, so now he feels that his emotions should be private.[6]

Even Reagan may have seen something in himself that lay beyond articulation, as the very title of his pre-presidential autobiography suggests: *Where's the Rest of Me?*

Beyond biographies and insider memoirs, writers have amassed a large body of classical political analysis of Reagan's approach to the presidency. In it he proves to be an elusive target. Reagan hardly fits the arch-conservative label given him. The whole notion of planting him somewhere on a spectrum from right to left unravels quickly, for his public persona showed just as much complexity and depth as his private one. As governor of California, for example, he tightened eligibility for welfare but made sure that recipients were protected against the ravages of inflation. As president he espoused laissez-faire economics and effected tight-fisted monetarist policies that tamed inflation; yet he helped bail out Chrysler, ran then-record budget deficits, and used fiscal stimuli like the best of Keynesians. He ran for office in 1980 on a platform that portrayed America as dangerously behind the Soviets in the arms race yet quickly became his administration's chief advocate of arms reductions. He called for the creation of strategic missile defenses yet promised to share them with the Russians. He saw the Soviet Union as evil yet reached out in partnership to the leader of that evil empire. This was not a president who could easily submit to ideological labeling—a point that infuriated conservative pundits, one of whom labeled Reagan's reaching out to Soviet leader Mikhail Gorbachev as both "ignorant and pathetic." Another leading conservative who opposed the easing of tensions with the Soviet Union put the matter even more sharply: "Reagan has accelerated the moral disarmament of the West. . . ."[7]

Reagan also defies classification of the sort attempted by the political scientist James David Barber in his framework for understanding presidential character. Barber argues that all presidents can be categorized in one of four clearly defined ways, based on combinations of two factors. The first is the amount of energy (measured in terms of their levels of activity or passivity) they poured into the business of governance and statecraft. The second considers their positive or negative emotional attitudes about politicking and the job of the presidency itself.[8] For Barber, Franklin D. Roosevelt was a classic "active-positive" president, the category he suggests is most linked to success in office. Richard Nixon was the quintessential "active-negative" personality, the type Barber thought most likely to get into trouble. (His other active-negatives include Herbert Hoover and Lyndon Johnson, who gave us, respectively, the depression and Vietnam.) Of the low-energy "passives"—who do not rate very highly according to this theory of character—Dwight D. Eisenhower epitomized the negatives while William H. Taft exemplified the positives.

Barber categorizes Reagan as a quintessential "passive-positive," but the evidence he employs in making this judgment—mostly commentary about Reagan's bonhomie, followed by a recounting of his penchant for short work hours—seems thin.[9] While it is clear that Reagan took a joyful approach to meeting voters and sharing his message with them, there is also much evidence of the emotional detachment that Peggy Noonan observed. It was as though Reagan, to protect himself, had to maintain a kind of professional distance from others—scarcely in keeping with notions of the classic "positive" personality. As to his energy level, Reagan was indeed famous for being caught nodding a few times and for not working long days in the of-

Figure 1.   Barber's View of Presidential Character

Energy Level

	Active	Passive
Positive	Franklin D. Roosevelt John F. Kennedy George H. W. Bush	William H. Taft Warren Harding Ronald Reagan
Negative	Richard Nixon Lyndon Johnson Herbert Hoover	Dwight D. Eisenhower Calvin Coolidge

Attitude

Sources: James David Barber, *The Presidential Character*. James MacGregor Burns et al., *Government by the People*.

fice. But this hardly speaks to the overall energy with which he approached the presidency. Any president who comes into office intending to reduce the size of government, improve the common defense, and bring down a great external enemy simply cannot be viewed as "passive." Beyond the sweep of the many new policies that he envisioned, we now know (largely through the research of Kiron Skinner) that Reagan also had an almost boundless intellectual energy that kept him writing—whenever he had a private moment—throughout his two terms.

In addition to Barber's notions about presidential character, a few other major theories about presidents and the presidency itself may prove useful in attempting to understand Reagan. Richard Neustadt's theory of presidential power seems at first particularly well suited to Reagan. Neustadt's basic point is that presidents are inherently weak, an artifact of the Constitution's design for divided policymaking powers. For Neustadt, a president is only as strong as his ability to persuade others and must husband this form of power by being especially mindful of the risk to his reputation posed by any decision.[10] Neustadt's core belief is that even a president is only a small part of a big government that will function well when persuaded and inspired, and will do more poorly when simply commanded.

Reagan is a puzzle to Neustadt, who says of his presidential attributes: "the Reagan combination [of traits] is not found in any other President of modern times, from Franklin Roosevelt to George Bush."[11] Neustadt proceeds to describe a president with outstanding persuasive skills but one, in his estimation, with virtually no substantive knowledge and little apparent desire to increase his intellectual capital. Neustadt then dwells at length upon Reagan's misstep into the Iran-Contra arms-for-hostages affair as evidence that he fits the pattern of presidential weakness. As with Barber's analysis, Neustadt's evidence seems lacking. For example, he quickly passes over Reagan's summitry with Gorbachev—which Barber fails to discuss at all—in less than a sentence. And Reagan's high public approval rating at the end of his presidency further belies the notion that this was a president who squandered his reputation and power.

One more leading theory to consider is that of Samuel Kernell, who built upon Neustadt's notions by pointing out that a president has effective options even when his legislature and civil administrators may balk at his ideas: he can "go public," speaking directly to the electorate.[12] By persuading the mass public of the worth of his ideas, the president may then induce others in government, through indirect pressure, to align themselves with his policies. Ronald Reagan, who earned the sobriquet the "Great Communicator," continually demonstrated his skill at persuasion—both in government and on the many occasions he took to speak directly to the American people about his hopes, dreams, and policies. Clearly these persuasive skills also worked well in his interactions with Mikhail Gorbachev.

These leading academic theories about presidents and the presidency probably bring us only marginally closer to understanding the inner Reagan, but they do suggest ways for us to evaluate his public persona that begin to give us at least some glimpses of the private man. After all, these are theories about individual character and interpersonal skills. In assessing Reagan's persuasive power, Neustadt takes on Barber's notion that he was a "passive" president. As

Neustadt puts it, "we will not look back on Reagan as 'passive' in policy terms."[13] He also shares insights about Reagan's complex character as lying outside traditional notions of conservatism or liberalism, noting that as president he was "the last Roosevelt Democrat" and that he reflected "the old-fashioned patriotism and the anti-Sovietism of a Truman Democrat."[14] In the course of analytic efforts such as these—which despite their flaws strive usefully to achieve a better understanding of his public life—the "private Reagan" finally begins to emerge more clearly. It may prove useful next to consider more of Reagan's public record as president, but without trying explicitly to crack the carapace of his psyche.

A more general approach to understanding the presidency and its various officeholders—one that eschews psycho-biography and the crafting of vastly detailed personal histories—includes studies that range far beyond dealings with Congress, the various government bureaucracies, and the mass public. Some look explicitly to the connections that a president must make with the wider world. One of the earliest and most important of these efforts was undertaken by Sidney Warren in his thoughtful study of "presidents as world leaders."[15] Warren argued that from the time the United States moved decisively onto the world stage as a great power—beginning with the war against Spain in 1898—its presidents have had to take on the mantle of world leadership. Before then American presidents did interact with the larger world, of course, but mostly in ways designed to keep the United States from becoming entangled in global political struggles, or to shield the Western Hemisphere from European colonialism, as the Monroe Doctrine sought to do. This "limited presidency" was changed forever at the beginning of the twentieth century, Warren argues, when under Theodore Roosevelt American leadership took the form of negotiating a peace in 1905 between Russia and Japan, ending the bloody war they were waging in Northeast Asia. A decade later, Woodrow Wilson attempted to end World War I, then sought to redefine the world system along more liberal democratic lines. Warren surveys each president in this manner, finding that the world leadership role grew larger with each succeeding chief executive. His study ends with John F. Kennedy, but the trend is clear: the burden of world leadership seemed only to grow heavier. By Reagan's time the stakes were exceptionally high, and his ability to act with fluidity and flexibility under such pressure reveals an important aspect of his character and emotional timbre.

Another important theory, recently advanced, is more about foreign policy than the presidency per se, yet it may prove the most useful in understanding a given president's character and actions. This is Walter Russell Mead's idea that American presidents relate to the world in ways that fall within four identifiable archetypes, three of which he associates with particular presidents, the fourth with one of the Founding Fathers.[16] First, Mead sees Woodrow Wilson as the model for those who would emphasize the spread of democracy and concern for human rights, and who would be most likely to emphasize the need for international consensus on matters of high statecraft.

Second are the ideas of our country's first treasury secretary, Alexander Hamilton, who is the intellectual polestar for those fundamentally concerned with economic issues. But it is important not to equate a focus on prosperity with any particular economic ideology. In the nineteenth century the Hamiltonians supported protectionist approaches to trade in order to nurture infant U.S. industries. In the twentieth century, however, they became far more supportive of free trade for reasons of national interest. Today Hamiltonians tend to be associated with ensuring that the United States is on the leading edge of economic globalization.

The American folk ethic that favors developing maximal military power while simultaneously upholding populist values would be the province of the third major strand of thought in American foreign policy, articulated by Andrew Jackson and his "descendants" in office. Jacksonians are thus seen as supporting both large defense *and* entitlements spending. In present terms, for example, they would favor both advanced weapons purchases and cost-of-living increases for seniors. Beyond pocketbook issues, Mead is careful to note that Jacksonians care a great deal about their country's reputation in the world. Yet they are not eager to intervene in foreign conflicts or crises—and are likely to be instinctively suspicious of strategies of regime change undertaken in the cause of nation-building and democratization.

Finally, those who care most about protecting individual civil liberties and imposing constitutional limits on the various uses of presidential power form the fourth pillar of foreign policy. They walk in the footsteps of Thomas Jefferson, whose beliefs are nicely summed up in his aphorism "That government is best which governs the least." In terms of foreign policy, Jeffersonians have little interest in imposing their ideas and values upon others, and their deep-seated worries about military institutions encourage them to embrace the use of force only as a last resort. In the context of the ongoing war on terror, the true Jeffersonian would most likely oppose intrusions on civil liberties at home (such as those of the Patriot Act) and would support, at best, a more limited, surgical approach to the use of force against terrorist hideouts and havens abroad.

Mead argues quite compellingly that the history of American foreign policy can be clearly and thoroughly explained by referring to these four basic ways of interacting with the world.[17] The Monroe Doctrine of the early nineteenth century can be seen as a skillful application of the Jeffersonian quality of "strategic elegance." In this instance the United States—at virtually no cost or risk to itself—persuaded Britain to use its overarching naval mastery to protect the Western Hemisphere from European colonial exploitation.[18] A century later the sharp debate about whether the United States should join the League of Nations after World War I reflects, in Mead's view, the continual pulling and hauling between the Jeffersonian and Wilsonian schools of thought, with the Jeffersonians prevailing again.

A decisive shift came in the 1930s, though, when Hamiltonians discarded their protectionist tendencies to help pull the country out of the Great Depression. At the same time the Jeffersonian preference for nonintervention led to a dangerous neutrality policy in the face of looming fascist threats from Germany and Japan. Indeed, the Jeffersonian role in dangerously slowing American entry into the war put this school of thought into an eclipse from which it has not yet fully recovered. The Jacksonian combination of power and populism finally came to the fore, creating both the military superpower that emerged from World War II and the simultaneous impulse toward building the "Great Society" that Lyndon Johnson dreamed about and that his successors have pursued.

Ronald Reagan fits seamlessly into this presidential progression. In many ways Reagan as president personified both aspects of the Jacksonian ideal of power and populism. His principal call when running for office was for the United States to regain its military pre-eminence in the world. Yet he also asked the public whether individuals felt better or worse off than they had at the onset of the Carter administration. Once in office Reagan relentlessly pursued a military buildup but also maintained social spending at levels that would "leave no one behind." Power and populism. And record budget deficits too. Reagan's landslide electoral victories suggested to Mead that "Jacksonianism had done more than survive; it was, and is, thriving."[19]

Beyond cataloguing the four main styles of U.S. foreign policy and providing a brief history of their various appearances in our history, Mead's remarkable study also conveys a powerful message about the need for each of these styles to continue. Even at a time when one or another type is paramount, it is essential, he suggests, for the others to form part of the U.S. policymaking process. Twenty-five years of near silence from the Jeffersonians, from the outset of World War II to the onset of the Vietnam War, contributed to the costly stumble into a Southeast Asian quagmire. Today Jeffersonians hope to find their voice again. They tried to slow the march to war with Iraq, a failed effort gallantly led by Senator Robert Byrd. In this instance the Jeffersonian voice was drowned out once more, this time by a Jacksonian rage against terrorists who managed in attacks on America both to outflank our traditional military strength and to strike directly at innocent civilians in our very "homeland."

The democratic ideals of Wilsonianism suffered a setback when Congress refused to allow the United States to join the League of Nations after World War I. But the dominant American role in the formation and activities of the United Nations after World War II represented a major rebound for this idealistic school of thought. It gained further ground when classic cold war realpolitik, which often saw the United States cultivating cozy relationships with putatively anti-Communist tyrants, gave way to the rise of rights-based policies. These policies began with Gerald Ford's stand for the protection of basic human rights—enshrined in the Helsinki Accord. Ford's stand was followed by Jimmy Carter and Ronald Reagan's joint recognition that the cold war had a fundamentally moral dimension. Bill Clinton's idea of "democratic enlargement" was essentially Wilsonian. And George W. Bush first picked up on this theme as one of the justifications for his invasion of Iraq, then made it the centerpiece of his second-term foreign policy.

For all this attention to Wilsonian ideals, U.S. foreign policy remains inconsistent about the spread of liberal political values. American-style democracy in, say, Algeria, Egypt, Pakistan, or Saudi Arabia would likely have quite unpleasant consequences for our interests. And even two long-standing democracies that we helped create—Germany and Japan—would generate a frisson if they invited American forces to leave their countries and announced their intentions to become fully "normal" countries with policies of their own and nuclear arsenals to reflect their great power. In short, it is hard for a president to adhere faithfully or consistently to any *single* strand of Mead's four schools of thought about U.S. foreign policy. It is probably not wise to try to do so, either.

A graphic representation of Mead's concepts serves as a useful way to categorize the presidents. Hamilton and Jefferson, so often at odds with each other in life, are diagonally opposite each other in this figure, given that the former's foreign policy preferences placed commerce as the highest value while the latter cared far more about individual liberty, constitutionalism, and nonintervention. Hamilton would love such notions as globalization and the goal of forging a "new world order." Jefferson, on the other hand, would be more likely to espouse the kind of "humble" foreign policy of which the younger Bush spoke before he became president. It is important to remember that Jefferson could still be an opportunist when circumstances permitted. Witness his picking of Napoleon Bonaparte's pocket with the Louisiana Purchase in 1803, which added enormously to the territory controlled by the United States.

The other two diametrically opposed styles of foreign policy are those of Wilson and Jackson. Wilson would without doubt support the spread of democracy and would possibly engage in uses of force to pursue that goal. Jackson would care far less about others' democratic instincts. Instead he would concentrate on maintaining and extending American power—and would surely emphasize taking good care of "homeland security" and of the tidal wave of baby-boom retirees about to make heavy demands on all forms of government-funded social services. For Jackson, the simultaneous pursuit of power abroad and progressivism at home was the sine qua non of governance.

In Figure 2, I have portrayed the foreign policy styles of our presidents from Jimmy Carter to George W. Bush—the presidents who held office from the wake of the Vietnam War to the onset of the war on terror. Carter is located so as to reflect his very deep Wilsonian commitment to democracy and human rights as well as his Jeffersonian concerns about constitutionalism in the post-Watergate era. So he is vertically located near the bottom of the diagram, horizontally closer to Wilson's corner than to Jefferson's. The dotted line angling toward Jackson's corner reflects his desire, late in his first term, to increase defense spending and begin taking firm stands against Soviet or Soviet-inspired threats and acts of aggression. Had there been a second Carter term, it would have been somewhat more Jacksonian.[20]

With Ronald Reagan, the American people elected a president who was ideologically closer to Jackson. Yet he was also in step with Jeffersonian notions of nonintervention and limited government and

Figure 2.   An Integrated View of Mead's Theory of Foreign Policy Styles

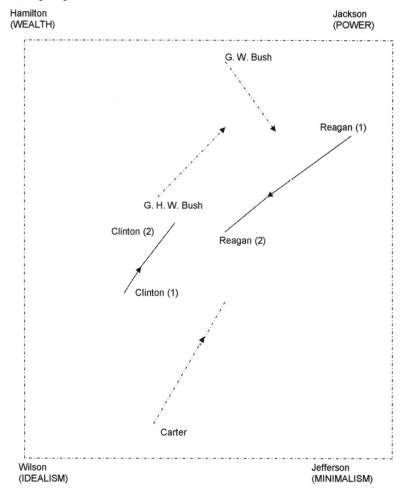

came into office with a great willingness to tolerate authoritarian allies. Reagan was quite taken with Jeane Kirkpatrick's notion that military juntas and other forms of dictatorship were much less objectionable than any kind of Communist rule and could prove useful in the fight against communism.[21] These traits place Reagan well over to the right side of the diagram and closer to Jackson than Jefferson. In his second term Reagan moved sharply to embrace Wilsonian values, as evinced both by his support for freeing Soviet satellite states and his abandonment of such roughneck regimes as those of dictator Ferdinand Marcos in the Philippines and of the apartheid-loving South African Broeders. By the end of his second term, Reagan is located near Carter's intended second-term position.

The elder Bush is positioned almost directly above Reagan's second-term endpoint—but angled slightly more toward Jackson. This location reflects both his sensitivity to international economic affairs and his evident willingness to use force in pursuit of American interests. In his single term Bush conducted a small war against Panama and a big one against Iraq. As to Bush's intentions for a second term, he clearly aimed to move sharply toward Jackson's corner. He intended to seize the period in the wake of the Soviet Union's dissolution as a time when American mastery of a "new world order" could be consolidated and the rise of new great powers prevented.[22]

That did not happen. Instead Bill Clinton entered office with a decidedly centrist agenda, albeit one that inclined in favor of both Wilson and Hamilton. At the national security level Clinton concentrated on what he called "democratic enlargement": the spread of democracies, which he believed were less war prone than other types of government.[23] In the world economic sphere, Clinton pursued a Hamiltonian series of economic initiatives, beginning with the North American Free Trade Agreement and concluding with the World Trade Organization. Whatever their practical effects, they were intended to encourage openness and job creation and smooth capital flows. Clinton remained devoted both to fostering democracy and free trade during his two terms, though he saw the need to use force—but always on a modest scale—on several occasions during his time in office. Clinton inherited an intervention in Somalia (1993) that he mishandled, neatly cowed dictators into submission in Haiti (1994) and Bosnia (1995), sparred with Saddam Hussein and Osama bin Laden (both in 1998), and conducted an air war for Kosovo (1999). As his uses of force grew somewhat in scale over the years, Clinton's second-term position moved slightly toward Jackson's corner. Nevertheless both placements for Clinton locate him close to Ronald Reagan's second-term position on the diagram.

Clinton's successor, George W. Bush, came into office at a point almost exactly opposite to where Jimmy Carter began. That is, the younger Bush can be located just about at the midpoint between Hamilton and Jackson and quite far from either Jefferson or Wilson. His concerns on assuming the presidency focused on the prosperity and security of the United States itself. Of all the presidents included in this analysis, Bush is the closest—by a small margin over his father—to Reagan's starting position. Once the war on terror began, Bush moved on a diagonal that brought him simultaneously closer to Jackson and Wilson. That is, his newly articulated doctrine of using "preemptive force" against terrorists and rogues was coupled with rhetoric about democratic nation-building.[24]

Visualizing Mead's ideas generates new insights by revealing much about the real Reagan. As presidential foreign policies have unfolded, Reagan's ideas and initiatives show him positioned much closer to Jimmy Carter and Bill Clinton than to either of the Bushes. Of all the presidents considered in this graphic, Reagan moved the farthest from his initial point of departure, confirming the notion that he had great flexibility of mind. Both of these findings illustrate his ability to adapt and embrace change. This flexibility may hardly seem surprising in a man who was a Democrat until he was fifty years old, then rose to lead the Republican party, his country, and the free world.

This somewhat theoretical analysis is useful in pointing up Reagan's intellectual nimbleness and his willingness to step out in new directions. But it is important also to note his continuity with his predecessors. The best way to do this is to reflect briefly upon the presidential doctrines embraced during the cold war, to see better how they fit together. Or to see if they do not, as one common criticism of American foreign policy is that a democracy has a hard time maintaining a steady course.[25]

Harry S Truman was the first cold war president. In the wake of World War II he became disappointed with Soviet leader Joseph Stalin when he was made fully aware of the USSR's true aggressive intentions toward Eastern and Central Europe. Truman had thought he understood Stalin as a leader similar—but on a larger stage—to Kansas City political boss Tom Pendergast, who had played an important role in Truman's early career. But when it became clear that Stalin wanted more than just to dip his beak in Eastern European affairs, Truman grew disillusioned, angry, and ready to react. The "long telegram" that George Kennan sent to Washington around this time, which both outlined Stalin's plans and identified a way to thwart them, gave Truman the ideas he needed to formulate his own doctrine of "containment." The Truman Doctrine that soon emerged was essentially defensive in nature, holding that Communist aggression had to be opposed wherever it arose, by military or other means. During Truman's time in office, this meant both the use of economic aid to those under threat, as embodied in the Marshall Plan, and the use of force, as in the costly three-year war fought to defend South Korea.[26]

During his two terms in office, Truman's successor Dwight D. Eisenhower largely followed the containment game plan. If there was any new departure, it was his desire to explore more fully the possible uses of nuclear weapons. Truman had ordered nuclear attacks on Japan at the end of World War II and had been aware of early U.S. military planning for subjecting the Soviet Union to nuclear bombardment in the event of a new war. But it was left to Eisenhower, the general turned president, to develop this concept. Early in his presidency Eisenhower made vague nuclear threats in order to speed up the negotiations that were to end the fighting on the Korean peninsula. Similarly nonspecific threats were directed against the People's Republic of China on the two occasions later in the 1950s when it threatened Taiwan.[27] These nuclear threats were part of a doctrine that came to be known as "massive retaliation"—the notion of responding to any sort of aggression by the most extreme means. Beyond these crises, Eisenhower also gave much thought to the idea of a preventive war against the Soviet Union, to deal decisively with the

Communist threat before Moscow could obtain a substantial nuclear capability of its own. Eisenhower thought seriously about launching such a war—but finally decided against it. As he noted in a press conference held on August 11, 1954: "A preventive war, to my mind, is an impossibility today. . . . [Frankly], I wouldn't even listen to anyone seriously that came in and talked about such a thing."[28]

When John F. Kennedy came to office in 1961, he too affirmed a devotion to containment, the only added wrinkle being his articulation of the notion that Americans would "pay any price, bear any burden" to uphold this strategy. In practice this implied a willingness on occasion to take the offensive against communism. Kennedy's successor, Lyndon Johnson, adhered to this formulation, which inspired him to commit U.S. forces to a long, hard—and ultimately losing—fight for Vietnam's future. Johnson also continued the presidential march away from freewheeling options for the use of nuclear weapons, overseeing the rise of policies more closely associated with "flexible response"—a doctrine that in practice meant trying to fight any war by conventional means and resorting to mass destruction only to avert final defeat.[29]

The first sustained shift in presidential-level doctrine during the cold war came from Johnson's successor, Richard Nixon, who introduced a softer version of containment. Nixon and his team devised a new approach that differed from his predecessors' readiness to employ U.S. forces to defend others against Soviet aggression. He explicitly rejected Kennedy's notion of paying any price in such struggles. Kennedy's activist approach had sought to seize the initiative in the cold war, using U.S. special operations forces to guide counterinsurgencies and more conventional forces to deal with the specter of Soviet missiles in Cuba.[30] Soon after Kennedy's assassination, Lyndon Johnson had reinforced both special and conventional forces in Vietnam as part of this activist approach. Coming into office as the war in Vietnam was going sour, Nixon wanted none of this.

He believed that containment might be practiced even more defensively and passively, primarily by means of helping others to help themselves. "Vietnamization," the replacement of U.S. combat troops with those of the Army of the Republic of Vietnam (ARVN), was the first practical test of this new Nixon doctrine. The success of the ARVN in halting North Vietnam's 1972 Easter offensive—albeit with considerable American air and naval support—was a hopeful sign. But when Vietnamization was put to a more rigorous test in the spring of 1975—when American fire support was withheld—South Vietnam was swiftly overrun.

This softening of containment strategy under Nixon included his introduction of an increasing element of direct negotiations in relations with the Soviet Union. In some respects this Soviet-American rapprochement had been foreshadowed by Nixon's earlier willingness to negotiate with China as a means of pressuring the Soviets to support the treaty ending the Vietnam War. But Nixon's next move went beyond grand tactics, an effort to craft a new strategy designed to tamp down disagreements between two parties who were inextricably bound by their nuclear stalemate. In some ways Nixon was the herald of Reagan's later summitry with the Russians. Nixon failed, though, due to the Watergate scandal that undermined his presidency. As Henry Kissinger has observed:

> In the absence of a morally persuasive presidency, many of those reared on the traditional approach to American foreign policy—in both the liberal and the conservative camps—joined forces in opposing Nixon's new approach. Liberals did so because they considered the new emphasis on national interest amoral, conservatives because they were more committed to the ideological competition with Moscow than to the geopolitical one.[31]

Although Gerald Ford would try to restore some momentum to this détente process in the wake of Nixon's resignation, he too would fail. And when Saigon fell and Cuban troops began deploying to Africa as an elite military force of the Soviet empire, all soon unraveled.

Amid all his travails, Nixon succeeded in putting his own stamp on nuclear doctrine. He was concerned that the nuclear war-fighting strategy embodied in the existing "single integrated operating plan" (SIOP) consisted of only one option—an all-out attack using everything we had. So he made it a priority to develop "limited nuclear options" covering many conflict scenarios, in the hope that any use of such weapons would not necessarily lead to a holocaust.[32] Nixon's successor, Jimmy Carter, continued to refine nuclear strategy, making a variety of limited war-fighting options formal policy in his Presidential Directive No. 59. But in other aspects of his presidential doctrine, Carter did little to amend what he inherited from Nixon, with the exception of making it clear to the world that U.S. forces would directly engage any threat to continued flows of Persian Gulf oil. Carter also built on the advocacy of human rights that Gerald Ford had advanced at Helsinki—another kind of foreshadowing of Reagan's strategic emphasis.

Overall, American presidents from Truman to Carter—with Kennedy a brief but important exception—stayed within the limits of the original containment concept. They even backed away from it a bit, to the extent of expressing a preference for simply helping other countries defend themselves against Communist aggression. This shift was no doubt due in large part to the costly, unsuccessful experience in Vietnam and the slight resurgence of Jeffersonian preferences for nonintervention that the Southeast Asian conflict had sparked. Yet even as American presidential doctrine on foreign policy was becoming more defensive and passive, security policy—the mostly military component of foreign policy—at the same high level was shifting toward ever more thinkable uses of nuclear weapons. This perilous phenomenon might also have been a product of the Vietnam War. For the apparent "hollowing out" of the U.S. military had bred new concerns—beyond those relating to the American public's willingness to support any new fight—about the ability of U.S. forces to keep Western Europe from being overrun by Russian tank armies.

The dangerous malaise that settled upon American foreign policy and national security strategy was swiftly dispelled in 1981 when Ronald Reagan came to office. Most remarkable about Reagan's initiative is that it was undertaken in open defiance of the sharply prescribed limits imposed by earlier presidential doctrines. Reagan did echo his support for the three-decades-old policy of containment, and he even held generally to the Nixonian notion of helping others help themselves. But he also differed radically, in some areas, with those who had come before him. Reagan saw no reason to allow existing concerns and constraints to force the United States to remain indefinitely on the defensive. Instead, in something of the spirit of Kennedy's vision, Reagan was determined to take the offensive in the cold war by helping others not just defend themselves but overthrow Communist rule. This shift in U.S. policy directly challenged the Soviet Union's "Brezhnev Doctrine," which held that once a nation had been taken into the Communist fold it would never be allowed to leave.

Thus Reagan turned American strategic thought on its head. While cognoscenti such as Kissinger and other members of the national security policy elite fretted that the United States had fallen behind in the cold war, Reagan saw ways to retake the initiative immediately by empowering others to confront communism around the world. As to more direct concerns about the effectiveness of the U.S. military, Reagan quickly began to rebuild American field forces—and encouraged the development of an innovative doctrine, "AirLand Battle," to accompany the new forces. He also began to turn radically away from existing strategic nuclear doctrine by stepping back from the nuclear abyss. That is, instead of thinking about how to fight and win limited nuclear wars, Reagan took the position that they "cannot be won and must never be fought." This was yet another striking difference between Reagan and his predecessors that would have profound consequences for world affairs.

What Reagan did at the highest levels of grand strategy, and how he strove to reshape the U.S. military, are deeply revealing about his character. Where others saw the nation as relegated to the defensive, Reagan sought the means to mount counterattacks on communism—on the battlefield and in a war of ideas. Where others despaired at the hollowing out of the post-Vietnam U.S. military, Reagan simply rolled up his sleeves and began rebuilding. And where others had become comfortably dependent on the nuclear koan of "security by means of the threat of mutual nuclear annihilation," Reagan wanted to make such indiscriminate weapons "impotent and obsolete." He intended to reduce their numbers—in fact to eliminate them if possible—and to build defenses against nuclear missiles, an ethically superior notion to the idea of holding huge civilian populations as "hostages in perpetuity" to threats of mass destruction.

So in his matter-of-fact, low-key manner, Reagan spun the ship of state around. And the change of course came quickly. Peter Robinson, one of Reagan's key speechwriters, notes in his memoir that from the very outset of his presidency Reagan took the position that the Soviet Union could be defeated and dismantled.[33] Caspar Weinberger, who served as secretary of defense for most of Reagan's two terms, makes the point that Reagan was "never afraid to challenge the conventional wisdom, and that is one of the reasons why he was so successful in changing the political agenda of . . . the nation."[34] In short, Reagan had both new ideas and the strength of will to act upon them. And these new ideas may tell us more about Reagan's character than any other aspects or analyses of his public life. For they tell us of his innovative qualities as a strategist, of his political courage, and of his profound ethical sense of the need to end a cold war that relied upon threats of mutual mass destruction in order to maintain the semblance of a peace.

It is enlightening to relate these broad matters of presidential style and doctrine to Reagan's successors and to the emerging contours of the twenty-first-century world. His immediate successor, George H. W. Bush, clearly intended to expand upon Reagan's pro-active notions of "rollback." Instead of simply helping others free themselves, the first Bush administration sought to seize a moment in world affairs when the United States could reshape global politics because of its military primacy. At the same time the elder Bush closely followed Reagan's game plan when it came to making further reductions in nuclear arsenals.

If Bush made any important deviation from Reagan's approach, it was probably in his subtle shift in emphasis toward hard military power and away from persuasive "soft power" in pursuit of American interests. A classified "defense planning guidance" written at this time—widely but mistakenly thought to have been written by Paul Wolfowitz—outlined the military means by which American primacy could be sustained and expanded.[35] Yet early on in the Soviet Union's period of dissolution, the Bush administration initially placed itself in the curious position of opposing the breakup. See, for example, then Secretary of State James Baker's famous "Chicken Kiev" speech, which favored holding the Soviet system together. All this said, though, policy toward the Russians soon returned to a more Reaganesque track aimed at bringing about the end of the old Soviet Union and its empire. And Bush's public diplomacy in crafting the large coalition that expelled Saddam Hussein from Kuwait in 1991 was a masterful example of information strategy rather than a simple demonstration of military primacy.[36]

With the presidency of Bill Clinton, Reagan's ideas about encouraging free markets and free peoples returned to center stage. And stayed there. The notion of leading with a strong military suit was relegated to the background as Clinton clearly preferred the application of purely diplomatic means. Although he often resorted to the use of force, his actions were always discriminate and quite limited. His bloodless success at coercive diplomacy against the Haitian dictator Raoul Cedras in 1994, for example, stands as a classic demonstration of the skillful blending of power and persuasion.

Yet there was also much sloppiness in the Clinton style. This became evident in the unraveling of U.S. policy in 1993 in Somalia, and in the 1999 decision to wage only an air campaign for Kosovo. In the latter case the approach to the use of force did nothing to protect the innocent Kosovars, for whom we were fighting, from the worst depredations of the Serbs. An earlier disjunction between a growing peril and the appropriate policy response to it had surfaced in 1998, when the threat from al Qaeda was made manifest in the embassy bombings in Kenya and Tanzania. In response to these acts, the true beginning of the al Qaeda war, military force was used in a primarily symbolic way—limited to missile strikes aimed at empty tents in Afghanistan—against Osama bin Laden. This weak response enabled the terrorist leader to continue the planning that would culminate in his attacks in 2000 on the *USS Cole* and in 2001 on New York and Washington. Clinton also had a Hamiltonian belief in the efficacy of economic sanctions and imposed far more of them than any other president in American history. Their effects were mixed at best, and often young innocents and the impoverished—in places like Haiti and Iraq—were punished most by such measures.

Reagan's first two successors in office provide an informative comparison. While the first Bush presidency neglected Reagan's "war of ideas" in favor of relying on more traditional military power, Clinton revived Reagan's information strategy while being somewhat negligent in his approach to the use of force as a tool of American statecraft. In particular, his decision to do nothing in the face of genocide in Rwanda in 1994, when even a modest show of force might have saved nearly a million lives, leaves him with a haunting legacy of inaction. Yet when we compare each president in overall terms to Reagan, Clinton lies somewhat closer to him philosophically. For Clinton never swerved from Reagan's ideas about the spread of democracy, and he stumbled militarily in ways quite similar to Reagan's own questionable decisions about the use of force. If Clinton presided over a debacle in 1993 in Somalia, it only echoed the massacre of Marines in 1983 in Beirut. And the ineffectual 1998 missile attacks on Afghanistan look much like Reagan's failed attempt to intimidate Libyan leader Moammar Qaddafi with the 1986 air raid on Tripoli.[37]

If the administrations of George H. W. Bush and Bill Clinton flip-flopped in their military-diplomatic emphases, the second Bush presidency showed the pendulum again swinging back toward the military side. Much less emphasis was given to "hearts and minds" during the first few years of the war on terror; far more attention was paid to confronting terrorism itself as a form of war and acting preemptively or even preventively. The strategy employed by George W.

Bush to head off the rise of new terrorist threats makes much use of the ideas about sustaining American primacy that were such a prominent feature of the defense planning guidance written during his father's term in office.[38] Even so, by the beginning of his second term, the younger Bush was downplaying the use of force in favor of the more diplomacy-oriented strategy of fostering democracy. Clear echoes of Reagan, and Clinton too.

This brief review suggests the continuing seesaw struggle over Reagan's legacy. The first Democratic president after him was deeply attuned to his notions about the primacy of ideas, whereas his Republican father-and-son successors both concentrated more on the use or threat of force in world affairs. None of the three managed to integrate information strategy with military strategy in a skillful way. The looming challenges that lie immediately ahead will determine not only the lasting impact of Reagan's legacy but also whether the twenty-first-century world will be one of light and progress or of darkness, terror, and perpetual warfare.

Additional insights into Ronald Reagan's presidency can be gleaned by looking at how he is rated in comparison to *all* his predecessors and successors. The most widely accepted of these rating systems include and weigh the opinions of many leading presidential historians and biographers, and the whole process, begun by Arthur Schlesinger more than fifty years ago, has taken on a commendable rigor extending to regular ratings updates.[39] In Ronald Reagan's case, this rating process has proven quite revealing. In 1994, just five years after leaving office, Reagan was listed at or around twentieth place among the forty presidents generally included in such ratings.[40] By 1996 he had dropped even farther, to twenty-fifth place in one poll.[41] But then something strange happened, and Reagan's stock began to soar in the various polls. By the turn of the millennium he had climbed to eighth place.[42] More recently, a Zogby poll (taken of the general public rather than of presidential scholars) found Reagan in fourth place. No doubt his death in June 2004 will stimulate further attempts by presidential

Figure 3. The "Top Ten" Presidents

1. George Washington (1789-1797) 2. Abraham Lincoln (1861–1865) 3. Franklin D. Roosevelt (1933–1945)	**"Great"**

4. Thomas Jefferson (1801–1809) 5. Theodore Roosevelt (1901–1909) 6. Andrew Jackson (1829–1837) 7. Harry S Truman (1946–1953) 8. Ronald Reagan (1981–1989) 9. Dwight Eisenhower (1953–1961) 10. James K. Polk (1845–1849)	**"Near-Great"**

Source: *President Society/Wall Street Journal* (last ranking prior to Reagan's death in June 2004).

historians to assess his performance in office and its impact upon the world.

But for now, Figure 3 lists those presidents who have been evaluated as "great" and "near-great" in the scholarly polls. What clearly ties the three in the highest class—Washington, Lincoln, and Franklin Roosevelt—to one another is that each confronted and mastered mortal threats to the Republic. Washington led a new country and resisted the temptation to turn the presidency into an authoritarian office. Lincoln saved the Union and pointed the way to a mending path in its wake. And Franklin Roosevelt played a vital role in the defeat of fascism. Reagan's success in ending the cold war and reducing the nuclear threat may eventually elevate him into their company.

Reagan's stock among presidential scholars may also continue to rise if the broad strategy he developed while in office remains relevant to future American statecraft. Reagan's game plan, in its most distilled form, was driven by three major beliefs: the world could be made less nuclear; tyrants were weak, not strong; and persuasion was at least as important as coercion. Using these beliefs as guideposts will help in understanding and analyzing how Reagan engineered such a remarkable reversal of American fortunes during his presidency. Keeping these principles in mind will perhaps also help us discern deviations from Reagan's strategy when they emerge. And will help us understand the various unintended consequences of his policies that have sometimes proved highly inimical to our national interests. Arms control, military affairs, and public diplomacy continue to be profoundly shaped by the policies of Ronald Reagan—generally, though not entirely, for the better.

In the following chapters I look at these key issues and determine the extent to which Reagan's ideas and initiatives have continued to exert their influence. Each issue bears upon important, persistent concerns of U.S. foreign policy and national security strategy. Presidents must remain deeply attentive to matters relating to the spread of weapons of mass destruction. And questions about dealing with rogue leaders also remain relevant, particularly the issue of when to use force. The manner in which these concerns are addressed has powerful implications for the overall viability of the international system.

Even the central strategic problem of our time—how to counter terror networks—has been profoundly shaped by Ronald Reagan's somewhat muddled approach toward this scourge more than two decades ago. But before examining all these continuing concerns, I focus on Reagan's role in ending the cold war on such favorable terms. For this was the signal achievement that has so significantly shaped the contours of the twenty-first-century world. This combination of historical reflection and more current (and sometimes even prospective) policy analysis may help uncover some of the still-hidden complexities in Reagan's character and thought.

2

The Turn of the Tide in the Cold War

I n April 1975 Saigon fell to the surging North Vietnamese Army, signaling the utter failure of long, costly American efforts to keep South Vietnam free from Communist rule. It was a stinging defeat for the United States and its cold war strategy of containment, one that had powerful ripple effects. Nearby Laos quickly came under Hanoi's control. Cambodia followed a few years later but only after nearly two million innocents were killed by the madmen of the Khmer Rouge. While this went on, the Soviet Union attracted new client states in Africa—Angola, Ethiopia, and Mozambique—and Communist insurgents took over Nicaragua and endangered El Salvador. Pursuing direct action themselves, Russian troops invaded Afghanistan in December 1979, a month after Iranian militants stormed the U.S. embassy in Tehran and took fifty-two American hostages. In April 1980, almost exactly five years after the fall of Saigon, an attempt to rescue these hostages by elite American forces was botched at a marshaling point in Iran called Desert One, with tragic loss of life.

Before this sorry string of humiliations, the first quarter-century of the cold war, from the late 1940s to the mid-1970s, had featured much thrust and parry, with victories and defeats fairly equally distributed on both sides. Eastern Europe had fallen under Soviet control, and Chinese Communists had won their war against Chiang Kai-shek. But in the meantime Greece and the Philippines had been saved, and an American-led alliance kept South Korea free, though at a heavy cost in casualties during the Korean War. Twice in the 1950s Chinese saber rattling toward Taiwan was thwarted, yet by the end of the decade Fidel Castro had installed a Communist regime in Cuba, just ninety miles off the coast of Florida. This back-and-forth continued throughout the 1960s, with the conflict in Vietnam gradually taking center stage in the global struggle. When that war went poorly for the United States, so apparently did everything else.

Those five fateful years between the fall of Saigon and the disaster at Desert One saw a steady procession of defeats for democracy. And more were seemingly in the offing, prompting Soviet leader Leonid Brezhnev to thunder at the Twenty-fifth Communist Party Congress: "There is no future for capitalist society!"[1] During this period the U.S. economy showed little growth, suffering both high inflation and unemployment—partly due to the heavy costs of Vietnam, partly as a result of sharp rises in world oil prices. These lean years began with the brief presidency of Watergate-weakened Republican Gerald Ford, then continued with a Democrat, Jimmy Carter, who spoke freely about "limits" and the sense of "malaise" that had taken root in the country. On the world stage, the United States seemed to exercise little beneficial influence, with perhaps two exceptions. First, the Ford administration played a key role in support of the Helsinki Declaration—which began to bring the issue of global human rights to the forefront. Then the Carter administration skillfully brokered a lasting peace at Camp David between Egypt and Israel. Beyond these glimmers of hope, though, the news was routinely grim. And it was not at all clear how matters could be set right.

Yet from the moment he came into office, Ronald Reagan began to turn things around. With roughly the same resources as his immediate predecessors at his disposal, he nonetheless invented a wholly new image of American power and will and harnessed it to an innovative strategy that seized the initiative in the cold war. He soon began to influence the course of events, making a huge impact on the decision-making of Soviet leaders and other adversaries. A tangible sign that change was afoot came in January 1981 on his very first day in office. Their humiliation of Carter complete, and fearing what Reagan might do to them, the Iranians allowed the hostages—whom they had been holding for more than fourteen months—to fly out of Tehran just half an hour after Reagan was sworn in.[2] This was but the start of a long, successful campaign. When Reagan left office eight years later, the Soviet tide was ebbing back out of Eastern Europe, on the heels of reverses in Afghanistan and Central America. Shortly after, the Soviet Union itself would dissolve. The cold war would end with the United States and its allies the clear victors. How this occurred forms one of the most interesting intellectual puzzles in world history.

It is quite rare for a great empire at the height of its powers and holding the initiative—as the Soviets did in the 1970s—to lie in ruins just a few short years later. One of the USSR's intellectual ancestors, the Byzantine Empire, took a thousand years to collapse after the fall of Rome. Even the nomadic Mongols, whose thirteenth-century imperial territorial limits were quite similar to those of the modern Soviet Union, took a few hundred years to come apart. By contrast, Napoleon's empire lasted only a decade (1804–1814) but required an enormous amount of carnage to be defeated. The Nazis were crushed in a relatively short time—along with their Italian and Japanese allies, who sported empires of their own—but defeating these three took several years of hard fighting by a global coalition that suffered several tens of millions of casualties. It almost always takes either a long time or a lot of blood to kill an empire.

One key exception to this rule was the ancient Assyrian Empire of the seventh century B.C., replete with proud warriors who fought well but far too often. The Assyrians had poor lands of their own, located as they were between the fertile soils of Mesopotamia to the south and the rich, wild Caucasus Mountains to the north—so they specialized in war. They won nearly all their battles and built the world's first true empire, but even victorious armies suffer casualties. Very simply, the Assyrians virtually wore themselves out of existence. The end came for them with stunning swiftness in 612 B.C., as a loose coalition of Medes from the south and Scythians from the north wiped them out in a single, surprisingly easy campaign. As Will Durant observed, "at one blow Assyria disappeared from history."[3] The Soviet Union, which some have called the "last empire," dissolved as swiftly and surprisingly as the first empire. The collapse was more surprising, given the absence of major warfare before its downfall.

The mystery about the causes of the Soviet collapse and the American-led victory in the cold war only deepens upon closer consideration. When Reagan came into office, for example, the weight of expert opinion in academia and in defense policy and intelligence circles was that the United States had fallen dangerously behind the Soviet Union. On the right, communism was seen as growing increasingly attractive to insurgents in the developing world, and the Russian military seemed ever closer to achieving knockout capabilities with either nuclear or conventional weaponry. No less an authority than Henry Kissinger thought the Russians were winning the cold war, confiding this to Elmo Zumwalt—whose duties eventually included serving as chief of naval operations—and noting that the Soviets were "Sparta to our Athens."[4] A troubling analogy, given that the militaristic Spartans won the nearly thirty-year-long Peloponnesian War against the democratic Athenians. Reagan himself was deeply worried about the way that the strategic balance had been mismanaged, noting during his failed 1976 run for the presidency that "[u]nder Nixon and Ford, this nation has become Number Two in a world where it is dangerous—if not fatal—to be second-best. All I can see is what other nations the world over see: collapse of the American will and the retreat of American power."[5]

On the left, there was less thought of being behind—and more thought of rough parity. Still, the need to engage in arms reductions felt urgent. The sheer numbers of weapons of mass destruction—which had more than tripled between 1969 and 1980—were undermining crisis and deterrence stability to a point where an accidental nuclear war was becoming much more likely. The left also evinced a weary fatalism about, and sometimes a profound sympathy for, the spread of Moscow-friendly regimes in the third world. And across the political spectrum there was strong agreement that high inflation and unemployment, the second oil shock in 1979, and continuing post-Vietnam malaise were having increasingly debilitating effects on American power and policy.

In short, the end of the cold war seemed a long, hard way off. Some, like Bernard Brodie of the influential RAND Corporation think tank, even mused that the concept of victory itself had lost meaning in a world over which the shadow of mutual assured destruction (MAD) loomed. Yet there was a vigorous effort to rebut Brodie and the large numbers of defense analysts and policymakers who agreed with him. Ironically the intellectual leadership for this alternate view also came from RAND,[6] in the person of Albert Wohlstetter, who held that even nuclear wars could have winners. Wohlstetter's line of reasoning inspired a new school of strategic thought about nuclear war, which argued that ensuring the security and improving the accuracy of weapons, along with deploying them skillfully, would make all the difference. Richard Nixon embraced this thinking by approving a multitude of "limited nuclear options," the so-called Schlesinger Doctrine. Jimmy Carter took this thinking further; his Presidential Directive No. 59 made it clear that the United States intended to be able to fight and win a protracted nuclear war.[7] Today Wohlstetter's thought lives on among so-called neoconservatives who think the United States should use its power to sustain global primacy. Two of the most influential neocons who have held senior defense policymaking positions are Richard Perle and Paul Wolfowitz, both of whom were graduate students of Wohlstetter in the 1960s.

The trouble with Wohlstetter's view was that it called for a strategy aimed at knocking out enemy missiles before they could strike. This strategy put nuclear matters on a more precarious hair-trigger basis than ever before, a situation made worse by the Russians maintaining a large advantage in numbers of highly accurate warheads capable of striking at such things as missile silos or nuclear submarines in port. The reason for this seemingly parlous situation was less due to the Soviets having superior numbers of weapons and more due to their possessing more land-based missiles which, in the 1970s, were far more accurate than the sea-launched missiles that made up the largest part of the American arsenal. Our submarines were relatively safe when at sea, but in a world before global positioning satellites it was too hard to know the exact location from which a sea launch was made. This lack of knowledge affected the ability to calculate a strike at, say, a particular missile silo in the Soviet Union. It implied that the United States was indeed behind the Russians and ever more vulnerable to a devastating surprise attack. It also implied endless arms racing and an ever-increasing risk that an actual nuclear war might break out.

Similar debates arose in the realm of conventional warfare. Here also the Soviets appeared to have a winning advantage in Central Europe as they could quickly surge more than a hundred armored and mechanized divisions through the Fulda Gap in Germany, overwhelming the much smaller NATO forces deployed there against them. American strategy in this theater focused on fighting a delaying action, holding on until reinforcements could be brought across the Atlantic. Most analyses concluded that NATO could not hold out and that nuclear weapons would be needed in order to stem the invading Red tide. NATO's regular war games, the so-called "Reforger" exercises, always ended with field commanders calling for authorization to use their battlefield nuclear weapons. So it seemed that all roads led to Armageddon.

Given the intractability of the nuclear dilemma, the political, economic, and military malaise that followed in the wake of defeat in Vietnam, and the broad appeal of Marxist-Leninist ideals to insurgents the world over, few in those days saw how the West could win the cold war. At best, defeat could be averted and a protracted struggle sustained in the hope that matters might eventually resolve themselves acceptably. If there was one great exception to this conventional wisdom, it came in the person of George Kennan, the diplomat and historian whose famous "long telegram" from Moscow after World War II had introduced the concept of containment to senior policy-makers. Kennan argued that Communist rule in Russia was a devia-tion, sparked by defeat in World War I, from the relatively orderly passage from authoritarian tsarism to representative democracy that had been under way. He believed that Soviet rule was a passing phase and that the containment of Communist aggression needed to focus more on the battle of ideas than on military confrontations around the world. In the end, he held, communism would "wither away" and Russia would return to a more normal path of political, economic, and social development. Kennan alone saw the true fragility of the Soviet empire and even made the prescient point, more than a decade before the actual events, that its downfall might be sparked by Eastern Eu-ropean "liberationist ripples that would carry into the Soviet Union itself."[8]

In addition to Kennan, there were a few other insightful, dissent-ing voices as well. In 1979 the French scholar Hélène Carrère d'En-causse wrote *Decline of an Empire,* in which she argued that ethnic tensions would tear the Soviet Union apart. Her main point, echoing Kennan, was that Marxists saw only class differences in the world (i.e., between capitalists and workers) and assumed that cultural fac-tors were of little import.[9] She correctly saw the Soviet attempt to "Russify" its empire as bound to fail. Another fascinating insight into the possible end of the cold war came from journalist Donald James. He wrote a speculative novel in 1982, *The Fall of the Russian Empire,* which forecast the implosion in 1986 of the Soviet Union. He was not far off. Beyond these two voices though, the pickings were quite slim, with only Senator Daniel Patrick Moynihan having the perspicacity and willingness to predict that the Soviet Union would die by the end of the decade. In the event, he was off by barely a year.

Then along came Ronald Reagan who, like Moynihan, believed that the end was near for the USSR because the West enjoyed a "supe-riority of the spirit" that had put the Russians on the horns of an in-soluble dilemma: they could only use force to make up for their lack of moral appeal; and the more force they used, the less appealing they became. Reagan sought from early on in his presidency to clarify what he saw as the real situation, one that was far simpler than that described by all manner of experts. As he said in an address to British Parliament in 1982:

> We are witnessing today a great revolutionary crisis, a crisis where the demands of the economic order are conflicting directly with those of the political order. But the crisis is happening not in the . . . West, but in the home of Marxism-Leninism, the Soviet Union. It is the Soviet Union that runs against the tide of history by denying human freedom and human dignity to its citizens.[10]

Initially Reagan stood virtually alone among policymakers in his belief that the Soviet Union was in a terminal crisis. Because of his modest educational credentials, lack of experience in foreign policy, and movie-actor background, his philosophizing tended to be dismissed. Today, as his voluminous private correspondence becomes public, it is apparent that Reagan had been thinking insightfully about big issues for decades and had gotten onto something of the utmost importance.[11]

Although we associate him with arch-conservatism, Reagan's thoughts on the cold war came much closer to Kennan's progressive notion that communism in Russia constituted an unnatural deviation from that society's normal path of political and social development. Reagan possessed a natural optimism about the idea of freedom taking root even in totalitarian states and believed in the kinds of failure-from-within possibilities that d'Encausse and James developed in their writings. But he also saw great opportunities for nudging along the process of internal dissolution from the outside, and he nurtured a strategy designed to do just this.

The elements of this strategy were simple and straightforward, and they resonated deeply with Reagan's own core beliefs about how to win the cold war. These points were advanced in Reagan's first national security strategy, made public in February 1982.[12] His belief that the Soviet Union was in fact quite brittle emboldened a small band of dissenters in the Pentagon and in the intelligence community to press their case that the Russians were actually teetering on the edge of economic collapse. They were shepherded along largely by Andrew Marshall, the Defense Department's director of "net assessment," the Pentagon's in-house long-range planning group. They soon began to provide crucial counterpoint to the prevailing view—championed by Henry Kissinger and Paul Nitze, the latter a leading defense intellectual respected and employed by both parties—that the United States was way behind, and still losing ground.[13]

Andrew Marshall is one of the legendary characters of the cold war era. An owlish-looking man of few words, Marshall is an economist by training and a former RAND analyst. Now in his mid-eighties, he took charge of the Office of Net Assessment in 1973 and was still running it more than thirty years later—a record of single-minded control matched only by Hyman Rickover, father of the nuclear navy. Marshall takes the "long view" of everything and has been involved in most of the great events of his time. Yet it is possible to see some clear patterns even in a record as varied as his. During the 1980s, for example, he and his staff focused on exposing and exploiting the brittleness that lay at the heart of the Soviet Union. Later, during the 1990s, Marshall inspired much of the thinking about what defense analysts came to call a "revolution in military affairs," i.e., the effort to transform the U.S. armed forces with smart weapons and new doctrines and forms of organization. Since 9/11 Marshall and his minions have been working on ways to counter terror networks.

During the Reagan years Marshall formed something of a bureaucratic "band of brothers" to help argue that official CIA estimates of the size of the Soviet economy were overstated by at least 60 percent. Two of his principal allies were Charles Wolf, an eminent economist at the RAND Corporation, and Harry Rowen, chairman of the National Intelligence Council during Reagan's first term. A fourth member of the team, Patrick Parker, former deputy assistant secretary of defense for intelligence during the Nixon administration, had done much to bring the whole group together initially and to find other allies in the many secret hamlets of the military and intelligence communities. The four hammered home their case that estimates of the size of the Soviet economy had been seriously mistaken going back as far as 1928, a time when leading economists still tended to look at the great experiment of the Soviet Union with more hope than clarity. Beyond wishful thinking, misestimates were due in part, they said, to the veils of secrecy with which Kremlin leaders routinely shrouded their doings. The lack of economic ties between the Soviet Union and more developed countries also made details difficult to obtain. And real economic output was difficult to gauge in a society that could hide inflation with long-standing price controls and accounting legerdemain. For Marshall, Wolf, Rowen, and Parker, though, long waiting lines for few products on the shelves were signs that cried out for proper interpretation—and action.[14]

Today we know that the estimates of the "Marshall Group" were right on target—conservative actually, as the CIA had overstated Soviet economic growth by 90 percent in the 1975–1980 period and by 200 percent in the 1980–1985 period.[15] When these errors were corrected for, it was evident that the portion of the USSR's overall economic output given over to the military was far higher than anyone had ever guessed—possibly more than a third of the whole Soviet economy. This was scarcely sustainable in the long run and even less likely to be possible when Reagan brought American defense spending to just over 6 percent of a much larger total economic output level, intending to cruise along at this rate of spending for the foreseeable future.[16]

The United States thus found itself in a position to ratchet up the pressure on an increasingly shaky Soviet economy. The concrete implication for policy was that the United States should pursue what Marshall called a "cost-imposing strategy" on the Soviet Union.[17] Wherever the Russians had commitments, the Americans should make them more costly to uphold. And they had many, as the "Brezhnev Doctrine" vowed that no Socialist country would be allowed to stray back to the capitalist side. For Marshall, it mattered little whether any single initiative led to a specific victory over the Russians or one of their clients. The strategy was really more about winning by means of attrition, bankrupting and bleeding the ever more vulnerable Soviet Union to death.[18]

In some respects the Marshall strategy unknowingly took a page from the Soviet playbook of the preceding decade. For during the long struggle over the fate of Vietnam, the Russians thought explicitly in terms of tying down huge American resources in Southeast Asia with an "economy of effort." That is, they believed that providing modest support for the North Vietnamese might generate huge returns. This was exactly how matters played out. As Adam Ulam observed of Russian aid to Hanoi during the war, "the cost of Soviet military supplies came to about $700–800 million per year, as against the $30 billion the United States was spending [annually] on the war."[19] This was clearly a kind of cost-imposing strategy that prefigured Reagan's approach.[20]

Marshall and Harry Rowen pitched this idea to Reagan in a meeting in 1981, quickly gaining the president's support for the strategy. Soon any defense funding request had to include a section stating exactly how the proposed initiative would pressure the Soviets to respond with higher levels of their own spending.[21] In this way, even in the absence of a clear victory in any particular cold war confrontation, there would still come a time when the Soviets simply could not keep up. As in a closely fought battle that ends in a rout, or nervous stock trading that ends in a crash, a "tipping point" would eventually emerge, beyond which the Soviet Union would lie irretrievably in ruins. As Malcolm Gladwell has noted in his classic study of such tipping points, they have a quality of "contagiousness," where many little causes eventually have one swift—rather than gradual—effect that is best described in political terms as a "social epidemic."[22]

Although Marshall and his minions had some allies in the defense and intelligence communities, they formed a distinct minority with their beliefs about the shaky state of the Soviet Union. Yet their ideas found little organized opposition, even from Paul Nitze who by then, though a Democrat, had become a senior adviser to Reagan. Nitze was the leading thinker among the majority stubbornly clinging to the idea that the United States had fallen dangerously behind the Russians. He and his supporters were soon mollified, however, because the Marshall strategy did not threaten their goal of increasing defense spending.

For his part, Reagan saw that both points of view could be quite easily accommodated. He came into office promising to beef up defense, and this he would do. But the perspective of the Marshall team provided him with an important opportunity to examine all spending initiatives to see just how efficient they might be in terms of forcing the Russians to greater levels of spending themselves. There would thus be a great deal of defense spending, but there would also be guidelines for spending wisely. By giving due homage to Nitze's fears while embracing Marshall's hopes, Reagan subtly kept the peace among all his cold warriors.

Beyond what the Americans were starting to do to them, the Soviets had been busily contributing to their own economic problems. First there was the matter of high-level party corruption, which saw vast sums skimmed off by key members of the ruling elite. There was much small-scale misuse and pilferage as well, of the kind so tellingly depicted in Alexander Solzhenitsyn's *For the Good of the Cause,* his short novel about the political machinations of party apparatchiks, each determined to appropriate a public building for his own preferred use. Corruption, high and low, was so rampant that ending it became one of the goals of Mikhail Gorbachev's *perestroika* (restructuring) strategy.

In addition to corruption, though, there were even greater costs and inefficiencies associated with the existing Soviet bureaucracy's balky, wasteful processes. The damage done by well-intentioned officials working in an increasingly obsolescent central planning system probably dwarfed the problem of pilferage. For Gorbachev, institutional redesign was the key to fixing the problem. He put the matter this way:

> Ever since the revolution there had been countless discussions . . . on the unwieldiness and inefficiency of our management apparatus and its rampant bureaucracy. Decisions had been adopted—but the bureaucracy continued to grow, since attempts to solve the problem simply resulted in the creation of new management structures. It was

therefore necessary to change the very system of economic management, keeping only social and scientific-technological strategies under central direction and leaving everything else to the discretion of the individual collectives.[23]

Apart from its internal problems, the Kremlin's strategic decision to try to press a geopolitical advantage against the Americans during the window of opportunity opened up by their post-Vietnam malaise turned out to be a case of overreaching. Thus the latter years of the 1970s became a time of substantial Soviet investment in third world client states and insurgencies, fueled financially in 1973 by the quadrupling of the price of oil and in 1979 by its further tripling.[24] For the USSR, one of the world's leading oil producers, the prosperity of this period was, as the historian Eric Hobsbawm put it, like having "a guaranteed weekly winning ticket to the lottery."[25] But the Soviets were immediately spending their windfall gains, a shortsighted strategy that soon had serious repercussions.

At the same time the Russians were pursuing expanded influence among poor countries—where success would only entail the need for endless subsidies—they were paying insufficient attention to goings on among their satellites in Eastern Europe.[26] So while the free states of Western Europe reduced energy consumption by 40 percent in response to the oil shocks of the 1970s, the satellites reduced theirs by only 20 percent. Further, the satellites were borrowing huge sums from the financial surpluses accruing to leading oil producers. They amassed petrodollar debts they could never hope to pay—in part because the loans were used to make products that the Soviets paid for with "nontransferable rubles," a currency good only for purchases within the Soviet empire, not for repayment of hard currency debts owed to the West. Beyond this "funny money" problem, the sheer size of hard money debts had grown to unmanageable levels. In 1974 the whole Soviet bloc owed only $13 billion. By 1978 this had grown to more than $50 billion and was closing in on $100 billion in 1985 by the time Gorbachev came to power. Poland, where unrest was greatest, alone accounted for over a third of total bloc debt.

Even in areas of relative success, like their relationship with Cuba—which provided Moscow with surrogate forces that fought well on many far-flung cold war fronts—the Soviet Union was financially bled. In this case the economic problem came in the form of the sale of Russian oil that was paid for by highly (and deliberately) inflated prices for Cuban sugar. By means of this systematic overpayment, the Soviet Union was providing Fidel Castro a straight subsidy amounting to between $4 and $5 billion annually to help prop up his regime and keep his forces available for new ventures. This was roughly ten times the size of the outright annual subsidy the Soviets gave to the Nicaraguan Sandinistas—a substantial sum in its own right. The whole rickety system was vulnerable to a drop in oil prices; and the means to engineer such a decline—with the acquiescence and connivance of the rulers of oil-rich Saudi Arabia—soon became a central part of U.S. planning.[27]

Among several other elements to the American cost-imposing strategy, a key one was the idea of funding insurgencies against pro-Moscow regimes, a notion that was enthusiastically supported by CIA director William Casey, who had been a clandestine OSS operator during World War II. This time around, instead of helping French and other Resistance fighters against the Nazis, Casey was figuring out how to put weapons in the hands of any group that would step up to fight a Moscow-friendly regime. Thus the "Reagan Doctrine" of helping others to fight for their freedom was born. The contras in Nicaragua and the *mujahideen* in Afghanistan became the best-known examples of this strategy. The situation in Afghanistan had the added benefit of allowing American proxy forces to strike directly at the Red Army. But some have argued that it was the initiative in Afghanistan that enabled the rise of al Qaeda itself, which would shift its aim to America after the campaign against the Soviets.[28]

In both these cases, Reagan's initiatives had roots in Jimmy Carter's own policies. Carter, who had at first been open-minded about the true intent of the Sandinistas, had become sharply opposed to them when their anti-democratic intentions were made clear. Arming the contras was a logical next step. With regard to Afghanistan,

Carter provided early support to the *mujahideen* with the intention of driving up the cost of Soviet occupation. Thus it seems he was pursuing something of a cost-imposing strategy of his own—though the Afghan case is more complex, in that Carter had begun assisting the anti-government resistance there *before* the December 1979 Soviet invasion. Indeed, Zbigniew Brzezinski has made it clear that American support for the armed overthrow of the Soviet puppet rulers (Hafizullah Amin and, after his death, Babrak Karmal) may actually have increased the chance that Russian forces would intervene in the country in the first place![29] So it seems that the "Great Game" played out in the Hindu Kush during the 1980s was just as complex and surprising as the one conducted a century earlier during the 1880s and chronicled by Rudyard Kipling.

Contrary to some of the more breathless assessments, neither of these Reagan-supported guerrilla movements ever won decisively on the battlefield against the Sandinistas or the Soviets. But with American support both were able to stay on their feet, compelling their opponents to continue to incur costs in blood and treasure. Attrition worked in both cases. Just four weeks after Reagan left office, Soviet General Boris Gromov became the last Russian soldier out of Afghanistan, ending more than nine years of costly, fruitless fighting in that sad land. The end for Communist Sandinista rule in Nicaragua came when the regime allowed free and fair elections in 1990—which it lost decisively.

The magnitude of the eventual victories in these cases, however, should not be overstated. The Sandinistas maintained control of Nicaragua's military—which they do to some extent to this day—and the illicit effort to continue funding the contras led Reagan into a secret arms deal with the Iranians that, when exposed, nearly unraveled his presidency.[30] In Afghanistan the final Moscow-installed regime, that of the single-named secret policeman Najibullah, held out against the *mujahideen* for years after the Soviet withdrawal. When Kabul finally fell to the resistance, the victors then viciously fought each other. One of them, the Uzbeg leader Rashid Dostum, eventually came to receive solid Russian support and retained control of a portion of northeast Afghanistan. In the fall of 2001 his forces, which were still linked to the Russians, became a central element in the American offensive against the Taliban and al Qaeda. Today American troops are engaged in a counterinsurgency in Afghanistan that has no end in sight. So it seems that neither in Central America nor in Central Asia were local problems ever fully resolved. But both campaigns did succeed at the strategic level, because each forced the Soviets to incur increasingly heavy costs in supporting their clients.

Aside from proxy wars, Reagan and his chief advisers believed that the United States could also force the Soviet Union into a costly defense spending spiral. In the wake of the U.S. defeat in Vietnam, there was a widespread belief among American conservatives that the U.S. military had been "hollowed out." In particular there was great concern that the Red Army could win a lightning conventional campaign in Europe against NATO before reinforcements came to the rescue from across the Atlantic. Fixing these problems would both eliminate a dangerous vulnerability and at the same time force the Soviets to respond by spending more on their military, incurring ever greater costs.

In some cases the Soviets could be forced to higher levels of defense expenditure without even the prior need for direct American spending. All it took was a willingness to use some parts of the U.S. military in new ways. Perhaps the clearest case of this was the articulation of the so-called "maritime strategy" during Reagan's second term. By this time it was obvious that his repeated first-term calls to build a six-hundred-ship navy would never be answered. Still, a new doctrine could be substituted for ships; and the maritime strategy, which envisioned a protracted conventional war against the Soviets—around their periphery and against their clients around the world—threw a great scare into the Russians. An especially chilling aspect of this new offensive doctrine, which replaced the earlier idea of using the navy simply to protect shipping lanes, was the publicly proclaimed U.S. ability to "make the oceans transparent" (Reagan's phrase). If such American claims were true, they suggested that the submarines that formed the backbone of the Soviet navy were in great and immediate peril. Even though these claims about being able to see Soviet submarines—from satellites and other platforms—were deliberately inflated, the Russians could not know this for sure, and they spent enormous sums that they could ill afford to develop underwater "bastions" in the arctic to protect their submarine fleets.[31] This was a signal triumph for the cost-imposing strategy.

Both in terms of declining economic growth rates, rising hard currency debts, and the share of overall government spending being devoted to the military, the 1980s proved to be a decisive period for the Soviet Union. Its economy continued to stagnate, its military burden grew, and the sharp fall in world oil prices—from both natural and artificially created causes—soon had extremely deleterious effects. Without the unifying thread of Reagan's "cost-imposing strategy," though, it is hard to see how this period could have been fully exploited in the cause of ending the cold war.

As seen in Figure 4, the economic underpinnings of the Soviet Union had come under great and increasing strains. This at the very time when the United States was enjoying a long economic boom after the sharp but short recession of 1982. Some of the economic dividends were being used to ratchet up the military pressure on the Russians. How different the reality of the situation was from the doom-saying of Kissinger and Nitze.

In another key dimension of Reagan's strategy, reducing the shadow cast by nuclear weapons, he pursued two main avenues of approach. The first was the attempt to halt and then reverse the arms race rather than simply trying to limit the rate of growth in numbers and types of warheads. Reagan's emphasis on getting rid of nuclear weapons ran strongly counter to the preferences of the American right wing, which continued to worry about the United States being "dangerously behind." But Reagan's ideas appealed to and were empowered by a mass public that saw things like the "nuclear freeze" and other arms reduction plans as eminently sensible policies. The second element in Reagan's plan to end the arms race was to create viable defenses

Figure 4. Two Views of Soviet Economic Collapse

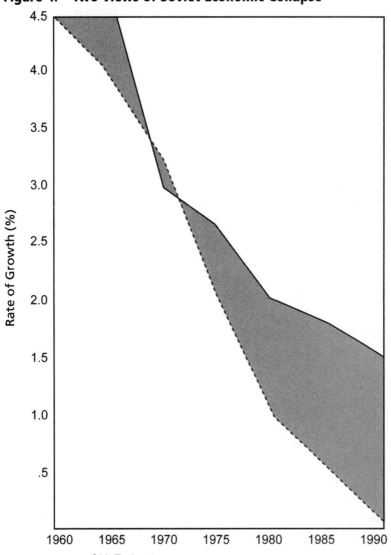

— CIA Estimate
- - - Soviet Economists' Estimates
▓ CIA Misestimates of Soviet Economic Growth

against nuclear attack—a notion then known as "Star Wars" and now called national missile defense. This issue remains highly contentious. Conservatives loved, and still love, Star Wars and missile defense; liberals worried, and still worry, that such weaponry, even if labeled "defensive," might spark a new round of arms racing.

The center and the left had concerns too—which also endure—about the feasibility, costs, and international political consequences (among allies and adversaries) of trying to field effective missile defenses. At the time America's NATO partners were seemingly as upset as the Russians by the prospect of missile defenses. Star Wars implied the possibility of the alliance waging a nuclear war in which America was protected while Europe and Russia were devastated. This fear was only amplified by the concomitant American initiative to locate substantial new "intermediate range" nuclear weapons in Europe, reducing the need to rely upon the United States–based strategic arsenal in the event of war. It made nuclear war more thinkable and gave the appearance of an American willingness to "fight to the last European."

Reagan's immediate results in this area were thus somewhat mixed, largely because his two-pronged strategy to make the world "less nuclear," which gave him cover on both the left and the right, included elements that the Soviets saw as threatening—and which even our allies found alarming. While the Russians were ready to talk about ending the nuclear arms race, the specter of Star Wars—a system that could seemingly disable their strategic rocket forces completely—encouraged them to try to offset the U.S. missile defense initiative by means of expanding their offensive capabilities. The Soviet theory was that even very good defenses could be overwhelmed by masses of real weapons and clever decoys. So, naturally, the Russians began to build more and better nuclear weapons and delivery systems.

These Russian increases were matched by growth in the American strategic arsenal, with numbers of missiles and warheads reaching all-time highs during Reagan's time in office. This folly was further fueled by the continuing efforts of some in policy circles to make the case that a protracted nuclear war could actually be fought and won, if only the United States built enough of the right sorts of weapons—a point with which Reagan had always disagreed. Nevertheless he acquiesced to pressures to keep expanding the American arsenal in the absence of arms control agreements. Despite these problems, there were successes as well, with both sides agreeing to make Europe free of intermediate-range missiles—the "zero option." And both sides agreed to keep talking about making strategic arms reductions (START), a process that would come to fruition in the 1990s.

On balance, the risks of a nuclear holocaust had been somewhat mitigated. As to the attempts of some analysts to link the prospect of missile defenses to the imposition of great new costs on the Russians, these seem quite overstated.[32] Costs incurred in trying to counter Star Wars did not break the Soviet Gosbank. Building and maintaining a first-rate arsenal of strategic weapons never required more than a tenth of Soviet defense spending. Increasing the number of warheads was a simple, cost-effective response to the threat that might be posed by even a fully functioning American Star Wars defensive system. Twenty years later this is still a fundamental fault line in the continuing debate about whether to try to build a national missile defense. And, as a hedge against the rise of such defenses, the Russians still maintain a large, capable strategic nuclear force equal to our own. Nevertheless the 1980s turned out to be the pivotal period in which a seemingly endless and scarcely controllable arms race was slowed, finally halted, then reversed.

As Figure 5 shows, numbers of warheads more than tripled during the 1970s, with the American arsenal rising from just under three thousand strategic warheads to more than nine thousand. During the same period, Soviet strategic warheads also tripled, from less than two thousand to about six thousand. This rapid growth was fueled in part by mutual antipathy but also by technological advances that made it possible to put several warheads on each missile, what are called "multiple independently targetable reentry vehicles" (MIRV). During the 1980s the rate of increase in warheads eventually slowed, then stopped (though at an all-time high in numbers of warheads), and finally reversed.[33] This happened because Ronald Reagan persuaded

Figure 5.   The Arms Race at a Glance

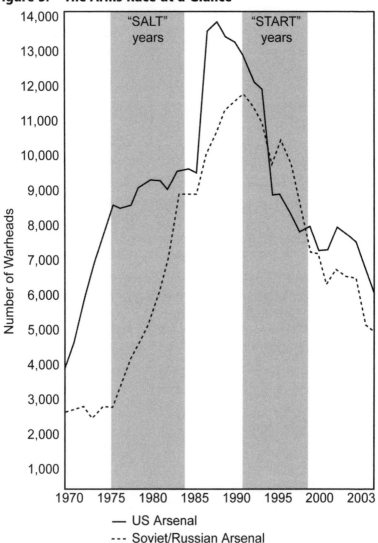

— US Arsenal

--- Soviet/Russian Arsenal

his own conservative supporters—as well as Soviet president Mikhail Gorbachev—that it was in everyone's interest to see an end to the arms race. As Reagan often put it, "a nuclear war cannot be won and must never be fought," a statement he frequently followed with the call to make nuclear weapons "impotent and obsolete."

At their Reykjavik summit in 1986, Reagan and Gorbachev even went so far as to call for the abolition of nuclear weapons. This prompted peace advocate Jonathan Schell, author of *The Fate of the Earth* and *The Abolition,* to claim that Reagan was the most effective president ever on weapons limitation, with his term in office representing a relative "golden age of arms control."[34] Clearly Reagan was the most dovish member of his own administration, though he remained aware of and sensitive to classic concerns about nuclear war-fighting strategies and even championed the notion of creating viable missile defenses—which he promised to share with all, even the Russians. His policies in the nuclear realm should therefore be seen against the backdrop of his own somewhat divided sentiments. And so, long before Bill Clinton would popularize the notion, Reagan succeeded in finding a "third way" to triangulate between the opposing schools of thought about Armageddon.

Even though advisers to both Gorbachev and Reagan managed to curb their leaders' initial enthusiasm for total nuclear disarmament, it seemed that finally everyone was listening to their call, and a true tipping point in the arms race was reached by Reagan's last year in office. Since then the numbers of warheads on both sides have continued to decline, with American nuclear forces currently reduced to the level of the arsenal thirty years ago. There is even much talk of taking arsenal sizes down further. If the gravest threat posed by terror networks is that one day they might possess even a few nuclear weapons, then it seems that Reagan's ideas about nuclear abolition and strategic defense may prove more timely than ever in the coming years.

With regard to persuasion, the "soft power" aspect of Reagan's strategy, the Great Communicator was most attuned to the notion of mobilizing the English language and sending it off into what he called the "war of ideas." Reagan's faith in the transforming power of the ideal of "free peoples and free markets" was unshakable, and he quickly set to work on this front. He was greatly aided by the willingness of most Americans across the political spectrum to support his hopeful views about a future world that would be democratic, peaceful, and prosperous. Reagan stayed well out in front in this "battle of the story," sometimes perhaps overstepping, as seemed the case when pundits and policy analysts on both right and left urged restraint or criticized him for labeling the Soviet Union "evil" or for demanding that the Berlin Wall be "torn down." Even his own advisers often tried—generally unsuccessfully—to tone Reagan down. When it came to his famous June 12, 1987, appearance at the Brandenburg Gate, for example, Dinesh D'Souza notes that "the State Department kept from Reagan's speech the reference to dismantling the Berlin Wall. Even the more hawkish National Security Council was opposed."[35] Reagan insisted on keeping his words in. As this and other events unfolded during his two terms in office, Reagan's convictions were borne out, and the realm of public diplomacy, a key element of what I would call "information strategy," turned out to be his strongest suit.

Perhaps the most important aspect of Reagan's public diplomacy was the boost in morale he gave to the millions living in the Soviet satellite states of Eastern Europe. The effects of nurturing a civil society that would undermine Russian rule were most quickly and profoundly felt in Poland—a theater in the "war of ideas" where Reagan received a great deal of support from Pope John Paul II. Together they reached out to the Solidarity labor movement, which mobilized Polish society and soon placed the Soviets in a terrible dilemma—whether to use force to repress an emerging democratic movement. The prospective costs of invading Poland and trying to keep its more than thirty million people under control were seen as prohibitively high by the Kremlin, which found a stopgap measure in the imposition of military rule under Polish General Wojciech Jaruzelski. This bought some time, but Poland eventually freed itself, as did the other captive nations of Eastern Europe, shortly after Reagan left office—as soon as it became clear that the Red Army would not be called upon to restore control in the event of trouble.[36]

This was the ultimate triumph of a bloodless information strategy whose operational costs were not much more than those associated with providing resisters with faxes, cell phones, and some other means for communicating in more secure fashion. The return on this investment came swiftly, as the six countries of Eastern Europe that had fallen under Soviet control after World War II—East Germany, Poland, Czechoslovakia, Hungary, Bulgaria, and Romania—freed themselves without bloodshed in a series of "velvet revolutions." They won their freedom, in the words of Czech playwright and statesman Vaclav Havel, simply by "acting as if they already were free."

And, as George Kennan had predicted, there were "ripple effects" that soon had the Soviet Union itself shaking on its foundations, and which were felt in other parts of the world as democracy began to spread. As Figure 6 depicts, the 1980s proved to be the political tipping point in the cold war as well—with continuing dividends from Reagan's political strategy being paid out during both the first Bush and the Clinton administrations. In the decade between the last Carter years in office and the period immediately following Reagan's second term, the number of free countries in the world rose by more than 40 percent. By the middle of Bill Clinton's second term, freedom had grown by 75 percent overall in the twenty years since 1978.

Yet there is need for caution in reflecting on these trends, as a good bit of the spread of freedom came in the form of new countries emerging during the period. And while the number of nations living under tyranny declined during the Reagan era by 20 percent, they began to nudge back up in the following decade. For communism, though, the Reagan years proved disastrous. In 1980 there were more than twenty Marxist-Leninist regimes around the world. By 1989 the number had been chopped nearly in half. Today there are only five Communist states remaining in the world: China, Cuba, Laos, North Korea, and Vietnam.[37] And each is under pressure—from within and without—to liberalize. What a far cry from Brezhnev's assertion of there being "no future for capitalist society."

Of all the elements of the Reagan strategy, firing the imaginations of subjugated peoples turned out to be the lowest-cost means of imposing pressure on the Russians. Solidarity in Poland, along with the social movements in the other Eastern European satellites,

Figure 6.   The Spread of Freedom, 1978–2003

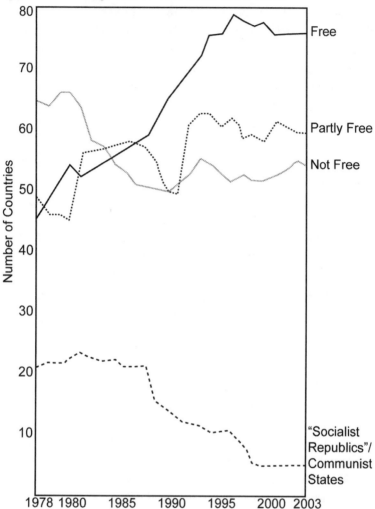

both restored morale among their peoples and simultaneously de-
moralized the Soviets and their satraps. Until recently this strategy
has continued to undermine dictators around the world. With the
coming of the terror war, though, some of the pressure that has been
exerted on authoritarians has been eased, as they have bought useful

"cover" for themselves by becoming involved in counterterrorist operations. Thus the struggle against terrorism has become like a latter-day version of the fight against communism, with the same result: the United States may "look the other way" if a dictator agrees to serve a broader American agenda. Couched in the euphemistic notion of "constructive engagement" during the Reagan years, the idea was that those who cooperated in dealing with the most serious threats to international security might continue in their undemocratic ways—for a while. There are problems with this approach today; but even during the 1980s it did not work very well. Ronald Reagan eventually found that he had to distance himself from the tyrant Ferdinand Marcos in the Philippines and the apartheid-loving Broeders who ruled South Africa. George W. Bush seemed to have made the same discovery at the outset of his second term, when in his inaugural speech he reasserted the primacy of human rights and democracy as the key values guiding American foreign policy.

Perhaps the most ingenious aspect of the Reagan strategy was that it lured the Russians into the serious negotiations that really ended the cold war. More than anything else, it was the reduction in antipathy between the two sides that finally made peace possible. But this could not have happened without the support of two other leaders who deserve much credit: Jimmy Carter and Mikhail Gorbachev. President Carter and his national security adviser Zbigniew Brzezinski determined to put U.S. foreign policy on the high ground of protecting human rights, a departure from the Nixon-Kissinger penchant for amoral *realpolitik*, which favored such actions as the 1973 violent overthrow of the Marxist-leaning Allende government in Chile. Carter and Brzezinski saw that the moral domain was a crucial fault line in the cold war and laid the groundwork for a policy of "power and principle" that Reagan later followed.[38] As Carter said in his January 1977 inauguration speech:

> . . . we can never be indifferent to the fate of freedom elsewhere. Our
> moral sense dictates a clear preference for those societies which share

with us an abiding respect for individual human rights. We do not seek to intimidate, but it is clear that a world which others can dominate with impunity would be inhospitable to decency and a threat to the well-being of all people.

For all his breadth of vision, though, Jimmy Carter was unable to achieve any of the sorts of gains that would accrue during Reagan's presidency. Carter may indeed have seen the way ahead correctly, but it was not to him to lead the way.

Mikhail Gorbachev should also receive high marks for striving to protect human rights. When the true meaning of his reforms began to be understood by the Communist governments in Eastern Europe— i.e., that they posed mortal threats to dictatorial rule—one after another of their leaders came to him looking for assurance of support for their continuing in power. Gorbachev made clear to each that "following the path of reforms begun in the Soviet Union meant the end of the system they embodied. No longer could they count on Soviet tanks to prop them up." Instead Gorbachev, from his point of view as a true believer in the good that communism had wrought in the world, chose to reach out to the mass publics in all the satellites. His strategy immediately alienated the leaders in these countries but had just as electric an effect on their mass publics. Very quickly, long-subjugated peoples' "aspirations and hopes found expression here—for revitalization of outdated forms of life; for democracy and freedom; and, probably most of all, for the long-awaited possibility of deciding the fate of their own countries independently."[39] Here at last was a Russian leader working on the same wavelength as Carter and Reagan. Gorbachev sincerely believed that the system he stood for could compete in Reagan's "war of ideas." It was a reasonable assumption. But from the perspective of the Soviet Union it turned out to be a mistake that proved fatal to their empire, as it spread an unstoppable "social epidemic" whose consequences will be felt for generations.

Just as the results of economic pressure tactics and military spending have been somewhat overstated, so too has the American "victory" in the cold war. The Soviets ended up *choosing* to retreat from their empire—largely bloodlessly, unlike many other empires (e.g., see the French, who made a similar decision to retrench only after fighting bitterly in both Indochina and Algeria). And while they may not have engineered the same kind of "soft landing" that the British Empire did—thanks to Britain's special relationship with the United States— the Russians at least survived a kind of "controlled crash." Today Russia remains rich in natural resources, is more politically lively than ever before in its history, and continues to be an important player in world politics. And it continues to have a great store of human capital in its well-educated mass public.

Russia is also still as well armed as the United States, at least in terms of strategic nuclear weapons, upon which it now openly relies for national security (having moved away in 1994 from its long-held "no first-use doctrine"). Even its conventional military forces, chronically plagued by tight budgets and manpower shortages, have shown signs of resurgence. After a humiliating defeat in the 1994–1996 war in Chechnya—which one journalist's eyewitness account prematurely labeled the "tombstone of Russian power"—the military performed far better in a second campaign there, regaining control over the breakaway republic.[40]

Thus the cold war should be seen as ending with a much more qualified outcome. The American-led West did win, but victory does not look anything like the end for the Axis powers in 1945, which saw all three of them devastated materially and physically occupied. Those who might equate the events of 1989 with the end of Wilhelmine Germany in 1919 are somewhat off the mark as well, given that the Russian military had not been ground down in a terrible conflict as the Germans had in World War I. Also there has been no modern analogue to the humiliating Treaty of Versailles with its many restrictive covenants and calls for financial reparations. Those who hold that both sides lost the cold war are mistaken as well. While they correctly note the wasteful spending that both sides engaged in for several decades, they do not emphasize enough the gains for both sides.[41] For the West and for the liberated satellite states, the receding of the

Soviet threat constituted a priceless gift. But the Russians also made amazing progress, as their own social revolution brought a degree of democracy and hinted at the possibility of new efficiencies in governance that can only revitalize their country in the long run. From this perspective, one could even say that the outcome of the cold war had something of a "win-win" quality.

Viewed through an even longer historical lens, the forty-year cold war seems to have much of the flavor of the first forty years of the struggle between the rising Muslim empire in the seventh century and the waning Byzantine Empire. By the end of this period Islamic forces were the clear victors, having liberated Arabia and North Africa from the Byzantines and conquering the last remnant of the Persian Empire. But still the Eastern Romans stayed on their feet, first repelling the determined Muslim attacks on Constantinople, then reconquering Anatolia (modern-day Turkey), their "near abroad." And in the centuries that followed they held on to their core domains and sometimes even dealt the caliphs of Mecca sharp, stinging reverses. Truly a cautionary tale, as the Russians still think of themselves as heirs to Byzantine traditions and strategic culture. They know that even a wounded empire still retains much residual power, and they must surely remember Alexis de Tocqueville's prescient assessment of the United States and Russia, made more than a century and a half ago in his *Democracy in America*:

> Their point of departure is different and their paths diverse; nevertheless, each seems called by some secret design of Providence one day to hold in its hands the destinies of half the world.

None of the foregoing is an attempt to diminish the importance of victory in the cold war. Rather, putting its outcome in proper perspective allows for a more accurate appreciation of what was achieved—which was quite a bit, from the freeing of millions from servitude to engineering a peaceful ending to history's most dangerous arms race. A true tipping point was reached, and at a most unexpected moment. In analyzing the waning years of this conflict, it may also be possible to sketch the strategy employed against the USSR more fully, and perhaps even draw out its implications for the challenges of our time.

But in order to do this we should first have a clearer understanding of just how such revolutionary change in world politics came about. The key questions are among the oldest asked by historians: Was change effected by the choices of one or a few individuals acting on the basis of their core beliefs? Or did change grow inevitably from mindless monolithic forces and mass movements? If the great events of history result from tidal surges, then the role of the individual and his favored strategy may matter less and an ability to understand the sweep of events will matter more. But much depends upon individual ideas, will, and choices; strategy becomes crucially important as an expression of the world-forming power of thought.

These different ideas about what caused such epochal change two decades ago mirror closely the questions that wise men were asking about the world-shaking events of two centuries ago, when Napoleon Bonaparte very nearly conquered Europe. For Thomas Carlyle, who articulated the "great man" theory of history, events were clearly driven by the individual. In *The French Revolution* (1837), Carlyle used the metaphor of the "ship of state," which he saw as near foundering until Napoleon took the helm, "steady as bronze." But Leo Tolstoy, writing some thirty years after Carlyle, looked beyond the opening shots of the revolution to the whole span of twenty years of war that Napoleon's "captaincy" wrought. He notes in the Second Epilogue to *War and Peace*:

> In 1789 a ferment rises in Paris; it grows, spreads, and is expressed by a movement of peoples from west to east. Several times it moves eastward and collides with a counter-movement from the east westward. In 1812 it reaches its extreme limit, Moscow, and then, with remarkable symmetry, a counter-movement occurs from east to west, attracting to it, as the first movement had done, the nations of middle Europe. The counter-movement reaches the starting point of the first movement in the west—Paris—and subsides.

Carlyle's and Tolstoy's perspectives should both be kept in mind in thinking about the end of the cold war and its aftermath, as it seems there are both tidal forces and forceful individuals evident—much as in the earlier era that they were surveying. For me, Tolstoy's mass movements theory advances a slightly more persuasive case than Carlyle's "great man" theory, at least in thinking about their theories in the Napoleonic context they were both observing.

But the end of the cold war is far murkier, with neither Carlyle's nor Tolstoy's view seeming to hold an immediately decisive edge. Interestingly, Carlyle's "great man" theory, so closely associated with broad Western ideas about the role of the individual, seems to have more appeal in Russia. There both Reagan and Gorbachev are seen as having played pivotal roles in the ending of the cold war and the dissolution of the Soviet Union. In the West, though, Tolstoy's classic Russian ideas about ineluctable "forces of history" seem to have taken firmer hold, as perhaps best exemplified by Richard Nixon's brusque critique of Reagan's role: "I'm not trying to minimize Reagan, but he was only part of what brought down communism. Communism would have collapsed by its own weight anyway."[42]

The evidence, such as it is, cuts both ways. Many in the United States and around the world saw the cold war as going very badly for the United States when Reagan entered office, for all the reasons stated earlier in this chapter. Yet just as many have joined Nixon in saying, since the dissolution of the Soviet Union, that it was going to happen anyway. Some have even intimated that Reagan's policies were unnecessarily costly and might actually have delayed the collapse of communism. Against this we have the immediate turnabout upon Reagan's accession to the presidency, and the remarkable changes that followed in the wake of an extraordinary series of summits between him and Gorbachev. This leaves us with a true puzzle to be solved.

We must consider next which of these two perspectives on the end of the cold war is more apt, for the answer to this question goes beyond its intrinsic worth and will likely provide some important clues to wise policymaking in the years ahead.

3

The "Controlled Crash"of the Soviet Union

On the Ides of March in 1990, almost five years to the day after he rose to power, Mikhail Gorbachev became the Soviet Union's first—and last—elected president under its newly amended constitution.[1] He had engineered the process himself by calling an emergency meeting of the Congress of People's Deputies in Moscow. He hoped that a "free and fair" election would both legitimize his continuing reform efforts and head off the devolution of power that had begun in the Eastern European satellites and was now, to use George Kennan's prescient phrase, "rippling through" the Soviet Union itself. An open vote affirming his personal power to govern, he thought, would also help to keep his chief political rival Boris Yeltsin at bay, and would pave the way for the constitutional reforms he sought to enact. As events played out, though, Gorbachev's election victory was Pyrrhic. He ran with no opposition yet could win only 59 percent of the votes cast. Of the nearly 2,100 deputies who had come to the Congress, 495 of them voted openly against his becoming president, and about 1,000 more abstained or simply left the Congress—hardly an electoral mandate.

In the following months popular discontent grew, even featuring an open demonstration against Gorbachev's March "democratic coup"—one that erupted in Red Square during that year's May Day parade. By the end of May, Yeltsin had been elected to the presidency of the Russian Federation. The election had been hotly contested and Yeltsin's margin was narrow—as he had had to confront and master Gorbachev's overt opposition—but he prevailed. Other republics of the Soviet Union were following suit with elections of their own, some even calling for outright secession, all in the name of the democratic right of self-determination. Meanwhile, the economic dislocations caused by Gorbachev's attempts to shift the Soviet economy from central planning to market-oriented mechanisms simply fanned the flames of dissent.

Yet even as his own country was falling apart, Gorbachev continued to be lionized by the world community, receiving particularly high praise in the United States. In June 1990, as Yeltsin was swiftly asserting his control over all state banks in the Russian Federation, Gorbachev was traveling in the United States attempting to drum up interest in business investments in the Soviet Union and was warmly welcomed at every stop. At Stanford University he received exceptionally friendly treatment. I was a doctoral fellow in politics there at the time and recall a colleague telling me that it was like receiving "a visit from Lenin himself." Gorbachev certainly had rock-star status among Americans, as supposedly jaded and worldly academics— myself included—lined up along campus roads on June 4 to wave as his famous Zil limousine passed by. Former Secretary of State George Shultz summed up the prevailing view that day, saying to the Soviet president in front of a large gathering: "You light up the landscape with your ideas. You are a great leader. You have a key role to play in this drama. We need you, Mr. Gorbachev."[2]

Then Gorbachev went home where he felt ever less appreciated and faced burgeoning financial and food distribution crises and increasingly testy relations with the various secessionist republics. Still he held to his reformer's course. A year passed in this increasingly tense fashion, with the growing unrest finally beginning to undermine Gorbachev's confidence. The pace of reform slowed, and Gorbachev eventually acceded to pressure to sack his right-hand man, foreign minister Eduard Shevardnadze. But Gorbachev's tactical retreats from *perestroika* both undermined his support among reformers and emboldened his opponents, and in August 1991 a brief coup d'état was mounted. The reactionaries—Communist party hacks for the most part—tried to supplant Gorbachev with his vice president, G. I. Yanayev, on the pretext that the president was "too ill to continue with his duties." Gorbachev was confined where he was vacationing in the Crimea while apparatchiks in Moscow tried to turn back the clock and restore the Soviet empire. They were defeated by the heroism of Boris Yeltsin and his adherents, three of whom were killed before the military came to its senses and backed the people rather than the so-called "State Committee for the Emergency." Gorbachev was freed within days, but the August coup had fatally sabotaged him. The Soviet Union had been mortally wounded too, and it winked out of existence on December 25, 1991, just a few months later.

It was now Yeltsin's turn to become the "first man" of Russia. Although he was initially regarded very lightly by the West—and much lampooned for his public drunkenness—he was deeply appreciated at home for swiftly stemming the tide of disintegration. Yeltsin made it clear from the outset that, unlike Gorbachev, he had no reluctance to use force liberally to hold Russia together. He resorted to military action in September 1993, attacking the Russian White House—the heart of his country's emerging democracy which he himself had defended in August 1991—to put down a brief rebellion against his rule. He also sent Russian forces into now "former-Soviet" republics like Georgia, Tajikistan, and Armenia to keep order.

Although the full-fledged war he launched from 1994 to 1996 against the separatist Chechens failed, Yeltsin made it clear that the price of secession from Russia proper would always be high. The example provided by Chechnya became even more of a deterrent when Yeltsin's handpicked (and popularly elected) successor, former KGB agent Vladimir Putin, sent Russian troops back in to reassert control over the breakaway republic a few years later. They are still fighting there today, much as imperial Russia fought for several decades in the mid-nineteenth century when it first imposed control over the Chechens. The Russian army's current attempts to quell Chechen resistance are, except for the newer technologies it employs, eerily similar to the actions depicted in Tolstoy's novella *The Raid*. Tolstoy had served in Chechnya as a young man and chronicled in this story just how hard it was to come to grips with guerrilla fighters motivated by a dangerous mix of nationalism, religious zealotry, and clan loyalty.

In the span of just a few years, then, the Soviet Union fell from being a superpower empire to very nearly being atomized by the organizational and market-oriented reforms of Gorbachev's *perestroika* and the openness of his *glasnost* policy. *Perestroika* created absolute economic chaos while *glasnost* shone an unflattering light on the practices of earlier Soviet rulers and on the Communist party itself. To the nations of the West, this deliverance from mortal threat seemed to verge on the miraculous.

Once the dissolution of the Soviet Union had occurred, however, analysts tended to say that such an end for totalitarian rule had been inevitable. If this view were the correct one, the shaping of the twenty-first-century world would have been largely the result of Tolstoy's ineluctable interplay of social mass movements, countermovements, and overarching economic trends. If, on the other hand, the outcome of the cold war depended on the interaction of specific strategic choices made in Moscow and Washington by Gorbachev and Reagan—and of course by their respective successors—a peaceful ending in the wake of one combatant's collapse was hardly foreordained.

When Mikhail Gorbachev came to power in 1985, Ronald Reagan was just beginning his second term. The idea of wearing the Soviets down by raising their costs of waging the cold war—primarily by inducing them to try to keep up with U.S. military advances and to fight American-supplied insurgents—had been the centerpiece of Reagan's strategy for some time. But as his second term unfolded, Reagan broadened his approach to include a major diplomatic element that for the most part concentrated on arms control. Following both of these tracks, Reagan hedged his strategic bets. The cost-imposing approach was a solid coercive strategy that would surely find any chinks in the Soviets' economic armor and exploit them to the extent possible; diplomacy afforded the chance to respond to any sincere peace feelers. And, like any good strategy, these elements were complementary, as pressures imposed by arms racing, technological challenges like Star Wars, and support for proxies fighting the Soviets and their clients might drive Gorbachev to the bargaining table.

In retrospect it is clear that *something* worked. But to determine whether it was military, economic, and psychological pressure or the more conciliatory aspects of American strategy that ended the cold war, it is necessary to examine the last decade before the USSR dissolved—and to consider several aspects of earlier Soviet and Russian history. As far as Reagan's role in these events is concerned, his direct control over the various cost-imposing initiatives that put so much pressure on Moscow was minimal. When it came to the diplomatic arena, though, Reagan ventured onto the front lines again and again, in a tour de force of sustained summitry. In the analysis that follows I assess both these strands of thought about the end of the cold war—and find that Soviet economic malaise was less pernicious than commonly thought, which put a premium on Reagan's relationship with Gorbachev. Indeed, absent the "Reagan touch," the cold war would surely have dragged on.

The most widely accepted argument about why the USSR was bound to fail is economic. The main hypothesis is that Soviet central planning was hugely inefficient, and the additional pressure imposed by the Reagan military buildup during the 1980s pushed the Russians over the edge.[3] Some have argued that *perestroika* itself was simply a desperate attempt to modernize a Soviet Union that could not otherwise compete with the West in general and with the United States in particular. Perhaps the most compelling voice raised in support of this line of reasoning is that of Mikhail Gorbachev himself, who wrote in

his "Crimea Article" composed in that vacation locale a few days before the August 1991 coup, of his

> profound conviction that we couldn't go on living as we were. . . . I
> have never, not once, regretted the fact that I was the initiator of a
> sharp turn in the life of our country. What came to light through
> *glasnost* about our past confirmed inexorably and brutally that a sys-
> tem created according to the rules of tyranny and totalitarianism
> could no longer be tolerated, not simply from the moral point of view
> but also from the point of view of the country's basic economic and
> social interests. It had already led the country into a dead end and
> brought it to the brink of an abyss . . . it was kept in place by force,
> lies, fear, social apathy, and also with the assistance of artificial injec-
> tions, which squandered resources and weakened potential for the fu-
> ture. Had we preserved the old regime for a few more years there
> would have been every reason to speak of the end of history for our
> great state.[4]

It is interesting to note in this passage Gorbachev's admission that the
old system could have been maintained. He chose not to try to do so,
or to undertake a course of less disruptive, incremental change, because he believed that the old regime was incapable of being propped
up for more than a few years anyway. But his assertion in the Crimea
article should be considered in light of the dire straits in which he
found himself late in the summer of 1991. There was simply no way
for him to go back to 1985, and he was fighting for his life (literally as
well as politically) when he wrote that revolutionary change was inevitable. So perhaps Gorbachev felt compelled to argue that no other
course was really open to him.

The first step toward analyzing whether his assessment was correct is to reexamine the pertinent economic data, which in this case do
not seem to square entirely with Gorbachev's and others' thinking
about the future prospects of the Soviet Union. For example, as Figure 7 shows, the overall economy continued to grow, though not by
much, right up until the Union itself began to break apart—a dissolution that Gorbachev himself opposed. Per capita income continued

Figure 7.   Key Soviet Economic Indicators, 1981–1991

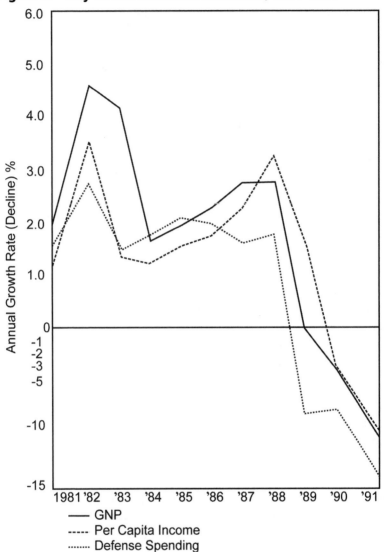

GNP
Per Capita Income
Defense Spending

to rise as well during the same period. As for military spending, it was actually dropping during these years, despite the pressures imposed by Reagan's various economic, political, and military initiatives. This trend hardly supports the idea that runaway military spending brought the Soviet Union down, or that the Russians had felt compelled to spend themselves into bankruptcy in order to stay in an arms race with the Americans.

It must also be noted that *perestroika*, the goal of which, according to Gorbachev, was "the introduction of a capitalist system throughout the economy," was hardly an anomaly in Soviet economic history.[5] From the very beginning of Communist rule in Russia, radical changes in the provision of goods and services had been periodically undertaken. When the newborn Communist regime found itself in dire straits in the early 1920s—partly the result of a costly, bloody civil war in which the Western powers had intervened on the side of tsarist "bitter enders"—it swiftly enacted a New Economic Policy. As Zbigniew Brzezinski has observed of it, the NEP "relied on the market mechanism and private initiative to stimulate economic recovery."[6] The NEP was a rousing success that breathed real life into the Communist system.

Twenty years later the Soviet Union was fighting for its survival against Nazi aggression. By the autumn of 1941, much of European Russia had been overrun and casualties suffered were already in the millions—the Soviet Union would eventually lose more than twenty million people—perhaps as many as thirty million—in the "Great Patriotic War." Moreover the areas lost to the German invaders included much of the industrial and agricultural heartland of the USSR. Without the skillful evacuation of equipment and workers and their swift reconstitution east of the Ural Mountains, the war would have been lost. The challenge for the brutal Soviet regime was to undertake the largest and most complex retreat in history, rebuild a shattered economy on the fly, and not lose control over the whole process. Mastering this daunting challenge would require "the creation of a special wartime system of administration and control—one that would facilitate operative decision-making and policy implementation, while, at the same time, permitting Stalin and his top associates to retain a fair measure of centralized control over the war effort."[7] The Soviets succeeded spectacularly in this, pulling off an economic and organizational miracle that, along with military *matériel* and other goods convoyed to Russia by Allied merchant ships, won the war.

Fast-forwarding another twenty years, to the 1960s, one can see yet another round of innovations under way in the Soviet Union, once again in an effort to coax more efficiency and productivity out of a system that may have become too centralized during the exertions of the Great Patriotic War. Yevsey G. Liberman, a professor from Kharkov, conjured up a way to blend a variety of market mechanisms into a system still controlled to a great extent by centralized planning. Writing about it at the time, the journalist Harrison Salisbury put it this way:

> Libermanism is an effort to introduce into the Soviet system the cost-price, supply-demand features of the capitalist market economy. Liberman proposed that factory managers be given authority to fix prices and determine product mix on a competitive basis—within certain overall limits. . . . Profitability would thus enter the Soviet economic system in a fashion quite similar to that in the West. Production bonuses, salaries, wages, raw materials purchases would reflect actual market conditions rather than simulated figures prepared by economic planning commissions.[8]

These innovations worked pretty well during the heyday of Leonid Brezhnev in the late 1960s and throughout the 1970s—contrary to the caricatured criticism of this period. As Eric Hobsbawm observed, "for most Soviet citizens the Brezhnev era spelled not 'stagnation' but the best times they and their parents, or even grandparents, had ever known."[9]

Hobsbawm's assertion seems well borne out by a comparison of the gross national products of the American and Soviet economies between 1945 and 1985. At the end of World War II, U.S. GNP was more than five times the USSR's. But the Soviets steadily chipped away at the American economic lead, which was just two to one by 1965 and was whittled down just a little bit further, right up until Gorbachev's accession to power.[10] Lest Leonid Brezhnev be given all the credit for these advances, it is important to mention the role played by Nikita Khrushchev, his immediate predecessor. Khrushchev oversaw some of the important groundwork for Brezhnev's reforms by decentralizing industry in the late 1950s, declaring, as he put it, "an end to the rigid, highly centralized economic machine concentrated in Moscow," as one historian observed at the time.[11] Considering the pertinent economic data for the period, it seems there was at least some basis for Khrushchev's confident speech at the UN about Soviet economic progress, during which he bluntly asserted, "We will bury you!" Put another way, he was not being delusional.

Keeping with the regularity of the twenty-year cycles of change, Gorbachev then appeared in the 1980s to fill a yawning leadership gap that had opened during the brief rule of Yuri Andropov and his weak successor, Konstantin Chernenko. Gorbachev came from a peasant background but had a sharp legal mind and was strong enough to work his way up through the hurly-burly of the Soviet system. He immediately sought to redress some of the corrupt excesses of the Brezhnev era and to stem the financial bleeding from the policy of heavy subsidies to poor third world countries whose only merit was their willingness to side with the Soviet Union in its conflict with the West. Much of Gorbachev's conception of *perestroika,* or "restructuring," was consistent with the ideals of the NEP of the 1920s and was observationally equivalent to the policies that flowed from 1960s Libermanism. His initiatives to improve labor discipline and crack down on waste, fraud, and abuse also echoed a number of top-down initiatives taken in the 1940s during the war years. But where he differed from those who had come before him during the Soviet era was in his insistence on going beyond economic reform in search of radical political transformation. This devotion to introducing democratic processes and free speech is what, in the words of John Dunlop, "unwittingly destroyed the Soviet Union."[12] Just why this happened must be carefully considered.

If one reflects even briefly on *perestroika* and *glasnost*, their internal contradictions quickly come to mind. Both aimed at trying to reconcile complete opposites. The economic restructuring of *perestroika* sought to blend socialism—and all the state control that attends it— with market mechanisms associated with the free enterprise system. Socialism enshrines equality of outcomes while markets are more about free choice and the willingness to live with sharp class disparities. And the trouble with *glasnost* was that its emphasis on open information flows and truly democratic processes ran head-on into the hegemony of the Communist party, long the sole source of rule in the Soviet Union. Thus these efforts to create "market socialism" and "one-party democracy" were at best long shots. Adam Ulam has put the matter succinctly: "The goal Gorbachev and his advisers set before themselves was unreachable."[13] Perhaps so.

Nevertheless Gorbachev strove mightily in pursuit of both these goals, trying to find the right pace for and mix of political and economic reforms. And while his failure might not have been inevitable, the principal source of his and his movement's undoing—bureaucratic resistance—seems unsurprising. The economic and political restructuring that Gorbachev envisioned posed a mortal threat to the security and power of a wide range of institutional actors who had held sway in the Soviet Union for many decades. They were bound to fear and resist the kind of change Gorbachev was seeking. This is hardly a new dilemma, as Machiavelli observed in *The Prince*:

> And it ought to be remembered that there is nothing more difficult to take in hand, more perilous to conduct, or more uncertain in its success, than to take the lead in the introduction of a new order of things. Because the innovator has for enemies all those who have done well under the old conditions, and lukewarm defenders in those who may do well under the new. This coolness arises partly from fear of the opponents, who have the laws on their side, and partly from the incredulity of men, who do not readily believe in new things until they have had a long experience of them. Thus it happens that whenever those who are hostile have the opportunity to attack they

do it like partisans, whilst the others defend lukewarmly, in such wise that the prince is endangered along with them.[14]

Machiavelli was writing about the situation in Renaissance Italy, but his words speak just as tellingly to Gorbachev's situation during the waning days of the Soviet Union.

Whether or not Gorbachev was well versed in Machiavelli, he acted from the outset in a way that demonstrated his awareness of internal threats to his plans. He accelerated the process—begun by his mentor Yuri Andropov—of replacing members of the Politburo likely to oppose reform. By March 1987, two years into his rule, Gorbachev's "humane purge"—i.e., those ousted were pensioned off rather than imprisoned or shot—resulted in a 70 percent turnover in Politburo membership. Gorbachev was also clever in not dropping all his veils at once, keeping the reactionaries off balance as to just how much change might be ahead. He also made it quite clear that he was a true believer in communism and in the USSR itself, making it yet harder for his critics to take aim at him. When he topped all this with a clear ability to negotiate with the West, it made him even more unassailable. For a while at least.

Aside from his natural institutional enemies among the government bureaucracy—who had been reasonably well preempted—Gorbachev also had to contend with powerful populist opponents in industry and agriculture. For example, the broad-based United Russian Workers Front stood firmly against private ownership of industrial enterprises—a view well articulated by Veniamin Yarin, a charismatic rolling-mill operator—in part because its members foresaw that huge income inequalities would emerge in the wake of privatization. The USSR Peasant Union similarly opposed efforts to privatize agricultural production. In this case, though, it appears that senior union bureaucrats also played a significant role in mobilizing resistance to *perestroika* among farm workers. As Marshall Goldman has observed of the leaders of this union, their principal fear was "that a breakup of the collective and state farms would mean an end to their prerogatives and power."[15] This sort of grassroots opposition to his goals proved extremely threatening to Gorbachev as it began to "bubble up" to higher-level government officials, revitalizing his long-quiescent bureaucratic enemies at the top of the Soviet government. Gorbachev had seemingly anticipated this threat, for at the same time his quiet purge of the Politburo was under way he had also systematically replaced nearly two-thirds of the party's district secretaries throughout the USSR.[16]

Even so, popular unrest continued to grow, sometimes prompted by policies that grated on all good comrades. For example, Gorbachev restricted sales of vodka in the hope of dealing with some of the social ills and lost productivity that accompanied alcoholism. But he failed to reckon with the fact that vodka—rather than religion, as Karl Marx thought—was the true "opiate of the masses" in the Soviet Union. Vodka was also a significant source of government income, the loss or serious reduction of which would have serious consequences for the overall economy. At the time Gorbachev imposed restrictions on vodka sales, they represented about 15 percent of total state revenues. The loss of these receipts was keenly felt.

The other major sources of opposition to reform came from the military and the KGB. Both feared the inherent social disorder that would inevitably come when Gorbachev acted upon his notions of decentralizing power. The military's particular complaints, though, had more to do with falling budgets, poor treatment of personnel—in terms of housing, pay, and other benefits—and the humiliating withdrawals from the Central European territories that had been won at such terrible cost in the Great Patriotic War. But for the KGB the greater threat came from *glasnost,* which might result in "outing" some of its more nefarious Stalin-era practices. Publication of long-suppressed novels like Anatoly Rybakov's wrenching *Children of the Arbat* did just this.

It is a testament to Gorbachev's coolness under fire that, for the most part, he pressed ahead despite opposition from so many directions. He was bolstered by the belief that he had true allies in his quest, in the form of the presidents of the now semi-sovereign republics and in the Russian mass public and its ever freer press. He also had faith in the rising new breed of military officers who understood the importance of rapprochement with the outside world and of democracy at home—and who were thinking innovatively about how to provide for Soviet security with smaller, nimbler, and much less expensive forces and new doctrines.[17] He had considerable praise for the role that all three of these sets of actors played in defeating the August 1991 coup against him. As he said of local political leaders, the public, and the media:

> I must mention the position of principle and courage taken up by the people of Moscow, Leningrad and many of the regions of Russia. The position of the presidents and parliaments of the majority of the republics and local Soviets was of great significance in defeating the conspiracy. They succeeded in taking a firm stand in the defence of the rule of law and their sovereign rights. At that difficult time the majority of journalists and the media made no mistake in choosing where and with whom to be: they did not take fright or behave as cowards or curry favor with the usurpers. Efforts on the part of the plotters to give the impression that the whole country supported them were seen to be pathetic and laughable.[18]

Gorbachev had special praise for his bitter rival, Boris Yeltsin, whom he said, with some magnanimity, "took up a brave position" and "acted decisively." Of the military role in defeating the reactionaries, Gorbachev noted that:

> The conspirators tried to do the most frightful thing: to turn the Army against its own people. But this didn't work for them either. Many commanders, officers and most soldiers, whole units and other formations refused to carry out their orders. They remained true to their oath and stood side by side with the brave defenders of democracy. . . . The Army showed that it is already a different army: as a result of very difficult and painful changes brought about by *perestroika* a new army is being born in our country. And we must give it its due. If it were not the case it would have been very simple for the plotters to carry out their plans.[19]

William Odom, who has written the definitive history of the waning days of the Soviet-era military, takes a much more nuanced view. He acknowledges that many units failed to follow the orders of the coup plotters; but he also uncovers much evidence that several officers at the highest levels were playing a bureaucratic "double game" as they waited to see which side was more likely to come out on top. This was perhaps best personified by the strange week-long odyssey of General Aleksandr Lebed, who was invited by senior army leaders to prepare an assault plan for rooting Yeltsin out of the Russian White House— a request with which he initially complied. But then later Lebed, a bluff, no-nonsense paratrooper, helped Yeltsin prepare his defenses to deal with the very attack he had planned.[20] Yeltsin's memoir of these tumultuous days adds an interesting detail about Lebed urging Yeltsin to declare himself commander-in-chief of all armed forces in the territory of the Russian republic—"compelling" the military to follow him rather than obey the coup plotters. Yeltsin made this declaration the day after Lebed suggested he do so.[21]

As events unfolded, the assault on Yeltsin and his supporters was never launched, a point that tends to support Gorbachev's view of the new role of the military. Yet in the end Odom makes the argument that the Soviet military did in fact support a coup—just not the one engineered by the grey men who wanted to bring back the old ways. Instead the military sided with Boris Yeltsin, helping him consolidate his own democratic coup—one that actually brought the Soviet Union down and ushered in the rise of Russia.[22]

In an odd way, then, it was the long-simmering ethnic tensions that had bedeviled the USSR that now played a key role in its dissolution. But the Soviet Union was not destroyed by the approximately twenty armed ethnonationalist movements around the Soviet periphery that were fomenting revolt against Moscow.[23] Rather, the USSR was humbled by the nationalistic aspirations of the largest and most powerful ethnic group in the empire—the Russians themselves. It was, as John Dunlop has argued, the rise of Russia that destroyed the Soviet empire. And the greatest symbol of and spokesperson for reborn Russian nationalism was the long-exiled literary giant Alexander

Solzhenitsyn, whose pamphlet *Rebuilding Russia* found followers across the social spectrum, from the military to the masses and on to disaffected intellectuals. Solzhenitsyn's basic message was that the USSR "had no future as a unitary state."[24] Yeltsin agreed with him for the most part, and soon after his accession to power the Soviet Union died.

But just because the Soviet empire did dissolve does not mean that it had to come apart. At least one thoughtful observer, David Pryce-Jones, saw the end of the Soviet Union as hardly inevitable; rather, it was "strange and unexpected."[25] To be sure, the late 1980s were a time of social travail and even more economic pain for the Russians. Yet the USSR could have kept ticking along. As in earlier crises, the situation could have been bettered by the introduction of economic reforms—just like earlier ones that had been undertaken throughout Soviet history, from the New Economic Policy of the 1920s to the innovative forms of "war communism" of the 1940s, and on to the "Liberman-ism" of the 1960s. It would not have been pretty but, as Adam Smith once noted about the resilience of states under economic pressure, "there is much ruin in a nation." But Gorbachev went beyond economic tinkering to introduce sweeping political reforms that soon threatened to bring the whole system down. He chose to pursue radical social change when it was not completely necessary and did so in the face of obviously strong and ever-growing opposition.

Gorbachev should be seen in the same light as other great "Westernizing" leaders in Russian history who also sought political change. The first and most important of these was Peter the Great, who ruled Russia from 1689 to 1725.[26] Peter was deeply concerned about the insularity and insufficiency of existing governance in his country, and sought to change matters very nearly single-handedly. He traveled extensively in Western Europe to study the workings of advanced economies. He also took a great deal of time to learn about shipbuilding, an obsession that led him eventually to build a navy along with the city of St. Petersburg, which he envisioned as a great port city on the Baltic that would give him a window on the West. It became Russia's new capital as well, symbolizing his emphasis on Westernization.

In domestic policy, Peter followed a consistent strategy of trying to decentralize power. In a country that had tended toward the concentration of power since the absolutist rule of Ivan the Terrible centuries earlier, this posed some stiff challenges, which have been carefully analyzed by the historian Bernard Pares. For example, Peter's effort to separate civil administration from the judiciary failed. But he had his successes. In consultation with Leibniz the philosopher, Peter advanced the idea of "ministerial colleges in which no single person had an absolute control"—a profound reform that greatly increased the efficiency of the state bureaucracy.[27] To help nurture the private sector and the process of commercial development, Peter also gave the merchant class some powers of self-government in the form of elected local leaders and assemblies. Needless to say, this engendered resistance among Russia's ruling aristocracy.

Thus Peter soon had to fight and overcome opposition from the powerful *boyars*—the apparatchiks and oligarchs of his time. He sometimes had to act quite ruthlessly, even allowing his own son to be convicted of treason for engaging in intrigues with them.[28] As for Russia itself, Peter's innovations did manage to outlast his lifetime, though soon after his death government offices began migrating back to Moscow from St. Petersburg, and policies and laws began to reflect latent resistance to rather than an open embrace of Western-style reforms. Yet there was much that endured, despite what Pares has described as "a series of talentless, vulgar and mostly foreign successors." Pares's final judgment on Peter was that "the structure of the State as he left it [in 1725] was in substance to remain until the revolution of 1917."[29]

Alexander II, who ruled Russia from 1855 to 1881, was Muscovy's second great modernizer. He came to power when his father, Nicholas I, died in the middle of the Crimean War (1853–1856), a conflict in which France and Britain aligned with the Ottoman Empire in an effort to reduce Russian influence in the Balkans. The course of field operations during the war made it clear to Alexander that Russia's armed forces were generally antiquated, leading him to infer that perhaps Russian society and industry were well behind the times.[30] He

soon sought to rectify matters, embarking upon a series of investments in railroad expansion and other aspects of industrial development and military reform. Alexander was also sensitive to the need for
social modernization: in 1861 he freed the serfs, dealing a staggering
blow to landed interests in Russia and to the feudalism that had served
them so well for centuries. At the level of local governance, he began
to nurture democratic practices while his central government began
to follow the policy of *glasnost* (the name he gave to this more open approach to the flow of information) that brought some previously se-
cretive decision-making into the open.

Alexander's foreign policy was equally innovative, beginning with
his decision to treat occupied Poland far more leniently than his predecessors had. The Poles immediately seized the opportunity to seek
their independence—as they would again in the 1980s when Gorbachev gave them the chance—but, in contrast to his successor a century later, he put the Poles down firmly. On the broader world stage,
he maintained the balance of power skillfully during the U.S. Civil
War, helping keep the British from intervening on the side of the
Confederacy. As Alexander saw it, the United States was the key
counterweight to overweening British power in the world and could
not be allowed to break apart. Russia was then engaged in an ongoing
cold war with Britain in central Asia—what Kipling would eventually
label the "Great Game"—and the breakup of the United States
would only give Britain a freer hand in dealing with Russia.[31]

Alexander's sweeping changes, like Peter's, engendered much resentment, both from those whose interests were threatened and from
a newly awakened intelligentsia that had grown ever more critical of
the whole notion of continued tsarist rule. So the great reformer soon
became a frequent target of assassination attempts, during which he
time and again demonstrated great courage. Even so, the continual
threats to his life did goad Alexander into rolling back some of his lib-
eralizing initiatives—which infuriated the intelligentsia even more.
Finally, in 1881, terrorists from the "People's Will" faction staged a
bombing in which Alexander was mortally wounded. In the years after his death, reactionaries took hold—much as they had tried after

Peter's death—and did manage to unravel many of his reforms. As Bernard Pares observed: "The bomb that killed Alexander put an end to the faint beginnings of Russian constitutionalism."[32] Yet this authoritarian reaction only fed greater unrest that broke out in 1905—on the heels of Russia's losing war with Japan—and then turned into the full-blown revolution of 1917, amid the chaos of World War I, that ushered in communism.

These earlier attempts at Westernization by Russian reformers seem eerily similar to Gorbachev's policies. Peter, Alexander, and Gorbachev all sought to reduce corruption and restructure their economies to achieve higher levels of efficiency. They all sought better relations with the West, and to emulate the West in ways that went beyond technology to include embracing liberal ideas and values. While Gorbachev enjoyed being compared with Peter, the similarities between him and Alexander go much further, as both were deeply committed to fostering democratic institutions and openness at home, and both sought to establish warm relations with the United States.[33] Beyond helping to keep Britain out of the American Civil War, Alexander smoothed relations with the United States in the North Pacific—a region where both countries had commercial fishing interests and where territorial issues had some potential to generate friction. In 1867 Alexander sold Alaska to the Americans. For Gorbachev's part, reducing tensions with the United States became the necessary first step in protecting his external flank while he dealt with the Soviet Union's internal problems.[34] For this strategy to have any chance of success, he needed above all good working relations with Ronald Reagan.

Like many able strategists, Gorbachev did not go after his objective head-on. Instead he took an indirect approach to Reagan by first introducing himself and his ideas to the West in a December 1984 visit to Britain. Although Gorbachev was still a few months away from being made general secretary of the Communist party, this trip to meet Prime Minister Margaret Thatcher took on all the trappings of a full-blown summit. Gorbachev and Thatcher hit it off from the start, as he convinced her that he was a man with whom, as she put it, the West "could do business."[35] Shortly after her meetings with this lively new Soviet leader who appreciated Savile Row suits and had a bright, outspoken Western-style politician's wife, Thatcher left for Washington to give Reagan a glowing report about him.

Gorbachev's opening gambit in Great Britain paid off handsomely as he had four major summit meetings with Reagan—one a year during the U.S. president's second term. Each built upon progress made in the preceding meeting. Taken together, they had an enormous cumulative impact on world affairs, ending the arms race and reducing the fear and hatred that had fueled the cold war. At Geneva in September 1985, the two men took each other's measure and liked what they saw. They met again in October of the next year in Iceland, discovering and appreciating their mutual abhorrence of nuclear weapons and of the illogical war-fighting strategies that went with them. At the conclusion of the Reykjavik summit, Reagan and Gorbachev went so far as to call for the abolition of nuclear weapons—to which the latter added a demand to cease all research into missile defense as well, a thrust that quickly went awry. Both their sets of advisers were appalled by the leap their leaders had made together and tried to frog-march them back a bit.

But both Reagan and Gorbachev were determined to continue to work together to make the world less nuclear. Both had seen the catastrophic effects of the Chernobyl nuclear reactor accident in the Ukraine in April 1986 as a sobering reminder that the use of nuclear weapons in conflict would wreak havoc on an unacceptably large scale. Thus they took a concrete step toward creating that "less nuclear" world in their December 1987 summit in Washington, where they agreed to abolish intermediate-range nuclear weapons. This issue had come close to poisoning Soviet-American relations earlier in the eighties. It had terrified many Europeans, who saw in such shorter-range weapons—to be deployed in their countries—an American design to fight a nuclear war while keeping the territory of the United States out of the target zone. Yet by the time of their final summit, held in

Moscow in the spring of 1988, almost all their differences had been worked out and Reagan was ready to say, to Gorbachev and the rest of the world, that the Soviet Union was no longer an "evil empire."

It was this reduction in mutual antipathy that ended the cold war and made possible Gorbachev's attempt to transform Soviet society. Such a sea change in relations can hardly be accounted for by thinking in terms of the classical considerations of *realpolitik*. For throughout the Reagan years both sides remained armed to the teeth, the Soviets continued a vicious fight in a country they had invaded (Afghanistan), and the United States was vigorously pursuing missile defenses that would, if they ever became operational, completely undermine the security strategy of the USSR. Yet during these same years Reagan and Gorbachev reached out to each other, pulling one another, and the world with them, back from the abyss. As Dinesh D'Souza has put it in his biography of Ronald Reagan, "no two other men could have produced the same result."[36]

To be sure, others like Margaret Thatcher, Lech Walesa, Vaclav Havel, and Pope John Paul II played important roles in Reagan's "war of ideas" against the Soviet Union. But in the end it was less a war of ideas and more a meeting of like minds that brought an end to what psychologist Ralph White called a pathology of "exaggerated fears and pride" that had fueled the cold war.[37] Interestingly, the ancient historian Thucydides also saw pride and fear as the key causes of the three-decade-long Peloponnesian War between democratic Athens and the very authoritarian Sparta more than two millennia earlier. It seems that individuals' beliefs matter more than any seemingly restrictive path that follows Tolstoy's ideas about "great tides of events," or Karl Marx's notions of "historical inevitability."

Beyond Reagan, Gorbachev, and the other heads of state and spiritual leaders who helped bring about peace, special mention should also be made of the American secretary of state, George Shultz, and Soviet Foreign Minister Eduard Shevardnadze. These two men had the daunting task of implementing the agreements that Reagan and Gorbachev reached. It was they who had to deal with the bureaucratic impedimenta that accompany and bedevil modern statecraft. Both men succeeded in this and went well beyond simply following the lead of their bosses. They developed a strong personal relationship with each other, and in their many contacts originated new lines of diplomatic reasoning that would soon be exploited to drive their countries' policies in more sensible, peace-enhancing directions.

A particularly important moment in the Shultz-Shevardnadze relationship came in the spring of 1987 when Shultz was visiting Moscow. After a mid-day session with Shevardnadze, Shultz had attended a Passover seder with Soviet Jews who were being denied permission to emigrate from the USSR (the so-called refuseniks). Then he went back to meet with Shevardnadze later that same evening—the seder having put human rights in the forefront of his mind. Shultz asked for and got a private meeting with Shevardnadze and Anatoly Dobrynin, the former Soviet ambassador to the United States. In the meeting, Shultz took a new tack in trying to persuade rather than coerce the Russians:

> I told Shevardnadze I had listened carefully to his comments and wanted to develop for him why a changed approach to human rights "was in the Soviet interest." I then went through carefully a line of argument in which I believed firmly and had introduced briefly, from a different perspective, to Gorbachev in the Kremlin in November 1985. I argued that the economic progress the Soviets sought from what they called "radical reforms" could not be achieved "unless the Soviet system is changed sharply, in ways that stimulate the creativity and drive of individuals. In the information age, success will come to societies that are open and decentralized and provide lots of room for individual initiative. Countries throughout the world are seeing this truth . . . [and] a society like yours is going to find, I believe, that the economic well-being of its people is likely to diminish to the extent that human rights are restricted."[38]

By Passover the next year, all of the refuseniks with whom Shultz met had been allowed to emigrate. In September 1989, after Shultz had left office, he and his wife dined in New York with the Shevardnadzes. Shultz asked Shevardnadze if he remembered their private conversation in Moscow. He answered: "Oh yes. I went over the notes carefully with Gorbachev and others in the leadership. What you said had a profound impact."[39]

The acute pressures that drove Gorbachev to craft a strategy aimed at reforming and revitalizing the Soviet Union do seem to fall in line, at least on some level, with Tolstoy's and Marx's notions about the larger movements in, or forces of, history. For example, the very basis of the USSR was an economic construct—communism—that ran fully counter to the foundations of market-based economic thought and practice. This factor alone suggests an enduring tension and a recurring need to tinker with the system. *Perestroika* could simply be seen as a part of a regularly required corrective pattern, as an updated New Economic Policy or a new form of 1960s-era "Libermanism." In short, reform and restructuring were processes that had to be undertaken periodically because of the very structure of the state.

Another important point along these lines about "forces of history" is that Russia is a divided "border empire," eternally riven by East-West tensions. Even though it nudges up to the West in Europe, it is at heart a land of the East. And despite the fact that most of its landmass and natural resources are in the East, the vast majority of its population lives in the West and develops its intellectual capital along Western lines. Yet those who have had the most profound impact on Russia have been the Eastern empires: the Byzantines and the Mongols. So it goes, as Eastern and Western influences have tugged continually back and forth throughout Russian history—and continue to do so today. It is not hard to see how Russia evolved a system of never-ending pulling and hauling between these disparate, almost always conflicting, influences.

Seen in this light, Peter, Alexander, and Gorbachev become archetypal examples of Thomas Carlyle's notion of the "great men" who try to take hold of history and move it by their force of will. Each succeeded in some ways—even Gorbachev who bloodlessly shrugged off the outer lining of a now unprofitable empire and conducted a social revolution at home. And this latest revolution is one from which Russia may well emerge stronger in the years to come. This last point was foreseen back in 1988 by Seweryn Bialer—once Khrushchev's principal speechwriter—and the American scholar Michael Mandelbaum:

> The consequences, in some cases unintended ones, of Gorbachev's changes thus may make the Soviet Union, from the Western point of view, a less forbidding and so less threatening place. The reforms could conceivably, however, have the opposite effect. Gorbachev's aim, after all, is to make the Soviet Union a vibrant, powerful, attractive country. Such a development could worsen the global rivalry by making Moscow better able to pursue goals that the United States opposes.[40]

The point is that post-Communist Russia may recover its power and exercise its renewed influence in ways that may actually threaten American interests in the future. Such a development would be very much in line with Theda Skocpol's theory that social revolutions sometimes occur simply because the nation-state itself occasionally needs "to burn away the undergrowth" by this means in order to revitalize itself.[41] The situation in Russia during the presidency of Vladimir Putin may have borne her ideas out, as the "controlled crash" engineered by Gorbachev—two decades after—has led to both a somewhat more democratic and certainly a more prosperous Russia. For the Russian nation has survived the loss of its foreign satellites and sister republics. The economy has recovered from the excesses of *perestroika* and the ruthless pillage of the country's key resources and infrastructure by so-called "oligarchs" during Yeltsin's presidency. Finally, the great diplomatic and military capabilities of the state are once again beginning to be asserted on the world stage—sometimes in ways that overtly oppose U.S. interests. As H. G. Wells put it, when alluding to modern Germany's travails in his *Outline of History,* "a great nation suffers, but does not die." So it is with Russia.

All this said, the cyclical need to patch and mend the economy scarcely required the overthrow of the entire system of governance in the Soviet Union. Dissolution of the USSR was not inevitable. Zbigniew Brzezinski observed it quite well back in 1989 when he noted that the end of communism was "almost as probable as the notion that it will endure."[42] It was a critical time, he meant, but one in which a continuance of the Soviet regime was still a likely outcome—just as likely as the path actually taken. Dinesh D'Souza also saw the end of the USSR as being very far from foreordained: "[T]he economic argument cannot explain why the empire collapsed when it did, when the Soviet Union was previously able to sustain itself in the face of comparable—and in some cases worse—economic conditions."[43]

An additional factor must also have been at work, one prompting Gorbachev to undertake the risky, radical, and ultimately transformational changes that were so closely akin to those attempted by tsars Peter and Alexander in their respective efforts to Westernize Russia. In Gorbachev's case that additional factor was the easing of tensions between Washington and Moscow. With his external flank secured against overt threats, he could operate freely at home. This he did, unleashing powerful social forces that he simply could not control. These elemental social forces are neatly personified by the example of Andrei Sakharov, the dissident nuclear scientist and political progressive, who had been kept in "internal exile" for years. When Gorbachev allowed him to come home from Gorky, Adam Ulam observes, "Sakharov returned to a triumphant reception in Moscow. While declaring his support for *perestroika,* he also demanded the release of all political prisoners and an end to the Soviet military intervention in Afghanistan."[44] The policy of openness thus helped make the system work better but, as the Sakharov case shows, also unleashed forces that strained the system's social fabric still further.

If the rapprochement with the United States made *perestroika* possible, it is among the greatest ironies of history. For it turned out that one of the two major adversaries in the decades-long, globe-girdling cold war imploded because of a *reduction* in tensions. There is simply no other case quite like this to be found in any era. The irony of the situation deepens when one considers that this happened during Ronald Reagan's presidency. Reagan came into office believing—along with the rest of the world—that the West had been doing poorly in the cold war and that get-tough policies were needed. But he also believed in his own ability to alter the course of this conflict profoundly. He knew that from his "bully pulpit" he could engage the Soviet leadership directly while simultaneously addressing his own people and the publics of the countries of the international community. This he believed would afford him his best chance of fostering real change in the world. That he succeeded in doing so was a major surprise, as much to observers in the West as in the East. John Lewis Gaddis, the great historian of the cold war, said about the impact of "the unexpected Reagan":

> The task of the historian is, very largely, one of explaining how we got from where we were to where we are today. To say that the Reagan administration's policy toward the Soviet Union is going to pose special challenges to historians is to understate the matter: rarely has there been a greater gap between the expectations held for an administration at the beginning of its term and the results it actually produced. The last thing one would have anticipated at the time Ronald Reagan took office in 1981 was that he would use his eight years in the White House to bring about the most significant improvement in Soviet-American relations since the end of World War II. I am not at all sure that President Reagan himself foresaw this result. And yet, that is precisely what happened, with—admittedly—a good deal of help from Mikhail Gorbachev.[45]

So it seems that one puzzle has been solved, but only by prompting us to consider another one. The Soviet Union did not blow up simply because it had to. Instead its dissolution was the product of choices made by a great man who decided to take even greater risks with his own and his country's future. But Gorbachev's willingness to play for the highest stakes was almost completely contingent upon gaining the reassurance he needed from Ronald Reagan that the United States had no desire to take actions that would in any way threaten the fundamental interests of the USSR.

That Reagan was able to convince Gorbachev of his sincere good intentions seems nothing short of miraculous, for the Soviet leader initially saw the idea of protracted summitry with Reagan as fraught with risk and unlikely to generate breakthroughs—because the American president was so "ideological." The first day of their first summit seemed to bear out his fears, as Gorbachev recalled that each man was quickly reduced to political posturing. But on the second day they finally began to "speak from the heart." As Gorbachev related the decisive moment,

> I realized by the end our two-day meeting that Ronald Reagan too was a man "you could do business with" . . . we were still clinging to our antagonistic positions, [b]ut the "human factor" had quietly come into action. We both sensed that we must maintain contact and try to avoid a break.[46]

Whatever "forces of history" had brought the two together, Gorbachev clearly states for the record that it was the personal connection between him and Reagan that made possible what followed over the next few years—a series of mutual decisions, agreements, and new policies that recast the world system.

The closest historical parallel to this kind of personal interaction at such a high level of state is the case of Winston Churchill's 1912 overture to Kaiser Wilhelm at the height of the Anglo-German antagonism. Churchill called openly for "taking a holiday" from the naval arms race in dreadnought battleships that was going on at the time. In this instance the kaiser took Churchill's overture as a sign of weakness and decided to redouble his efforts to overtake the British. World War I was soon in the offing.

Unlike Churchill and the kaiser seventy-five years earlier, Reagan and Gorbachev refused to see weaknesses to be exploited; rather, they chose to work together to end a long, bitter conflict, to reduce the shadow cast by nuclear weapons, and to free tens of millions of people from totalitarian rule. Both men deserve much of the credit for this, but it was Reagan's role in creating maneuvering room for his opposite number that proved to be the key ingredient.[47] As Gaddis implies, it was this "unexpected Reagan" who substantially shaped the post–cold war world that soon emerged in his wake.

4

Confronting the Perils of Proliferation

The nature of the "unthinkable" has changed radically. During the cold war, it meant the possibility that salvos of hundreds or even thousands of nuclear warheads would be fired in any major conflict—either wittingly or out of hypervigilant fear of surprise attack. Countless millions would die, civilization would grind to a halt, and even the global environment would likely be mortally wounded in such an exchange. Thanks to the arms reduction process initiated by Ronald Reagan and embraced by his successors in office, this particular variant of Armageddon no longer worries us.

Instead our concerns now cluster around the possibility of one or a few weapons of mass destruction being used for malign purposes by a mad tyrant or a terrorist. While the sheer amount of carnage created by this new threat would be but a shadow of what might have been in a total nuclear war, the prospect of such an incident is far more chilling because of its greater likelihood. Even at the height of the cold war, neither Russian nor American leaders would likely ever have chosen to "go first" in an apocalyptic confrontation, given that the deadliest retaliation would have inevitably followed. But today a dictator with nothing to lose by raising the stakes, or a terrorist with no territory of his own that could be targeted for retaliation, would be far more likely to use these ultimate weapons if he ever came into possession of them.[1]

The assumption of there being a greater propensity among some types of actors to use such weapons overturns most of the strategic logic built up over the past half century. For example, arsenal size becomes almost meaningless. When Russian and American military planners slaved over complex calculations of "first-strike survivability" and "hard-target kill capability," they acted on the belief that even small variances in force ratios could have huge effects—what Albert Wohlstetter once called "the delicate balance of terror." And yet, as his RAND colleague Bernard Brodie had observed before him, neither side had any real coercive bargaining power due to the inescapable threat of retaliation, a situation that would come to be known as "mutual assured destruction" (MAD).[2]

But in a world replete with stateless terror networks there can be no such "balance." If a terrorist comes into possession of even one nuclear warhead, he will immediately have a huge capacity to issue demands with every expectation that they will be met. This would be the case with only one qualifier: that the terrorist's target actually believed the nuclear blackmailer had such a weapon. Nothing else weakens his position, as the terrorist escapes the classical numbers game simply by not having a home territory against which retaliation can be credibly threatened. Simply put, if al Qaeda comes into possession of nuclear weapons, its various demands for the withdrawal of U.S. forces from parts of the Muslim world would likely be met—as we would have no reasonable retaliatory threat.

The situation for the leader of a rogue state is a bit more complicated—in that he has a country that can be "rubble-ized" in retaliation—but he too may prove able to slip the bonds of traditional nuclear force-on-force calculations. One strategy would be to engage in conventional aggression, most likely a swift campaign of conquest aimed at presenting the world with a fait accompli, then threaten to escalate to the nuclear level in order to deter a counterintervention. This type of problem would have been highlighted in 1990 had Saddam

Hussein been in possession of a nuclear deterrent before his invasion of Kuwait. A similar situation could develop in the future on the Korean peninsula should the North ever elect to launch a conventional offensive to occupy Seoul, other border areas, or even all of the South. In this case, possession of even a few nuclear weapons by the regime in Pyongyang would greatly complicate American decision-making about how to respond properly to an act of conventional aggression backed up by nuclear threats.

Another strategy—open in this case to any nuclear power, not just to small rogue states—would be to try to attack anonymously. The aggressor would likely use the same sorts of delivery means that terrorists employ (e.g., trucks, tramp steamers), in an effort to avoid leaving a telltale trail that would lead inexorably to retaliation. This anonymous approach to conflict was anticipated by the science-fiction writer Frederik Pohl in his chilling 1979 classic, *The Cool War*. In Pohl's dystopian world the great powers, fearful of direct nuclear confrontations, *all* make war in this secret fashion. Yet another troubling variant would be to make an attack look like the work of an innocent third-party country or group, fomenting a larger war out of such an incident.[3] Least likely would be simply to pass a nuclear device—or biological weaponry—to a private third party. This would engender a blackmail risk, as the terrorists in question could either threaten to expose the handoff or to use the weapons against those who had armed them in the first place.

In short, the threat posed to the twenty-first-century world by weapons of mass destruction may have diminished in overall scale, but this reduction is more than offset by the increasing propensity to use such weapons—and the huge coercive power enjoyed by those who come into possession of them. This means that it is now possible to think in terms of the rise of a "nuclear Napoleon." Where enthusiasts among the professional military—air force General Curtis LeMay being the archetype—all failed to make the case that nuclear weapons could be mastered like any others, it may now fall to a terrorist in some remote cave to craft the first truly usable nuclear warfighting doctrine.[4] A mind-numbing thought.

Thus the central question to be considered in this chapter revolves around the role Reagan played in trying to head off this dark nuclear future, not to mention its biological weapons counterpart. Whether and to what extent Reagan's ideas about making the world "less nuclear" still obtain and continue to inform security policy and strategy will, of course, be considered as well. Reagan's ideas about both making arms reductions and crafting strategic defenses to ward off mass destruction will necessarily form a large part of the discussion. But it is his view of proliferation itself—specifically about how to prevent or otherwise cope with the spread of such weapons—that must first be scrutinized.

The problems posed by proliferation of weapons of mass destruction can be approached in three basic ways. First is the diffusion of nuclear weapons to other countries—what is generally called "horizontal" proliferation. Next comes the matter of trying to control the sheer numbers of such weapons that are being produced and deployed—"vertical" proliferation. Last are concerns that relate to the introduction of innovative new types of mass destructive weapons and delivery systems. I call this third aspect of the problem "diagonal" proliferation, as it forms a distinct kind of activity that may be on the rise even when overall numbers of weapons are falling, or even after some nations may have renounced nuclear weapons (as, for example, Libya did in 2004). Thus the whole issue area can be described along three axes, as seen in Figure 8. But let us first consider these three aspects of proliferation in order, from horizontal to vertical to diagonal, then try to depict Reagan's counterproliferation strategies, their impact at the time, and their continuing consequences for the twenty-first-century world.

After the United States introduced nuclear weapons to the world in its attacks on Hiroshima and Nagasaki at the end of World War II, serious efforts were made by the nascent United Nations to prevent the spread of such weapons. American security policymakers, though generally sympathetic to this goal, refused to place the then-tiny U.S.

Figure 8.   The Three Dimensions of Proliferation

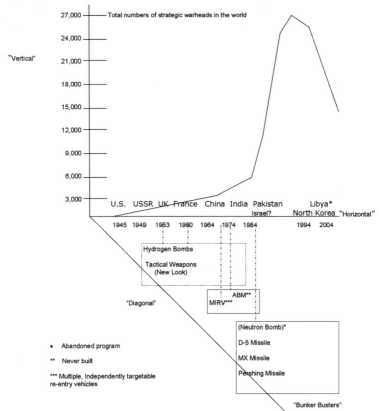

arsenal under international control in return for the rest of the world's promises to eschew the pursuit of nuclear weapons. As a result, other nations began to develop their own arsenals. The openly acknowledged nuclear club expanded to include the Soviet Union (1949), Britain (1953), France (1960), China (1964), India (1974), and Pakistan (1994).[5] Israel is a nuclear power as well—fielding, according to some accounts, an arsenal that grew from a few warheads in the late 1960s to several hundred today—but has never openly declared its status.[6] The North Koreans claim to have a small arsenal of their own—and it is believed that at least since 1994 they have had some sort of nuclear weapons capacity.[7]

In the late 1940s, when it became clear that an international-community-based solution would not be achieved, the notion of launching a preventive war began to generate considerable interest. Under presidents Truman and Eisenhower, plans were developed to take military action—with nuclear weapons—against the Soviet Union before it could develop a sizable arsenal of its own.[8] In Eisenhower's view, the costs and risks of failing to act preventively—i.e., allowing an enemy to become armed with weapons of mass destruction—might be prohibitive. Viewed this way, the problem might be one where, as he put it, "we would be forced to consider whether or not our duty to future generations did not require us to initiate war at the most propitious moment we could designate."[9]

This preventive-war option was debated back and forth for quite some time, but Eisenhower finally decided, in the fall of 1954, that it was simply not in the American character to engage in such attacks.[10] Instead he decided to rely upon deterrence as the principal pillar of security against other nuclear powers, though he was not at all reluctant to make direct nuclear threats in response to acts of conventional aggression. This was the so-called doctrine of "massive retaliation" which, as Thomas Schelling has observed of it, "was in decline almost from its enunciation in 1954."[11] It was a doctrine that had little credibility when aimed at non-nuclear states and even less when considered for use against those who had nuclear weapons of their own. In the latter case, having an adversary that could be "destroyed but not disarmed"—one capable of retaliating even while suffering its own death throes—sounded the death knell of "massive" responses and the birth of mutual deterrence.

Even though the attempt to put nuclear arms under international control had failed and the United States had chosen not to use its preeminent position in the world to wage preventive war, some good things were happening to slow the horizontal spread of atomic weapons. In 1967 the Non-Proliferation Treaty took effect, with sixty-two nations quickly signing on to it. An overwhelming majority of the nations of the world are signatories today—a real triumph in the struggle against the spread of nuclear arms. Several cases of quiet diplomacy have resulted in nations choosing to end their own proliferation efforts, the best-known being South Africa, Brazil, Argentina—all influenced by the Reagan administration—and, most recently, Libya. Attempts to link Reagan to the rollback of Argentina's nuclear weapons program have tried to show a darker side, alleging that he somehow duped that country's military junta into attacking the Falkland Islands in 1982. The idea is that Reagan knew the Argentines would lose the ensuing war, assumed the junta would fall, and believed that the democratic government that would subsequently come to power would end its nuclear weapons program. A fascinating notion (are we really that smart?) but one with insufficient evidentiary support.[12]

Overall the world's record in dealing with the lateral spread of nuclear weapons has been pretty good—with two troubling exceptions. The first is Pakistan, an unstable Muslim country that has, since its inception in 1947, veered dangerously between democracy and dictatorship. It has also fought several losing wars with India. In the wake of its defeat in the 1971 conflict that lost East Pakistan (which became Bangladesh) Pakistan decided to develop nuclear weapons. Little progress was made in this effort until a decade later when the Reagan administration decided to cultivate Pakistan as a haven for Afghan guerrillas resisting Soviet occupation. In return for Pakistani help in the fight against the Russians, the U.S. government, for the most part, "looked the other way" while Pakistan moved ahead with its nuclear weapons program. As the Reagan administration's official report on foreign policy strategy at the time put it, very softly:

> Pakistan has been developing a nuclear capability. The United States is concerned by this development because of our opposition to the proliferation of nuclear weapons among nations. However, we believe that we should use quiet diplomacy to indicate our concerns, rather than cut off bilateral assistance.[13]

Needless to say, quiet diplomacy failed, and the Pakistanis eventually succeeded in building a small but functional nuclear arsenal of their own. In the current war on terror the fate of Pakistan has thus become crucially important to efforts to keep its nuclear weapons out of the hands of terrorists. The failure of the Reagan administration to stop Pakistani proliferation may also have spawned the equally nettlesome North Korean nuclear dilemma. For it was A. Q. Khan, the father of Pakistan's weapons program, who turned out to be the hub of a clandestine international nuclear proliferation network that for many years funneled materials to rogue regimes like that in Pyongyang.[14] Even today, parts of the network still operate, continuing to provide assistance to Iran and other suspected proliferators.

For all his positive contributions to arms control, Reagan must still bear some responsibility in these cases. His willingness, in the name of *realpolitik,* to court Pakistan's support for an insurgency had the practical consequence of allowing the further spread of nuclear weapons to one of the most volatile areas on the planet. As to whether looking the other way while Pakistan proliferated was worth it, in terms of keeping the Afghan *mujahideen* on their feet against the Russians, former Senator John Glenn had this to say some years later:

> We not only turned a blind eye. . . . In some cases, we even abetted what they were doing by following up with additional sales and not cutting off shipments of things—of equipment—and not stopping the flow of technology, which American law says we have to do. How could it be in our best interest, no matter what our requirements were for shipping through Pakistan into Afghanistan during that war, or whatever? There certainly was a far, far greater danger here in Pakistan's efforts to get nuclear weapons than there was in what we were opposing in Afghanistan.[15]

Beyond the nuclear realm, Reagan also made a similar choice with Iraq. During the 1980s the Iraqis were involved in a long conflict with Iran, a war whose outcome bore sharply upon American interests in the Persian Gulf region. To preserve the local balance of power, the Reagan administration tilted toward Iraq, providing intelligence and other forms of support. Some of this assistance came in the form of direct military action, as in Operation Earnest Will, a campaign that defended commercial shipping against Iranian light coastal forces, and which included navy SEAL raids on forward outposts from which their attacks were being launched.[16] But perhaps the most telling support came, as with Pakistan, from an American willingness to look the other way as the Iraqis developed and used chemical weapons to restore their faltering fortunes on the conventional battlefields of the war.

The apparent imperatives of power politics led the Reagan administration to suffer yet another serious breach in the wall of its nonproliferation policy.

With regard to vertical proliferation, Ronald Reagan's overall impact, both during his presidency and upon our world today, is far more positive. Although he initially faced Russian recalcitrance, by the end of his second term the path back from the nuclear brink had been identified and was carefully followed. The initial problem had been caused by Reagan's dogged devotion to missile defense, a matter discussed in detail later in this chapter. But the clear, sensible solution to the arms race—to begin making reductions—was not lost on the Soviets, and because of Reagan today's strategic arsenals are less than half their levels at the height of the nuclear rivalry.

Both Reagan and Gorbachev were fierce "reduction hawks," going so far as to become joint spokespersons for the nascent nuclear abolition movement. They began speaking out along these lines at their Reykjavik summit in October 1986 and soon had their respective advisers pitching fits in protest. In Gorbachev's official statement at the press conference at the end of the summit meeting, he clarified that he and Reagan were committed to abolition but only after years of deep reductions and with "triple verification."[17] For his part, Reagan noted afterward that Gorbachev's willingness to discuss abolition was probably part of a gambit to derail missile defense research. This thought angered Reagan but did not get in the way of his continuing determination to push "for an agreement to ban nuclear weapons."[18]

Of all his ideas about making the world less nuclear, Reagan's fundamental devotion to nuclear abolition remains most relevant—perhaps most seductive—today. The abolition argument has many compelling aspects, the most important of which is that, if successful, it would virtually eliminate the problem of "loose nukes" falling into the hands of terrorists. From an American strategic perspective, abolition would also guarantee U.S. military primacy. Absent any weapons of mass destruction, American air and naval mastery would truly usher in a new world order unattainable while others still possess even a few nuclear weapons. In short, a world without weapons of mass destruction would be incontestably an American-led world.

Yet there are also reasons why abolition should still be viewed with great caution and concern. The most obvious is that a cheater could achieve world mastery if everyone else disarmed and he did not. Imagine, at the conclusion of the abolition process, that Russia (or any other nuclear country) announced that it had secreted away a few hundred warheads in order to ensure "reasonable" behavior by the United States and others. The risk of this happening means that verification of total nuclear disarmament would require the most intrusive, open-ended inspection regime ever devised. While not impossible to achieve, such a high-reliability approach to monitoring would undoubtedly prove both difficult and unendingly nerve-racking.

Before zero levels were reached at the end of abolition process, the period of drawdowns would also be unstable. The concept of mutual assured destruction is easy to understand when each side has thousands of warheads. But when both have only a few hundred, each is far more vulnerable to a disabling first strike by the other side. Even a well-intentioned reduction process could unwittingly undermine both deterrence and crisis stability. The period of deep reductions could also be a tempting time for some countries, allowing them an easy chance to achieve true parity with the leading nuclear powers. The nuclear era has been characterized as a Russo-American duopoly—that is, the two have always accounted for more than 90 percent of the world's nuclear weapons—100 percent between 1945 and 1953.[19] If the United States and Russia were to reduce their arsenals to the few hundreds, it might prove an irresistible temptation to others to keep what they had—since the two leading nuclear powers would have retreated to their level. Even more troubling, some advanced countries without such weapons might find the prospect of almost immediate equality with the "leaders" very attractive. Think of Germany or Japan, or any number of other advanced industrialized countries that might find such a move in the interest of their "strategic independence."[20]

The point here is that Reagan began a process of reducing the numbers of nuclear weapons that were the crux of the world's most difficult strategic dilemma. Reagan made it abundantly clear that he believed in abolition, which placed him squarely in line with the intentions of the framers of the Non-Proliferation Treaty. By the terms of that agreement, signatories agreed to forgo development of nuclear weapons, in return for which those who already had them agreed to strive for their elimination. Reagan believed in following both the letter and the spirit of the treaty, and stewards of American foreign policy in the twenty-first century can do little better than to follow the trail he blazed. But, as I have suggested above, the path should be followed with great care, given the surprisingly destabilizing consequences of the final round of deep reductions that comes at the end of the trail.

On balance, Reagan's record at dealing with vertical proliferation is quite strong. He did very well at engineering agreements to reduce the sheer numbers of weapons of mass destruction—and provided the world a blueprint for the abolition process. This was far better than the desultory results of his administration's efforts to control the horizontal spread of nuclear weapons—which saw Pakistan making huge strides toward attaining its own atomic arsenal and then seeding the North Korean program. In the realm of chemical weapons, reasons of state encouraged a willingness to allow Iraq to develop and use them during and after Reagan's time in office. This willingness resulted in the horizontal spread of ugly weapons that were used to kill tens of thousands of innocents in defiance of existing international law.

It seems then that Reagan batted "one for two" when it came to the horizontal and vertical dimensions of proliferation policy. What remains to be considered is how he performed in the qualitatively based "diagonal" dimension of arms control, and his devotion to the concept of strategic missile defense—both matters of continuing importance to global security.

The ability to hold seemingly contradictory positions and to find a way to keep them in balance was one of the hallmarks of Reagan's approach to statecraft. Nowhere was this more apparent than in his belief that reductions in nuclear arms had to be accompanied by simultaneous modernization of the strategic arsenal. For Reagan, the whole matter seemed straightforward despite the often-sharp opposition he faced from the outset:

> Over the next few years, many of my critics would claim it was contradictory and even hypocritical to embark on a quest for nuclear peace by building more nuclear weapons. But it was obvious that if we were ever going to get anywhere with the Russians in persuading them to reduce armaments, we had to bargain with them from *strength*, not weakness. If you were going to approach the Russians with a dove of peace in one hand, you had to have a sword in the other.[21]

This passage explains Reagan's unswerving devotion to making several of the qualitative improvements that experts deemed necessary for securing the U.S. strategic arsenal and keeping deterrence robust. In practical terms this meant that Reagan supported the development of new strategic bombers and intercontinental ballistic missiles—including a sea-launched missile that would have nearly the same level of accuracy as a land-based weapon. He would also come to favor the development of shorter-range missiles, to be deployed in Europe with the possibility of localizing a nuclear war if one broke out there. Along these same lines, Reagan championed the development of the neutron bomb, a weapon intended to generate lethal radiation but with a much lower blast effect. Jimmy Carter had been a proponent of the neutron bomb as well but had been dissuaded from his support for it largely by public distaste for the weapon, especially as articulated in Europe.

The idea was to use it against advancing Soviet forces, decimating them without destroying Europe in the process. Few believed in this sunny assessment, though, and even Reagan had too hard a time trying to revive the weapon.

Needless to say, these initiatives made for vigorous diagonal proliferation and put both NATO allies and Warsaw Pact adversaries in an uproar. Both saw that these qualitative improvements made nuclear warfare more "thinkable"—thus weakening deterrence—and both launched efforts to derail some or all of these new weapons systems. As events played out, the record looks mixed. It was increasingly difficult to deploy land-based missiles securely—only twenty-nine of the new MX missiles were ever made. They began deployment in 1986, and some remained "on station" until deactivated in September 2005.[22] The neutron bomb notion, on the other hand, was killed outright by popular protest. The D-5, a highly accurate submarine-launched missile, did move ahead and sharply reduced American vulnerability to a disabling first strike by the Russians—still the only country capable of mounting a major, counterforce-oriented strike against the United States.

Reagan used the threat to deploy the intermediate-range Pershing missile in Europe as a means to achieve agreement on local elimination of nuclear forces on both sides—his so-called "zero option." Finally, in terms of advances in strategic bombers, new radar-evading Stealth aircraft technology became the principal means of keeping the notion of strategic "penetrators" alive. It was the concurrent development of far-ranging cruise missiles that could be launched from older B-52 bombers that kept alive the idea of aerial bombardment during the 1980s. Today both Stealth bombers and air-launched cruise missiles remain the sine qua non of twenty-first-century air power.

In the midst of the ongoing war on terror, there continue to be strong incentives to pursue diagonal proliferation. A central war aim of those allied against terrorism is to keep weapons of mass destruction from migrating into enemy hands, and some think that the best way to do this is to strike at facilities where such weapons might be under development. In 1981, for example, the Israeli Air Force mounted a raid against an Iraqi nuclear facility at Osiraq. While a success, the Israeli action encouraged other proliferators to burrow deep underground to shelter their illicit activities—so deep that no conventional bomb can reliably knock out such facilities, of which there are now quite a few in the world.[23]

This problem prompted George W. Bush to accelerate research into developing a type of nuclear weapon designed specifically to destroy weapons laboratories located deep underground. This "bunker buster" notion is the major manifestation of diagonal proliferation in the world today.[24] Whatever the intrinsic merits of being able to "go deep," the fact that the United States continues to consider development of a new type of nuclear weapon can only have deleterious effects upon horizontal proliferation. Others can now ask why they should forgo nuclear acquisition while the United States is allowed to continue producing nuclear weapons of its own. Perhaps the political problem posed by bunker busters should induce us to consider other options against deep underground facilities, such as forcibly securing them for inspection by means of raids conducted by special operations forces.[25]

For Ronald Reagan the whole notion of mutual assured destruction rested upon an immoral premise—that it was acceptable for peace to be predicated on the perpetual vulnerability of innocent civilians. He refused to accept this as a given of the nuclear age and moved decisively during his first term to begin development of defenses against ballistic missile attack—the principal delivery system in any vision of nuclear holocaust. He put the matter succinctly in a speech to the American people on March 23, 1983:

> I call upon the scientific community in our country, those who gave us nuclear weapons, to turn their great talents now to the cause of peace, to give us the means to render those weapons obsolete. . . . My fellow Americans, tonight we are launching an effort which holds the promise of changing the course of human history.

It is important to note that, for all his zeal in pursuing strategic defenses, Reagan was not the first president to look closely at the issue. By the late 1960s Soviet nuclear capabilities had become robust, and a great deal of attention was beginning to be paid to the possibility of defending against nuclear attacks. This swirl of interest prompted Lyndon Johnson to call a high-level meeting in 1967 to discuss the possibility of developing anti-ballistic missile systems. LBJ brought together the Joint Chiefs of Staff and the past three Department of Defense directors of research and engineering, along with his own and the three previous presidential science advisers. One of the Pentagon research directors, Herbert York, recalled that Johnson asked them just two questions about an ABM system: Will it work? Should it be deployed? All those in attendance answered "no" on both counts.[26]

By the time Reagan came to office in 1981, the scientific limitations on ballistic missile defense had not begun to be overcome. Even today, early in the twenty-first century, the daunting challenge of trying to intercept an inbound missile is like trying to "hit a bullet with a bullet." The problem remains far more complex and intractable than defending against manned bombers, which had trouble penetrating determined defenses as early as 1940 in the Battle of Britain. But for Ronald Reagan, technological limits were simply obstacles to be overcome in the effort to bring an end to an immoral balance of terror that had been holding civilians hostage for decades. As he saw the matter, "It was like having two westerners standing in a saloon aiming their guns at each other's head—permanently. There had to be a better way."[27] And where the scientific advice President Johnson received in 1967 was unremittingly opposed to building missile defenses, by 1983 Reagan had found a wide variety of experts who thought it reasonable to undertake a serious program of research in this realm of inquiry.[28]

All this said, strategic defense created powerful political problems during Reagan's time, problems that persist. The first is that what we conceive of as protective in nature can be seen by others as quite threatening. A truly functioning missile defense system in effect disarms our opponents, throwing them wide open to nuclear devastation. If we have the ability to strike them while they have no hope of retaliation, our capabilities must appear frightening. As Gorbachev noted at his summit with Reagan at Reykjavik, the Russians perceived the negotiations there as an attempt to fulfill the American hope "to obtain military superiority through SDI [the Strategic Defense Initiative]."[29] Thus Gorbachev made it clear that American deployment of a missile defense system would set off a new spiral in the arms race—as the Soviets would have little choice but to try to overwhelm our defenses with swarms of new missiles and warheads. Our continued pursuit of national missile defense still strikes the same responsive chord in Russia—which continues under the leadership of Vladimir Putin to develop launchers and warheads designed to overwhelm our defenses—and in other countries as well.

Reagan took these concerns to heart and offered sincerely to share SDI research with the Russians—and the rest of the world.[30] In his view a nuclear war "could never be won and must never be fought," so all would benefit from the spread of missile defenses. Beyond the Soviet-American nuclear rivalry was the matter of rogues or madmen who might get their hands on one or a few weapons of mass destruction—strategic defenses would be especially good protection against them. This last point of Reagan's is particularly timely today, as the most serious nuclear threats are posed by rogue states and by the chance of a stateless terror network obtaining such a capability. All nations have an interest in defending against this possibility.

Yet it is important to realize that missile defense by itself would form only a partial solution to the mass destructive threat that may soon be posed by the rogue or the terrorist. Thus, in the coming years, when we think of "strategic defense" we should envision something much more far-reaching than just the ability to intercept missiles. We must also defend against bombs secreted on a tramp steamer or a truck, rowed ashore in a small boat, or even carried overland across one of our long, still largely underpatrolled borders. The current notion of "homeland security"—which contemplates the whole spectrum of threat, from missiles to madmen—should perhaps be seen as a much more fully articulated notion of the concept of "strategic defense." Cultivating this broader perspective would reconnect us with the concerns raised just after World War II by J. Robert Oppenheimer who, in a closed Senate hearing in 1946, laid out the seriousness of the threat that would one day be posed by nuclear terrorism. Oppenheimer, who led the scientific team that developed the first nuclear bomb, made it clear just how daunting a challenge defense was.[31] It still is.

There is one other approach to countering the proliferation of weapons of mass destruction: reciprocal behavior, or acting as you would have others act. A famous example of the power of this principle of reciprocity was the decision in 1985 by deeply impoverished Ethiopia to send aid to those suffering from that year's earthquakes in Mexico City. Despite their own travails, the Ethiopians were motivated to do this because, fifty years earlier, Mexico had been one of the few nations to send aid to Ethiopia after Mussolini's forces invaded the country.[32] In the realm of weapons of mass destruction, reciprocity's power has been best illustrated in global endeavors to reduce the chances of chemical or biological warfare. So far the record has been reasonably good.

Chemical weapons such as mustard gas and blister agents, which cause terrible suffering and painful deaths, came into their own during World War I. They were widely used on both sides during that conflict, with the Germans in particular integrating them into their battlefield doctrine.[33] After the war, though, in 1925, the use of chemical agents in combat was outlawed by the Geneva Convention. And in World War II all sides adhered to this behavior-based form of arms control and refrained from the use of chemicals.[34] With only a few very rare exceptions—Saddam Hussein being the principal culprit—this normative prohibition has remained in place and has been solidified in recent years by the Chemical Weapons Convention. Scores of nations could be making and using such weapons, yet virtually none do.

Modern biological warfare has been slower to emerge, being largely a by-product of the cold war era. To the extent to which germs have been on the cutting edge of conquest in the past—as Europeans brought their microbes to indigenous peoples around the world, beginning in the sixteenth century—the practice of biological warfare can be seen to have begun unwittingly.[35] But by the mid-twentieth century, systematic research was under way and deep plans were being laid for biological warfare. Despite a sharp Soviet-American antipathy, and the overarching prospect of nuclear havoc that made all other weapons pale by comparison, a universal sense of revulsion remained about the use of "bugs." And so a ban was enacted under international law in 1972, the Biological and Toxin Weapons Convention. For more than thirty years this ban has generally been observed, the greatest violation possibly occurring in the 1980s by increasingly desperate Soviet forces during their occupation of Afghanistan. Today, though, there are some signs that behavior-based controls may be in the process of breaking down. If this trend continues, biological warfare will grow into a much more serious threat.[36]

Despite the fact that the barriers to entry for those who would want chemical and biological weapons are quite low—scores of nations could easily field such weapons—only a few rogues and terrorists are experimenting with them. In these areas Ronald Reagan's ultimate goal of abolition is very reachable and perhaps even sustainable with full cooperation from the global community. Without question, abolition is desirable in the case of these sorts of weapons; and the type of cooperation needed for enforcement might have to entail the use of preventive force in certain cases. Such a drastic measure might prove necessary because the spread of these weapons to stateless terror networks would be only slightly less dire than terrorist acquisition of one or a few nuclear warheads.

As to nuclear weapons themselves, little behavior-based restraint was shown by the United States at the outset of the atomic age. Hiroshima and Nagasaki were bombed as soon as these weapons became available. After World War II, plans for nuclear strikes against the Soviet Union—to prevent its rise as a nuclear power—were bruited about for years. During the 1950s, nuclear threats were made against North Korea and Communist China, and a complete "New Look" was contemplated for the U.S. Army, one in which it would increasingly depend upon battlefield atomic weapons. In each case, though, American policy eventually backed away from crossing the nuclear divide as it had in 1945. Plans for a preventive war against Russia were discarded in favor of deterrence and a policy of containment. The idea of massive retaliation with nuclear weapons for acts of merely conventional aggression was scrapped, and the so-called "pentomic" division of a nuclear-oriented New Look army never really came into being. In short, U.S. policy in action did begin to look like it was following a series of self-imposed behavioral controls.

Ronald Reagan built upon this—and included the Russians directly in the process—with his success in the 1980s in calling for the elimination of whole classes of battlefield and theater nuclear weapons. Yet in one area of behavior-based arms control Reagan failed—a failure he shares with all his predecessors and successors from Truman to George W. Bush—the simple matter of pledging never to be the first in a conflict to use nuclear weapons. During the 1950s and early 1960s, for example, it was thought that NATO was inferior in conventional forces to the Soviets, and that a threat of nuclear first use was necessary to keep the peace. Yet from the outset this notion made little sense. In a variety of NATO field exercises and policy-level simulated war games, two conclusions kept reappearing: use of tactical nuclear weapons on both sides actually benefited the Soviets; and escalation to all-out nuclear war could not be avoided.[37] As early as 1960 Henry Kissinger agreed with this point, confirming that in his view even a "limited" nuclear exchange was likely to escalate and lead to mutual destruction. Further, he held that trying to compensate for numerically inferior conventional forces with nuclear weapons was an idea that "had lost a great deal of its validity." Finally, Kissinger considered the notion that the Soviets had anything resembling a permanent edge in ground forces both "fallacious and exaggerated."[38]

From NATO exercises to Kissinger's and others' analyses, the evidence continued to mount against the viability of the doctrine of nuclear first use. This prompted retrenchment, the first move being to back away from massive retaliation—the use of tactical nuclear weapons in response to a conventional invasion. Instead Robert McNamara, then President Kennedy's secretary of defense, created the notion of having a range of "full options" available. This meant the ability to choose a conventional or a nuclear defense; but the policy was clearly headed toward trying to defend first without weapons of mass destruction.

Within a few years, full options gave way to "flexible response," which made it even clearer that there would be no reflexive nuclear riposte to any Soviet invasion of Western Europe. During Reagan's time in office, doctrine was refined still further, conveying the deepening sense that nuclear options would be considered only as a last resort. Even during this period, as the end of the Soviet Union neared, decision-makers in his administration clung to the idea of reserving the right to use nuclear weapons first—although more and more Europeans were appalled by this prospect. Interestingly, at the higher end of the policy debates, it was actually Americans—former senior government officials—who argued for no first use while a group of influential German intellectuals championed the retention of the flexible-response doctrine (the right to initiate the use of nuclear weapons).[39] The formative power of Reagan's position on this point—articulated at such a pivotal time—has been such that all of his successors have reasserted the right of nuclear first use.

But if preventing the lateral spread of nuclear and other weapons of mass destruction is a central element in American security policy today, it is most unseemly for us to continue to claim our own right to the first use of nuclear weapons in conflict. By stubbornly clinging to this doctrine we may be tacitly signaling others that, if they really wish to secure their interests, they may need to possess similar weapons and issue similar threats. The irony of the situation is that there is simply no need for the United States to use nuclear weapons except in *response* to a nuclear attack. Today there is no sole power or group of states that can pose a serious conventional military threat to American national security. The U.S. Air Force dominates the skies of the world, the Navy its seas, and the Army simply cannot be challenged in open battle.

Yet by insisting on the right to use nuclear weapons first, the United States may encourage others to enunciate a similar doctrine, posing grave threats to American forces and overall global security. In the past decade both the Russians and the Chinese have moved away from their long-standing doctrines of no first use of nuclear weapons—a development that abolition-minded Ronald Reagan would view with much sadness. Further, North Korean and Iranian intransigence in curtailing their own nuclear and other weapons programs may also be tied to their perceived need to deter the United States. All this might be avoided or at least mitigated if the United States fully appreciated the importance of "role modeling" with its own behavior an approach to seeking security without relying on weapons of mass destruction—reserving only the right to use them in a retaliatory fashion. For if Americans want the less nuclear world that was so central to Reagan's strategy, we must wean ourselves now of unnecessary dependence upon these weapons.

In at least one area we have come close to taking a behavior-based declaratory stand against the first use of a new type of device: the realm of weapons of "mass disruption," or cyber-attack capabilities. This is the world of logic bombs, computer viruses, and "Trojan horses," the bits and bytes capable of crippling national infrastructures, making money in banks disappear, or even disrupting the ability of advanced militaries to deploy and fight. All the advanced technologies that make nations prosperous and their armed forces powerful also make them vulnerable. Virtually all states, terrorist and criminal groups, and disaffected individuals have access to these disruptive new weapons—and some are using them already.

For example, where the claims for physical damage from the 9/11 attacks on America amounted to just over $40 billion, cyber attacks inflict more costs than this every year. Yet in this new type of warfare, the United States has refrained from acting first, seeking instead to induce others to show restraint as well. Some years ago I co-chaired a meeting between senior Russian and American officials who were grappling with this issue. By the end of the week-long gathering, both sides had responded warmly to the prospect of exercising mutual restraint—a restraint the United States soon after demonstrated during the Kosovo War by not trying to mount electronic raids upon the bank accounts of Slobodan Milosevic and his cronies. America did not wish to set a precedent for this kind of disruptive war making. So, at least in the area of mass disruption, where attempts to prevent acquisition of attack capabilities are likely doomed to failure, there is much hope for this exemplary kind of behavior-based arms control. And there is every reason to believe that what works to curtail the use of weapons of mass disruption might apply just as well to problems posed by weapons of mass destruction.

Clearly Ronald Reagan's impact upon the shaping of the twenty-first century world has been and continues to be enormous. The most positive aspects of his legacy can be seen at the broadest conceptual level, where he believed that arms reductions could replace arms racing and that government was ethically obliged to defend people against missiles, much as an earlier generation had defended against manned bombers. Today we live in a world where the sheer numbers of nuclear warheads have fallen far below their levels at the height of the cold war arms race. And while missile defense remains a distant goal, its scientific feasibility seems to grow ever clearer.

Despite these positive developments, problems persist, to a great extent because of Reagan's choice not to take a hard line against Pakistani proliferation during his time in office. He neatly brought to an end the quantitative arms race between the United States and the old Soviet Union; but today's nuclear threat comes more from the lateral spread—largely the product of the A. Q. Khan network—of even just a few of these weapons to tyrants or terrorists. And such actors are far less likely to use ballistic missiles, which can be easily tracked back to their point of origin. Instead rogues and terrorists will employ various, mostly covert means of attack in an effort to maintain their anonymity and avoid retaliation. This means that strategic defense as a concept must now move well beyond its initial focus on ballistic missiles to identify the whole host of delivery means against which we must defend. Reagan certainly foreshadowed the coming of nuclear defenses; but he did not envision the breadth of measures that would have to be mounted.

The increasingly dire threat of this sort of horizontal proliferation means also that more active steps must be taken to minimize the possibility that weapons of mass destruction may "leak" into dangerous hands. In the case of Russia, for example, such initiatives as the Nunn-Lugar law—which provides material support for the dismantling of portions of that large arsenal—are most appropriate and need to be extended and fully funded for as long as necessary. The situation with regard to Pakistan is different in that the arsenal in question is so much smaller but the political risk of upheaval and loss of control is far greater. Thus the indicated strategy toward Islamabad runs more along the lines of helping the Pakistanis to maintain positive control over their weapons—with devices such as "permissive access links" (PALs)—and having special operations contingency plans ready in the event the government comes apart. It is an odd irony of our time that, though we extol the virtues of democracy, fostering true democracy in Pakistan would likely place nuclear weapons in the hands of freely elected but rabidly anti-American Islamists.

These problems aside, the greatest remaining impediment to dealing with the perils of proliferation is our own stubborn refusal to devalue weapons of mass destruction. As long as we continue to assert our right to use nuclear weapons first—a key policy point championed by Reagan even as he saw the Soviet military begin to fall apart at the seams—others will want such weapons too. And they will get them; whether nuclear, chemical, or biological. If these others are nation-states that can strike us anonymously, or are stateless criminal or terror networks, we will face a problem far more complex and dangerous than anything that arose during the cold war. What is most needed now is the willingness to be an exemplar of the proper kind of behavior toward all the forms of weapons of mass destruction; yet it seems this is the most difficult initiative for us to take. Even Ronald Reagan, the hawk who sought reductions and then abolition, could not bring himself to renounce the first use of such weapons. His successors have followed in his path, perpetuating and deepening the problem. Perhaps one day a successor of Reagan's will see the illogic of insisting on this contradictory position toward the possession and use of such weapons.

Meanwhile the contours of the twenty-first-century world, as they manifest themselves in this realm of exotic and most highly destructive weapons, have been molded—for both good and ill—by the ideas and actions of Ronald Reagan. Yet these are hardly the only weapons that can simultaneously protect and imperil our world. There are many other tools of the art of war, as good or as bad as those who wield them. These weapons systems, Reagan's influence on how they were reshaped, and how they are continuing to affect the world, are considered next.

5

Transforming the American Military

Beyond deterring an all-out war between great powers, nuclear weapons have had surprisingly little enduring effect upon military and security affairs. In the 1950s and 1960s they may even have had a stultifying influence on strategic thought, in that war planners became unduly focused on new mass destructive capabilities rather than upon innovative operational and doctrinal concepts. Yet the stalemate imposed by mutual nuclear deterrence eventually returned matters to more classical forms of warfare, and conflicts—albeit of limited scope and intensity—soon sprouted up around the world. As Kenneth Waltz, the leading academic advocate of the "realist" school of thought about power politics, put the problem at the outset of this period, "Mutual fear of big weapons may produce, instead of peace, a spate of smaller wars."[1] He was right, and we have had that spate of smaller wars ever since, the world averaging between ten and twenty deadly conflicts at any given time—the overwhelming majority of them fought within rather than between states.

During the last half of the twentieth century, most of these wars were fought in and over states that had once been colonized or controlled as satellites. These so-called wars of liberation often involved the United States or the Soviet Union or both, who eagerly and often bloodily played out their rivalry in diverse settings. The two super-powers never directly confronted each other's forces but rather conducted the conflict largely through or along with proxies—in places like Korea, Vietnam, Angola, and other theaters across a sad global tableau. The Soviet-American antagonism was particularly sulphurous in Europe, where the common horror of nuclear war helped keep the peace yet prompted each side to create ever greater capabilities for waging protracted conventional warfare. Between the global competition occurring at the periphery and the more central confrontation in Europe, the need for arms—lots of arms—was great and would seemingly only continue to grow. For as the United States learned better how to counter Moscow-backed insurgents, or how to move forces across the Atlantic faster in defense of Europe, the Red Army grew larger, the Soviet navy more potent.

In every respect the costly nuclear arms race was mirrored in the conventional realm. At the height of this spiraling situation, Ronald Reagan entered office, having to shoulder, beyond the existing range of serious strategic problems, the added burden of nurturing a wounded military that had been recently defeated and to some extent discredited in Vietnam. Although Donald Rumsfeld, George W. Bush's secretary of defense, would later popularize the phrase "military transformation" during his tenure, it was Reagan who knew, twenty years earlier, that he had to oversee the fundamental transformation of the American military. His success in this undertaking reshaped the U.S. armed services and has had a huge and continuing impact on world politics. In retrospect it seems quite surprising that so much change, in ourselves and in the world, came about in the wake of so little actual fighting. And the conflicts that directly involved our forces during the 1980s did little to suggest that a sharp new instrument of statecraft was being forged.

One of the greatest ironies of Ronald Reagan's presidency was that, for all the efforts to paint him as a trigger-happy cowboy, he used force sparingly. He undertook no major wars with American forces, landing

Figure 9.   Rating Reagan's Uses of Force (including by proxies)

troops on foreign shores only briefly, in 1983 in Lebanon and Grenada. A one-shot air raid on Tripoli in 1986 and some naval skirmishes in the Gulf of Sidra, the concurrent escorting of reflagged Kuwaiti oil tankers, and the small advisory mission in El Salvador round out the thimbleful of direct military involvement during his two terms. The other armed struggles during the 1980s in which the United States took a close interest were waged by American proxy armies—in Afghanistan, Nicaragua, and Angola. This record pales next to George H. W. Bush's invasion of Panama and liberation of Kuwait during his single term; Bill Clinton's resort to the use of force during each one of his eight years in office; and George W. Bush's open-ended "war on terror," which has already featured major military campaigns in Afghanistan and Iraq.

The outcomes of Reagan's few military interventions were not particularly impressive. American involvement in the Lebanese civil war, for example, led to the slaughter of hundreds of Marines in their barracks in Beirut—at the hands of a suicide bomber—and to the subsequent withdrawal of U.S. forces. This incident was undoubtedly both inspiring and informative to other terrorists, who must have perceived in it a glaring American weakness. Yet our willingness to withdraw may have also showed the world that the United States was capable of making flinty-eyed strategic choices about its goals and interests. This view may have been reinforced in 1990 when Lebanon was allowed to become a Syrian protectorate—the political price paid at the time to gain support from Damascus for our first Gulf War. The story line came full circle in 2005, though, when George W. Bush successfully used veiled military threats to pressure Syria to retreat from Lebanon.

Reagan's other direct military interventions featured quite spotty results. The invasion of Grenada in 1983, to depose a "Marxist" government and expel a battalion-sized Cuban mission there, turned out to be a sloppy success that highlighted many of the problems in the post-Vietnam American military. Three years later the air raid that Reagan ordered on Tripoli missed Colonel Qaddafi, and may even have goaded the latter to seek retaliation in 1988 in the skies over Lockerbie. Only the interception of the *Achille Lauro* terrorists, the small military advisory mission in El Salvador, and naval escort operations in the Persian Gulf went reasonably well—especially navy SEAL actions against Iranian light coastal forces. The more successful military actions in the Persian Gulf were overshadowed by incidents that saw the *USS Stark* gravely damaged by an Iraqi attack aircraft and an innocent Iranian Airbus wrongfully shot down by the *USS Vincennes*, killing all 290 passengers and crew aboard.

As to the three principal proxy forces Reagan backed, their results were also mixed. The *mujahideen* in Afghanistan did wear down Russian will after more than eight years, and Soviet forces did depart. But the legacy of that liberation was chaos, civil war, and terrorism—all of which led to an American invasion in 2001 and a new period of occupation that continues today. The contras in Nicaragua were never able to control territory, but the fact that they kept on their feet at all may have induced the Sandinistas to agree to hold free and fair democratic elections—which they promptly lost. Finally, the rebel forces of Jonas Savimbi, struggling against Angolan government troops and their Cuban allies, never achieved either their political or military goals. In this case the conflict was further muddied by the presence of powerful American oil interests—whose facilities in Angola were sometimes protected by Cuban forces against the very rebellion fomented and funded by Washington.

A further irony of Reagan's slight, somewhat mediocre military record is that it was compiled during a period of relative plenty for defense spending. Reagan entered office determined to "rebuild" the U.S. military at any expense. And he had bipartisan support for this aim, as Jimmy Carter had already begun to increase defense spending toward the end of his term. The Carter administration used this additional funding wisely, starting along the path (that Reagan followed) of developing precision-guided munitions, fast supply ships, and Stealth aircraft, among other innovations. Democrats as well as Republicans thought it was time to cast off the demons of the debacle in Vietnam and return to a great-power status.

In practical terms this meant that a window of opportunity for increasing military spending quite substantially had opened. As seen in Figure 10, the rise that began under Carter took on an even steeper upward slope with Reagan in office. Yet this period of rapid defense budgetary growth was over almost as soon as it began, with real spending increases leveling off early in Reagan's second term. His image as military spendthrift may have to be somewhat, but not completely, revised. Still, the sheer amount of spending increases set a new baseline for the defense budget that continues to have powerful ripple effects today, as neither Republicans nor Democrats have

Figure 10.   U.S. Defense Spending, 1970–2005 (in 2002 dollars)

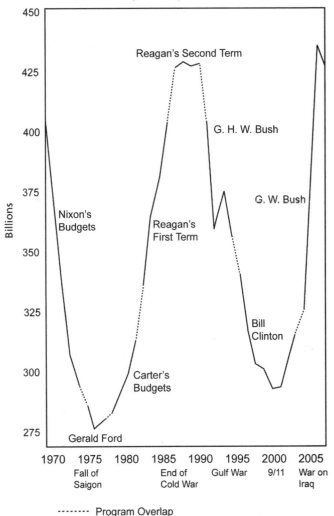

spoken meaningfully about radically cutting back military procurement.

Even George H. W. Bush's and Bill Clinton's budget cuts provided only a temporary respite brought on by the end of the cold war. Their lower spending was almost completely the result of a one-third reduction in the manpower of the armed services—from 2.1 million service members at the beginning of Bush's presidency to 1.4 million by the end of Clinton's. By way of contrast, few high-cost weapons acquisition projects were killed, a pattern that has continued as George W. Bush has overseen during his presidency the demise of only two systems: the Crusader self-propelled artillery piece and the Comanche helicopter. The rest of the legacy systems from the cold war era remain in the pipeline. Most of these weapons acquisition programs originated during the Reagan administration; they lie at the heart of the more than $1.3 billion the Defense Department now spends *every day*.

As in other aspects of his presidency, the domain of military affairs yields a complex if not outright contradictory set of insights into Ronald Reagan. For it appears that commonly held beliefs about his bellicosity and budgetary largesse are not wholly true. Yet the U.S. military that emerged by the end of the 1980s would soon be acknowledged as the preeminent armed force in the world. The proof that it merited this status was the huge, lopsided, and nearly casualty-free victory over Iraq in the 1990–1991 Gulf War. Although the Iraqis were hardly the Prussians of the Arab world, they were handled with remarkable swiftness and sureness. Something very good had happened to the American armed forces after Vietnam, and Ronald Reagan had a great deal to do with it.

Our constitution makes the president the commander-in-chief of military forces, a role Reagan assumed with relish. For years before his election he had been increasingly concerned about the deepening post-Vietnam malaise that was infecting the armed services and the American people. And he understood that the more serious aspect of this crisis was growing self-doubt rather than any sort of material insufficiency—though he was concerned about the latter as well. Even before entering office, Reagan focused on the need to set this morale matter right if we were ever to turn the tide in the cold war, noting in one of his radio commentaries at the time that "We stand in greater danger of defeat from lack of will than from any mistakes likely to flow from a show of purpose." This is an almost eerie foreshadowing of the Lebanon fiasco in 1983, where our "show of purpose" came at such a high cost. Reagan concluded this broadcast emphatically, making the point that "Only by mustering a superiority, beginning with a superiority of the spirit, can we stop the thunder of hobnailed boots on their march to world empire."[2]

Close observers of the U.S. military at the time were also focusing on this deep and growing malaise, concurring with Reagan about both the moral and material dimensions of the problem. At the time the articles that became Arthur T. Hadley's incendiary classic, *Straw Giant*, had become something of a guiding commentary for Reagan, who highlighted Hadley's ideas about "drift" and "bureaucratic incompetence" in a number of his radio commentaries. Another journalistic account of the hard times for the U.S. armed services, this one by James Fallows, echoed Reagan's concerns, considering it the "first task to restore the military spirit."[3] So Reagan did his best to treat the fall of Saigon in 1975 and the disaster at Desert One in 1980 as but the bookends to a brief, unhappy interlude. He set about systematically to salve the Vietnam wound, finding it, even in defeat, "a noble cause." And he saw the confusion and chaos in the Iranian desert as a call for military "revitalization" that became a key part of his 1980 platform.

When Reagan became president, senior leaders of all the services and defense-minded members of Congress knew they now had a true champion in office. So they quickly set to work, service by service, senator by senator, to articulate their needs and to seek an audience with the new president. In their interactions with Reagan, they and he together reshaped the military into an instrument of statecraft as preeminent as the legions that had once controlled so much of the world at the height of Rome's power. As the Roman military once had, the American armed forces during the 1980s would consolidate the shift away from a conscript army to a professional one. Like the Roman legions, U.S. forces would master the problems posed by competing states but, also like the Romans, would continue to have difficulty in grappling with the types of problems posed by unconventionally organized opponents. For Rome it was the barbarians. For the United States it would be the insurgents and stateless terrorists who—even as we were improving our forces—were crafting an entirely new mode of war. It is against this backdrop that the whole matter of military transformation must be considered, one service at a time.

The U.S. Army had emerged from Vietnam having suffered most of all the services. It had fought hard for several years, pioneered an entirely new sort of military doctrine based on heli-borne mobility and "vertical envelopment," and inflicted heavy losses on its enemy. Yet it was still defeated, in the end proving unable to keep South Vietnam from being conquered by the North Vietnamese army. It was the most stinging failure of arms in American history, far worse than the disastrous invasion of Canada during the War of 1812 or the wildly reckless advance to the Yalu River—from which our forces were also decisively thrown back—during the Korean War. While there have been some attempts to blame the defeat in Vietnam on hostile media coverage, political meddling, and fickle public opinion, careful studies of these charges—some by the army's own Center for Military History—have found them to be almost wholly baseless.[4] Perhaps the most trenchant critique of this "stab in the back" line of reasoning was provided by the anonymous "Cincinnatus" (more echoes of the legions). He was a senior field-grade officer whose analysis of the war formed both an indictment of the military response to an opponent who waged an irregular war and a guide to reform:

> The Vietnamese conflict, like all wars, was indeed a political war. Politicians did place certain limitations upon the United States Army's freedom of action. All armies face such restrictions. Within the bounds of these political restraints, America's military had wide latitude of action and a clear opportunity to win in Vietnam. It met defeat because it failed to "know the enemy" and therefore could not adopt the strategy and tactics that were specific to the particular enemy it faced, and because it forgot vital lessons learned in its own history. Vietnam showed clearly that our strategic and tactical military thought can be shamefully shallow and palpably wrong. It further demonstrated that, as the war dragged on, the army acted as though it was more interested in self-perpetuation and self-aggrandizement than in the efficient fulfillment of its mission. . . .
>
> The Army chose not to adapt to the unique environment of Vietnam. It conducted big-unit operations against bands of guerrillas. It

sought to achieve victory through attrition. It was uninterested in providing greater security for the people of the countryside and cities. It repeatedly relied on tactics already proven inadequate. It seemed not to understand the need for pacification and when it belatedly tried out that approach, it combined pacification with combat operations, thus negating both. It relied too heavily on technology and the lavish use of firepower. It refused to adopt more primitive tactics that could have dealt effectively with the sort of enemy it faced. It ignored calls for change that came from within. It continued to function as if it were pursuing units of the Warsaw Pact across the plains of central Europe. Stated simply, the army made too many mistakes in its years in Vietnam.[5]

By the early 1980s army leaders were ready to make a comeback from the dark days of the recent past. They reveled in having a new president who shared their pain and promised all the moral and material support they required. And they responded with a will, identifying key new technologies that would empower their forces and developing a fresh military doctrine—AirLand Battle—for their proper use in future wars. They also turned their backs almost completely on the problems posed by irregular and guerrilla warfare, fixing instead on visions of a climactic clash with the Red Army on the plains of central Europe. Thus the least likely conflict scenario was nevertheless the one that got the most attention. This was without doubt the bureaucratic preference of the army, as it justified the huge continuing expenditures associated with keeping 300,000 to 400,000 troops in Europe and entailed preparations for moving an equal number of ground forces across the Atlantic very quickly in the event of a Soviet attack. Such a war would also give the U.S. Army the leading role.

The key operational problem was how to prevent a Russian fait accompli. That is, a quick knockout blow from an armored Soviet blitzkrieg—occurring before reinforcements from the United States could arrive—somehow had to be averted. At the time we were well aware of Russian thinking on the subject of a campaign in central Europe—as aware as they were of our thinking.[6] And both sides believed that the next war would be fundamentally driven by attrition. Therefore the path to victory, each thought, lay in winning a kind of "battle of the buildup." For the Russians this meant assuring that their initial assault forces were swiftly followed by wave after wave of fresh tank and motorized rifle divisions, which could move by road and rail to the battlefront far more easily and quickly than American forces could be shipped across the Atlantic.

The strategic dilemma was further complicated by political considerations within NATO, which made it difficult to plan responses to an invasion that were driven strictly by military logic. For example, good strategy might imply that outnumbered NATO forces should make a fighting withdrawal at the outset of a conflict, trading space for time and forcing the Russians to stretch their supply lines and to wear down their best troops, making them more vulnerable to counterattack. But such a concept would entail conceding much—if not all—of Germany to the invader, a politically unacceptable plan. So actual NATO defensive planning relied instead on a "forward defense," which immediately guaranteed higher losses for both sides—and which would have greatly benefited the numerically superior Soviets.

The solution to this seemingly intractable problem came from the rise of a whole new breed of conventional weapons that featured both "deep strike" and "precision guidance" capabilities. Just as Reagan was coming into office, the information revolution was in its infancy. In the realm of military affairs this meant that weapons were no longer simply a mix of mass and energy hurled at the enemy. Now they would also include greatly enhanced information content, giving missiles—and eventually even artillery shells—an accuracy unheard of in the history of warfare. For the first time, the tight, age-old linkage between the range and accuracy of weapons was severed. In practical terms it was now possible to strike with extreme accuracy at both Russian assault forces—undermining their initial material advantages—and at second- and third-wave troops and tanks making their way from the Soviet Union to the front in central Europe. In this manner the battle of the buildup could be won decisively as long as the Atlantic sea lanes remained open.

Despite deep concerns expressed by many critics about the reliability of the new weapons, Reagan embraced them and championed their adoption.[7] At the Pentagon's Office of Net Assessment, Andrew Marshall—progenitor of the "cost-imposing strategy" against the Russians outlined in Chapter 2—began to see in these new weapons the possibility of an emerging "revolution in military affairs." Many in the Pentagon chose to view this strictly as a "military-technological revolution," keeping the focus on technical matters; but Marshall insisted on ensuring that the strategic, organizational, and doctrinal implications of the new technology be explored. In this he echoed the ideas of Michael Roberts, the British historian who, in a series of lectures at Oxford in the 1950s, introduced the idea that military revolutions were driven only in part by technology. Instead Roberts looked beyond machines and weapons to the new plans, tactics, and combat formations that would fully empower the new weapons.

At the same time the Russians too were beginning to consider the value of the newly emerging information systems and technologies, with some of their top military leaders developing at least as keen an appreciation of the situation as Marshall and other Western RMA (Revolution in Military Affairs) advocates. Marshal Nikolai Ogarkov in particular seems to have grasped the most profound implications of the new technologies for both deepening the battlefield and empowering even smaller forces to do far more than ever before.[8] Ogarkov is best remembered for a speech that summarized the future path of development in military affairs and took the position that, because of economic constraints, the Red Army could not make the changes necessary to bring itself effectively into the information age. The speech is known to this day as "Ogarkov's Lament."

The U.S. military also developed a doctrine of its own to go with the new precision weapons, calling it AirLand Battle to emphasize the close connection between ground operations and air support. Although it has been depicted as a completely innovative approach to warfare that among other things optimizes the use of advanced telecommunications and sensing and guidance technologies, AirLand Battle looks much more like German panzer-era blitzkrieg than what

I like to call information-age "bitskrieg."[9] The core concepts articulated in the Army's *Field Manual 100-5,* which introduced the Air-Land Battle doctrine, are observationally equivalent to the operational techniques pioneered by the Germans in World War II and imitated—with varying degrees of success—by the Allies.[10] Many analysts saw the American victory over Saddam Hussein's forces in the first Gulf War as a watershed in military affairs. Yet General Norman Schwarzkopf's marvelous 1991 "left hook" around the Iraqi army was little more than a mirror image of General Erwin Rommel's 1941 "right hook" around British forces in Cyrenaica (northeastern Libya).

The development of Army doctrine in the Reagan era can be said to reflect, more than anything else, the bureaucratic preference for waging a classical form of mechanized warfare, and a tendency to pour new technology into the organization's existing conceptual understanding of conflict. Then, a few years after AirLand Battle was introduced, an opponent—Saddam Hussein—was actually foolish enough to deploy his 500,000-man field army in static positions in the open desert where U.S. forces could destroy it. This was just the sort of fortunate scenario needed to reinforce the seeming validity of the approach taken during the 1980s. That a doctrine designed to fight on the flat plains of central Europe worked in the tank-friendly deserts of the Middle East was seized upon as an indicator that it could be applied in a general way to all types of conflicts. The unraveling of American policy in urban fighting in Somalia in 1993—just two years after the humbling of Saddam Hussein—was not seen as too troubling. But ten years after Mogadishu, as an urban-based insurgency was beginning to erupt in a now-occupied Iraq, the limits of the doctrine the U.S. military had taken into the twenty-first century could be clearly seen.

Despite its conceptual limitations and derivativeness, AirLand Battle did serve Ronald Reagan's larger national security strategy in one concrete and crucially important way: it helped widen the firebreak between conventional and nuclear war. For decades the key problem facing the United States and its NATO allies had been the seemingly inevitable need to resort to tactical nuclear weapons in order to thwart a Soviet invasion with conventional forces. Now a doctrine had emerged, the basis of which was the formulation that conventional attacks could be confidently thwarted by conventional means. Thus the pressure to escalate to the nuclear level—or to maintain what George Ball once called the "cosmic bluff"—had abated, making it possible to think about arms control initiatives such as removing all short- and intermediate-range nuclear missiles from Europe.[11] Even this kind of progress, though, could not convince Reagan to eschew the doctrine of "first use" of nuclear weapons.

Beyond the direct effects of the new approach to battle on an out-of-control nuclear arms race, the decision to focus on developing robust conventional military operations may, ironically, have indirectly helped reduce the overall Soviet-American antagonism. For Armageddon was no longer perceived to be on a hair trigger, threatening to go off with the first volleys between ground forces. The same calming effect was not achieved by the new naval doctrine that emerged during the Reagan years.

The U.S. Navy emerged from the Vietnam War with far less damage to its organizational psyche than the army had suffered. To be sure, there had been a serious drift away from some of its core competencies, but none of these were pernicious. For example, the primary training of naval aviators since World War II had been to attack ships. But during the Korean War (1950–1953), there were almost no targets to hit at sea, so carrier aircraft quickly shifted to providing close support to hard-pressed United Nations troops on the ground—where their help was sorely needed. Carrier aircraft also became involved in the bombardment of North Korea, striking at bridges and other strategic targets—an aspect of their operations that was the subject of James Michener's classic *The Bridges at Toko-Ri.* After the war, naval aviation returned to its focus on striking other ships. Things stayed this way until the start of the conflict in Vietnam, another war with an opponent who provided few naval targets. This brought matters back to the close support of U.S. forces on the ground; and carrier attack aircraft were also deeply involved in the strategic aerial bombardment of North Vietnam. Carrier aircraft mounted heavy strikes on bridges, railroads, and other infrastructure, perhaps to a greater extent than had been the case during the Korean conflict. Yet in a world without a naval rival possessing a fleet that could be easily attacked from the air, it made sense that the navy would shift its mission emphasis toward bombardment of targets ashore.

The navy's elite commando teams, its SEALs, were also drawn away from their core mission—supporting the fleet by providing hydrographic reconnaissance and undertaking other amphibious-related tasks.[12] Instead of these chores—which had been the main role of their World War II "frogmen" forebears—SEALs soon found themselves deeply committed to counterinsurgency operations. They worked closely with the navy's light forces that were operating on the rivers of South Vietnam—where the enemy did have some small vessels that could be targeted—but SEALs also often went far afield from strictly "brown-water" settings. As in the case of aircraft carrier operations, naval special warfare had undergone a major shift in emphasis that, as seen from the perspective of today's ongoing war against dispersed terror networks, turned out to be a step in the right direction. Even though attempts were made to return the SEALs to their original focus on fleet support during the Reagan years, counterinsurgency and the other various missions undertaken by special operations forces seem to have gotten into the SEALs' bloodstream.

The SEALs' first major post-Vietnam test of their capabilities came in 1983 in Grenada, where they were assigned a number of important tasks, including the rescue of a high-level political figure. They accomplished few of their objectives, and one entire assault element was accidentally drowned when it was air dropped into rough Grenadan coastal waters with loads that were far too heavy to bear.[13] But SEAL performance improved substantially from 1986 to 1988 during Operation Earnest Will in the Persian Gulf. There U.S. naval commandos played a key role in thwarting attacks by Iranian speedboat teams that were preying on oil tankers and other shipping—an attempt by Iran to hurt Iraq's economy during their ongoing war, but one that also imperiled Kuwait and other Gulf states. In this extended operation, SEALs worked well from their own swift boats and also raided bases—mostly offshore oil rigs—from which the Iranians were attacking Gulf shipping.[14]

This pattern of mixed results for the SEALs continued for years and featured a clumsy effort to secure the Paitilla airfield during the invasion of Panama in 1989—which cost four SEAL lives and dozens wounded. But there were also highly successful outings, such as the SEAL-led countersniper operations in 1993 in Somalia. More recently, SEAL performance in the war on terror has smoothed out at a generally high level, and command of important special operations task forces conducting counterinsurgent activities in Afghanistan and elsewhere—forces mostly comprising army personnel—has been held by SEAL officers.[15] Even so, restrictive rules of engagement and turf fights with the elite, super-secret Delta Force over control of certain types of missions kept the SEALs from actualizing their remarkable potential. This led to a precipitous drop in reenlistment rates of SEALs, posing the prospect of a serious meltdown in this elite force's human capital.

Beyond new thinking about how to employ carrier aircraft and special warfare teams, the navy's biggest change during the 1980s was its rekindling of classical strategic notions. The process of reintroducing these strands of thought about the use of American sea power began when Reagan selected John Lehman—himself a naval aviator—as secretary of the navy. Lehman quickly grasped the key implication for the navy of Reagan's desire to avert nuclear war by means of a large conventional buildup of forces: a bigger fleet could undertake bold amphibious operations and shore bombardments against peripheral targets on the edges of the Soviet Union itself as well as against client states and related Russian overseas naval bases located around the world.

This maritime strategy alerted the Kremlin that the American response to any invasion of Western Europe would be to strike back in a variety of places where Soviet forces and their allies might be outnumbered or isolated. Lehman's ideas were consonant with those of the great American naval theorist of a century ago, Alfred Thayer Mahan. His best-known work, *The Influence of Sea Power Upon History*, chronicled especially well how Britain responded to the Seven Years' War in Europe mostly in an indirect fashion, by striking at French colonial holdings in the West Indies, North America, and South Asia. As a stalemate emerged on the battlefields of Europe, Britain took hold of the vast territories that were to form its world empire.

Lehman decided to update Mahan's insights about the course of this conflict, waged from 1756 to 1763—which Winston Churchill once called in his writings the real "First World War."[16] Lehman reasoned that our naval mastery put us in a position similar to Britain's in its struggle with France for global supremacy two centuries earlier—which meant that we had an enormous potential advantage that only needed exploiting. Making this vision a reality would require, in Lehman's view, an enormous increase in the fleet, to as many as six hundred ships, a third larger navy than when he entered office. An armada of this magnitude would be necessary, Lehman believed, in order to continue securing the Atlantic shipping lanes *and* undertake offensives against the Soviets and their allies around the world.[17] Reagan was deeply drawn to this notion, as it was yet another means of keeping a war with the Russians conventional. He became the most ardent supporter of Lehman's plans, which were summarized in a speech given by the navy secretary at the Naval War College in April 1981, celebrating the "return of strategy" in place of simpler planning for a nuclear apocalypse.[18] Unfortunately the cost of this huge naval expansion would likely have been astronomical, and the dream of a six-hundred-ship navy was never realized by Lehman or any of his successors. It soon fell afoul of budgetary constraints.

In retrospect this may have been for the best. Once such a naval building plan were completed, all those new ships would exist for a long time and would carry with them huge continuing (and of course growing) operating costs. Given that the Soviet Union unraveled just a few years after this expansion was under consideration, the United States is fortunate not to have invested too heavily in ships at a time when our principal adversary was scrapping much of its own fleet. Even in the absence of the fleet Lehman and Reagan wanted, the U.S. Navy today dwarfs all others in the world. We have more than enough ships and should be thinking about the size of our fleet in relative rather than absolute terms, as the British did in their naval heyday. At the height of its power in the early 1900s, Britain followed a policy for the Royal Navy that granted it funds sufficient to make sure that the empire would be protected by a fleet as large as the next two leading navies of the world combined. Were the United States to adopt such a two-power rule today, it would require drastic cutbacks and mass mothballing of ships. We have—and have had—enough for our needs.

In addition to the huge, unhealthy budgetary demands that went with the vision of a fleet capable of carrying out the maritime strategy, there were several other reasons to question its usefulness—some of which raised the specter of a war that would end in nuclear escalation. First, the diversion of resources from the central strategic problem of holding the line on the ground in Europe might return NATO to the position of having to use tactical nuclear weapons to stave off defeat there. Next, even if the peripheral warfare strategy worked, Russian leaders might, out of desperation, feel that in this instance *they* had no choice but to resort to the use of weapons of mass destruction. They might well see such an option as the only way to reverse their fortunes in a conventional war that was going badly for them worldwide. Finally, one of the types of attack called for by the maritime strategy could have seriously undermined the stability of nuclear deterrence. This was the notion of sending U.S. hunter-killer attack submarines into Arctic waters to search out Soviet ballistic missile–firing submarines in the underwater bastions where they cruised in seeming security. Such an action—if it were ever actually carried out—might well have forced the Russians into a use or lose mind-set, placing the prospect of nuclear holocaust on a real hair-trigger.[19]

An additional problem was that the *types* of ships the United States was building then—and to a great extent now—were such that they would burn to the waterline if hit by an anti-ship missile. As a reference point, recall the grave damage done by fire to the *USS*

Stark when it was hit in 1987 by just one Iraqi missile in the Persian Gulf.[20] Throughout the cold war the governing idea in naval ship-building was to design fast, lethal, but poorly armored vessels. It was thought that they would conduct their battles far out to sea, against opponents who would be detected and destroyed before they ever got a shot off. Given that the maritime strategy called for lots of inshore operations, where they would be subjected to heavy missile fire from ashore, this lack of defensive armor posed a serious practical problem. For the kind of more heavily armored fleet capable of waging close-in "littoral warfare," as envisioned by Lehman and Reagan, would not have had the agility necessary to fence effectively with Soviet attack submarines ranging throughout the North Atlantic. And the notion of building two separate, special-purpose fleets—one for fighting when at "eyeball range," the other strictly for mid-ocean engagements—would have been an extremely inefficient use of resources.[21]

This problem was only deepened by that fact that the Soviets had decided *not* to imitate the U.S. Navy's emphasis on aircraft carriers and other types of surface combatant vessels. Instead the Red Navy, under the inspired leadership of Admiral Sergei Gorshkov, concentrated on developing its submarine arm as the principal means of challenging the United States for naval mastery. In effect, Gorshkov held that submarines were the true "capital ship" of the nuclear age: they were stealthy, capable of independent operation virtually anywhere, and packed an enormous punch.[22] The Soviet approach to naval strategy was thus a major refinement to the German conceptions about U-boat fleets before and during both world wars. The Germans—during the kaiser's day and then later under Hitler—made the mistake of investing heavily in surface combat vessels, resulting in their entering both great wars with relatively small submarine fleets (having just a few dozen at the start of each war). The Russians, on the other hand, would have begun a World War III with hundreds of submarines, and would have mounted a mortal threat at sea from the outset.

Reagan's second secretary of the navy, James Webb, resigned in part over what he thought was the administration's failure to address this concern. And military historian John Keegan also argued that the submarine had overtaken the aircraft carrier in naval affairs.[23] For what it is worth, the only real naval war of the past generation—fought in the South Atlantic between Great Britain and Argentina in 1982—featured just two Royal Navy attack submarines completely bottling up the entire Argentine surface navy. Fortunately a more rigorous test—in the form of a Soviet-American sea war—of just which type of vessel was the true capital ship of the age never happened.

In many respects the U.S. Navy, initially given substantial new resources by Ronald Reagan, reacted much as the army had. It rekindled a vision of naval strategy that came straight out of World War II, with twin emphases on aircraft carriers and amphibious assault operations. Much as the army looked back and rediscovered classical blitzkrieg doctrine. The best news about both of these responses to budgetary largesse was that our sea and land services bought enough and built enough new weaponry to make the idea of waging a straight conventional war far more palatable. And feasible. This meant that the firebreak between old-style warfare and nuclear holocaust had been widened yet again—a very good thing. The problem, of course, was that this blast-from-the-past approach to military and naval affairs made the United States dependent on the ability to find opponents, after the fall of the Soviet Union, who would agree to fight us conventionally. With the exception of Saddam Hussein, there have been no takers.

Instead a kind of "global intifada" mounted by a dispersed network of terrorists has erupted. And the navy that Reagan built, along with the army, entered the twenty-first-century world somewhat ill prepared for the war on terror and other odd new kinds of conflict most likely to emerge in the years ahead. A similar problem has bedeviled the air force.

From its birth nearly one hundred years ago as the Army Air Service, the United States Air Force has suffered something of an identity crisis. Created to provide reconnaissance and close-in fire support for ground troops, the air service and its organizational descendants nonetheless strove—from very early on—to carve out an independent role for air power. This search for a distinctive mission led to the concept of strategic bombing—the notion that air attacks alone, concentrated on enemy civilian populations and infrastructure, could win a war. This highly seductive idea implied that an adversary might be mortally wounded even if his land and naval forces had not yet been engaged, much less defeated. Instead they could simply be bypassed. As the range and payload-carrying capability of aircraft improved, particularly after World War I, the society-shattering potential of bombing, such as had been envisioned in H. G. Wells's prescient *The War in the Air* (1908), appeared within reach.

Thus began the long organizational romance—and not only in American military circles—with an idea that was at heart truly a terrorist conception, an idea that would lead to more than one million German and Japanese civilians being deliberately incinerated during World War II and to equally brutal bombing campaigns against civilians in the Korean and Vietnam conflicts. For all the killing that has been done in this fashion, though, it is hard to point to any strategic bombing campaign that has ever succeeded, by itself, in winning a war. Nations under such attack quickly learned to decentralize their industries and services, and their civil populations did not collapse emotionally. Rather, bombing kindled great hatred toward the attacker. But such poor material and moral results did little to dampen the ardor of air strategists, who continue even today to seek out the ultimate refinements to a process that will, they hope, one day gain them their holy grail.[24]

But there have been some bumps in the road for the bombing lobby. By the time Ronald Reagan entered office, the air force— which had not become independent of the army until after World War II—was returning to the idea of providing close support to ground forces as its principal mission. The recent failure of strategic bombing in Vietnam—both the Rolling Thunder campaign early in the war and the later Linebacker air offensives—had had a sobering effect on the air force's top leaders, who returned to basic battlefield support. Thus the air force came to provide the air part of the new AirLand Battle doctrine introduced during the early 1980s, which in many ways simply revisited the ideas of German *Luftwaffe* leaders who had done so much to enliven the concept of blitzkrieg forty years earlier, much as the ground-oriented aspects of AirLand Battle resembled the panzer tactics of that earlier period. But there was also something new, something that would soon revitalize thinking about strategic bombing: the rise of a new generation of precision-guided munitions of ever greater range and accuracy. These weapons, in the form of air-launched cruise missiles and laser-guided bombs, now made it possible for even a slow, relatively clunky bomber like the B-52 to mount attacks from safe airspace well outside enemy defenses.

Beyond the idea of strategic bombardment from a distance using smart weapons, the air force also experimented during this period with several types of aircraft designed to penetrate hostile territory by flying fast and coming in low, "under the radar." But none of these really seemed to work as, since the Battle of Britain in 1940, electronic means of detecting the numbers and direction of attack aircraft had given an inherent advantage to the defenders. Even in Vietnam, a struggle between a superpower and an underdeveloped third world country, losses to the strategic bomber fleet had proved unacceptably high. It was only when two new ways to defeat enemy sensors had been crafted that strategic bombing made a comeback. The first measure was to improve our ability to jam enemy radars or otherwise confuse them, combined with new anti-radar missiles that could destroy air defense sites as soon as their radars were switched on. The second innovation was to develop aircraft made with material that absorbed or deflected radio waves—so-called Stealth technology.

During the Reagan years, both these measures were vigorously pursued. By January 1991, during the administration of Reagan's immediate successor, George H. W. Bush, the U.S. Air Force was ready once again to test the whole idea of strategic bombing as a warfighting concept. Guided by an updated version of the classical ideas of Billy Mitchell and Curtis LeMay, the air force proceeded to pound the hapless Iraqi Army—and the rest of Iraq—for six weeks before a half-million-man ground force attacked.[25] The overwhelming victory in the field drew attention away from the fact that the strategic bombing of Iraq had done very little by itself to break the will of Iraqis. The conflict was hailed as ushering in a revolution in military affairs—even though more than 90 percent of the munitions dropped on Iraq from the air were "dumb iron bombs."[26]

Since its first Gulf War, the United States has mounted three major aerial offensives: against Serbia (1999), Afghanistan (2001), and a second time against Iraq (2003). Of the three, the air campaign against the Serbs is the case that comes closest to being a possible success for strategic bombing. The goal in this instance was to force the retreat of Serbian troops from Kosovo, and a U.S.-led NATO force waged a seventy-eight-day air war (no ground troops were employed in combat) in the spring of 1999 that ended with the Serbs withdrawing. At least one serious scholarly study has labeled this a clear success for strategic bombing.[27] Other studies have made the point, though, that the Serbs may have retreated when President Clinton began talking seriously about mounting a ground invasion—at a time that also coincided with the Serbian loss of Russian diplomatic support.[28] So the Kosovo case may not be clear.

The second major strategic bombing campaign, conducted in Afghanistan in October and early November 2001, was designed to topple the Taliban—the al Qaeda terror network's host and protector—from power. For more than a month, air force bombers roamed the skies over Afghanistan, striking at will but to little effect. It quickly grew clear to Secretary of Defense Donald Rumsfeld that bombing alone would not work; so he called in his theater commander, General Tommy Franks, and asked him what other options he had available. Franks responded that special forces could be used to lead indigenous resistance groups against the Taliban, and that they could also act as ground-air liaisons that would greatly improve the effectiveness of the air assets involved in the campaign. Rumsfeld ordered Franks to unleash the special forces and to shift the emphasis in the air operations to close support of these irregular, horseback-mounted troops.[29] In all, just a few hundred special operators led the way against the Taliban on the ground; but they were closely networked with attack aircraft and unmanned aerial vehicles which struck repeatedly and with ever greater effect against Taliban and al Qaeda formations. The lessons of the Afghan campaign were twofold, for it showed both the limits of air power alone and the enormous military potential of even small combat groups, properly interconnected with aircraft and armed drones above. The success of the special operations forces—after the failure of straight strategic bombing—suggests this campaign was something of "a war to change all wars."

But this was not to be the case. The next war, the second with Iraq in twelve years, began in the spring of 2003 with yet another application of massive strategic air power. This time using the catchphrase "shock and awe," derived from the title of a group-written think-tank study whose authors, among other things, lauded the psychological effects of the use of nuclear weapons on the Japanese civilian population in World War II.[30] Like so many previous aerial bombardment campaigns, this one did little to intimidate the enemy—either Saddam Hussein's hard-core supporters or the general Iraqi populace, several thousands of whom were killed in the bombing. Instead it was the advance of U.S. ground forces, in a lightning march up Mesopotamia, that brought down Saddam Hussein. And even though regular Iraqi forces melted away rather than confront the combined air-ground punch of the U.S. troops—where air power was extremely effective in its close support role—an insurgency soon arose that gave the occupiers fits. No shock, no awe. Just raw anger and resentment that spilled over into sometimes brutal acts of violence leading to new spirals of killing. As to the impact of the strategic bombing, the sheer amount of destruction seriously complicated the task of post-conflict reconstruction and also undermined our friendly story that we had come as liberators.

Despite all the failures of bombing campaigns that Reagan had witnessed during his lifetime, he remained a strong supporter of strategic air power and possessed a sophisticated understanding of the major issues. He knew of the remarkable opportunity posed by cruise missile technology and supported its further development. But he also knew that cruise missiles had serious range limitations and were susceptible to several types of countermeasures, so he favored development of a fast new bomber, the B-1, that could penetrate deep into enemy airspace. That the B-1 might eventually be countered by the Soviets was a likely outcome Reagan admitted and accepted. But this hardly daunted him because he saw in the development of a new penetrator a weapon that fit in with his own emerging ideas about pursuing a cost-imposing strategy against the Russians. As Reagan put it during one of his radio broadcasts, "We know the Soviets will have to spend more than the B-1's cost to develop a defense against them—and what's wrong with that?"[31] This was the attitude he took into the presidency and that guided much of his strategic thinking during his two terms in office. It seems hardly surprising, in light of his thinking about the value of the B-1 in forcing greater expenditures by the Soviets, that Reagan so warmly embraced Andrew Marshall's broad concept of a cost-imposing strategy when it was presented to him.

Reagan's successors would continue to value air power highly, even after the cold war. For George H. W. Bush, and even more so for Bill Clinton, American aerial mastery opened up a host of opportunities for the skillful use of force in the pursuit of greater goals. The excessive bombing of Iraq itself, along with the slaughter of thousands of hapless Iraqi troops (recall the infamous "highway of death") demonstrated how the United States could use overwhelming force from the sky in ways that made the military task on the ground far simpler to contemplate. For the first President Bush, this was a way, as he put it, to "exorcise" the demons of Vietnam.

Bill Clinton took this notion even further, using force frequently during his two terms but relying on air power as much as he possibly could. In the case of the Kosovo War, this meant trying to conduct an extended exercise in coercive diplomacy using *only* air power—which left the mostly defenseless Kosovars on the ground vulnerable to the worst sort of unfettered Serbian barbarism. But for Clinton, the ability to use force in this manner, and to reduce American casualties nearly to zero, made it a worthwhile exercise in what Michael Ignatieff has called "virtual war."[32]

Thus air power has taken center stage in the early twenty-first century as the most usable military tool in the American arsenal. The U.S. Air Force has global reach and can be employed in ways that reduce the likelihood of many American casualties. But the usability of air power should not be confused with its *utility*. Strategic bombing has a checkered past, including its most recent applications in our various conflicts. On the other hand, the use of air power in close cooperation with ground forces continues to have profound effects on the battlefield, as it has since World War II. And this remains true even when the ground forces consist of small numbers of special forces on horseback as opposed to large numbers of tanks operating on open plains or deserts. Yet senior military and political leaders, out of their habits of mind and institutional interests, keep reaching for massive strategic bombing, even when the historical record compels caution.

On the matter of air power, Ronald Reagan did little to shift emphasis from the use of one of its two basic applications over the other. Instead he supported both, seeking a return to the close-support roots of the air arm and the development of new means to keep strategic bombardment a viable option. Close support, he knew, allowed the United States a good chance of being able to wage any new war conventionally, virtually eliminating the need to think about resorting to nuclear arms except *in extremis* or in retaliation for a Soviet first strike. In this way air power could contribute to making the world "less nuclear." As to the emerging new tools of strategic bombardment, they would, Reagan reasoned, impose greater costs upon the Soviets than upon ourselves—in terms of the disproportionate response the Russians would have to make just to maintain the balance of power.

Reagan's support for the use of air power in close coordination with ground forces contributed much to the overall revitalization of the U.S. military and to the towering efficiency on the conventional battlefield that it still exhibits. His second strand of thought seems simply to have shored up the strategic bombing lobby, which had largely grown moribund in the wake of defeat in Vietnam. Although some air power diehards believed that "had the raids continued the North Vietnamese would have had to accept total military defeat," they were a distinct minority.[33] But thanks to the rehabilitation process begun under Reagan and continued by his successors, these "latter-day LeMays" seem to be with us to stay. This is a most troubling development for the twenty-first-century world, given the clear record of military ineffectiveness of this sort of bombing and the grassroots reaction of hatred that it tends to breed among the civilian populations that inevitably bear the brunt of aerial bombardment.

Aside from various changes in the land, sea, and air services, three other interesting developments in military affairs during the Reagan years merit notice. All three spoke to both organizational and doctrinal matters of the highest importance. And there have been problems in adopting and adhering to all three as well—though to varying degrees. Just how these three matters finally unfold will likely play a determining role in the shaping of the twenty-first-century world.

The first development has to do with the "revitalization of the special operations forces," the phrase that found its way into Reagan's 1980 presidential platform because of his belief (like Kennedy before him) that these elite troops were ideally suited to taking the initiative on several fronts against the Soviets.[34] This area was receiving attention largely because of the tragic and embarrassing failure of the April 1980 attempt to rescue American hostages held in Iran. Beyond that cathartic event, though, some in the Defense Department and in Congress believed that the Pentagon's obsession with the notion of a massive war in Europe dangerously neglected the fact that most wars were smaller and more irregular in nature. For them the doctrinal lessons of Vietnam were not to be ignored in favor of focusing on great tank battles against the Soviets in the Fulda Gap. Rather, the crucible of that lost war in Southeast Asia, it was thought, should have galvanized a true transformation toward a lighter, nimbler, and more lethal military.

Led in the Pentagon by mid-level civilian officials such as Lynn Rylander and Noel Koch, and with a political "product champion" in Senator William Cohen (R-Maine)—who later became secretary of defense under Bill Clinton—momentum soon built in support of enhanced special operations capabilities. No one initially wished to create a separate, servicelike institution. Rather, the focus was chiefly on how to improve tactical mobility so as to avoid another disaster like Desert One. But the uniformed conventional war-fighters in the Pentagon and their panoply of supporters in the Congress fought a vigorous bureaucratic battle to keep special operations forces "in their place." For several years the conventional forces' lobby succeeded, compelling the supporters of the special operations elite to resort to ever more extreme measures. These culminated in a sulphurous public debate and in the passage of federal legislation mandating the creation of the Special Operations Command, which was, in the end, to become a "servicelike" entity.

All this took six years to achieve, and the command was established in Florida rather than ensconced anywhere near the Pentagon.[35] In the end, though, this professional distance from the conventional forces may have allowed the new command to develop more independently and innovatively—just in time to breed a new generation of soldiers attuned to the vagaries of the emerging forms of conflict. Although they would be used for the most part in a conventional fashion during the invasion of Panama (1989), were kept on a very short leash in the first Gulf War (1991), and were humbled in Somalia (1993), the special forces would soon come into their own. They carried off an "immaculate invasion" of Haiti (1994), then blossomed in Afghanistan (2001), a campaign that was virtually all theirs until the fall of the Taliban. In the second U.S. attack on Iraq in 2003, special forces successfully undertook a wide variety of tasks. They knocked out the "Scud Box" missile firing grounds in Western Iraq; saved Iraqi oilfields in the southern part of the country; secured the approaches to Baghdad for the conventional forces' march up Mesopotamia; and mobilized the Kurds in the north. All this was achieved with limited numbers and resources—less than 5 percent of the total "force package" employed.[36] And even more was done that will remain classified for a long time.

The second major organizational development during the Reagan years was also embodied in legislation, the 1986 Defense Reorganization Act, or as it is more commonly called, after its congressional sponsors, the Goldwater-Nichols Act. This legislation contained a curious mix of centralizing and decentralizing initiatives. For example, it elevated the chairman of the Joint Chiefs from being first among equals with regard to the heads of the services to being instead the "principal military adviser to the president and the secretary of defense." The law also gave the chairman direct control over the Joint Staff, so that he had both the people and the resources to pursue his agenda. Goldwater-Nichols also greatly empowered regional commanders, who could now interact directly with the secretary of defense—and de facto directly with the president. Admiral Bill Owens, former vice chairman of the Joint Chiefs, put the matter succinctly:

> The congressional intent behind the Goldwater-Nichols Act was to make "jointness"—the formal concept of interservice cooperation and planning—the law of the land. Service on a Joint Staff, long regarded (accurately) by officers as a career-ending assignment, now became mandatory for advancement to senior rank.[37]

Jointness may have become the law of the land, but in practice this law has done little to tamp down service parochialism. The defense budget, which now well exceeds $400 billion annually, remains roughly equally divided among land, sea, and air services. And the dual empowerment of the chairman and regional commanders has created new possibilities for bureaucratic stalemate reminiscent of earlier eras. The 1999 Kosovo War is the prime example of this kind of infighting, which saw General Wesley Clark, the theater commander, at odds with the chairman, General Henry Shelton. In this case, one salient dispute centered on Clark's demand for deployment of a 250,000-man field army as a prerequisite for undertaking ground operations. Shelton, on the other hand, wanted to use special forces much as they would be used two years later in Afghanistan: with indigenous forces on the ground and in close conjunction with U.S. air power. In the event, it turned out that neither had the power to carry the day in the bureaucratic infighting. So a sloppy air-only war was fought—and yet somehow won.[38]

But the greatest problem caused by the increased empowerment of the chairman and the regional commanders had little to do with budgets or turf fights. Rather, the new system conveyed real power to make lasting doctrinal change; and when Colin Powell became chairman in 1989 he seized the moment to enshrine his belief in using "overwhelming force" as *the* governing doctrine. Regional commanders could hardly object to this, as it meant they now had reason to ask for as much as possible to wage any conflict, so internecine feuds were quieted. In practice the Powell Doctrine meant that Iraq would suffer six weeks of unnecessarily heavy bombing in January and February 1991 and would be subjected again in 2003 to similar "shock and awe" tactics. Adoption of Powell's doctrine meant that, in any conflict, U.S. military planners would always reach for the heavy hammer first—as happened in October 2001 in the fruitless first month of bombing in the Afghan campaign. In this case, however, the shift to small special forces teams turned the situation around—an operational necessity given Afghanistan's landlocked remoteness and the time it would have taken to gain basing rights and deploy a large force. The few hundred special forces soldiers on the ground hardly constituted an overwhelming force, yet they accomplished the job of toppling the Taliban in high style. The Afghan campaign, at least in those few shining months late in 2001, suggests that in the twenty-first-century world a legacy like the Powell Doctrine will likely prove to be a counterproductive, bothersome, and unnecessary burden.

The idea of applying overwhelming force in an era when opponents refuse to fight stand-up battles with the United States is a notion bound to cause heartache in the coming years. Quite simply, the Powell Doctrine is a cold war artifact that cries out for amendment as we face the rise of terrorism as a form of war in its own right. No longer do we require overwhelming force, but rather nimble networked forces that know how to rip apart terror nodes cell by cell.

With this in mind, the third major conceptual/organizational innovation of the Reagan era may prove useful as something of an anti-
dote to the Powell Doctrine. The Weinberger Doctrine, which preceded Powell's by some years—it was introduced in 1984—still
stands as a basic way to think about the use of force. Caspar Weinberger, who was Reagan's secretary of defense for seven years, devised a curious mix of notions, drawn both from ethical "just war"
theory and realpolitik, which held that six tests had to be passed before going to war:

1. Our vital interests must be at stake.
2. The issues involved are so important for the future of the United
   States and our allies that we are prepared to commit enough forces
   to win.
3. We have clearly defined political and military objectives, which we
   must secure.
4. We have sized our forces to achieve our objectives.
5. We have some reasonable assurance of the support of the American people.
6. U.S. forces are committed to combat only as a last resort.[39]

Many of the ethical notions of Saint Augustine's *City of God* and
Thomas Aquinas's *Treatise on Law* are echoed in Weinberger's Doctrine. The first test relates to their ideas about "right purpose." The
fifth test refers to the support of the people, which speaks in a modern
way to the classical requirement that a decision for war had to be undertaken by a "duly constituted authority." The sixth test draws directly from these theologians' injunctions to use force only when all
other efforts at dispute resolution have failed. The third test is the only
one that remains wholly steeped in realpolitik; but even this formulation relates to Aquinas's idea that any decision to wage a just war must
be taken only when the probability of success is high. This leaves the
second and fourth tests, which progress beyond initiating a just war to
waging it in a just fashion. While the core of Thomist thinking on this
point—*jus in bello*—is that noncombatants must be kept safe, just
war–fighting also requires "proportionality," or refraining from the

use of excessive force. The second and fourth tests speak directly to this last point and should serve as a reminder and a caution to those who instinctively reach first for overwhelming force, the bastard child of John Foster Dulles's "massive retaliation" idea in the 1950s.[40]

As a guide to national security policy in the twenty-first century, the Reagan-era Weinberger Doctrine will prove far more useful than Colin Powell's preference for the massive use of force. For we are likely to confront many situations in which a small amount of military action may achieve great ends. Even so, it is important to note the irony that Weinberger first elucidated his doctrine in rebuttal to the emerging call—coming from Secretary of State George Shultz—to commence a de facto war on terror. Weinberger disliked this notion, on both practical and ethical grounds, and a bureaucratic battle ensued—one discussed later in some detail in Chapter 7. Suffice it to say Weinberger managed to derail much of Shultz's policy initiative—a success that was perhaps a triumph of ethics but that had deleterious effects on counterterror policy for many years.

If, instead of minding Weinberger's call to use force in a proportionate manner, we stick to Powell's approach, we will use force less often, but when we do so it will be with much larger "packages"— which will be of little use against dispersed terrorists or insurgents. In the early years of the war on terror we have seen the tug between these two views played out. The Weinberger approach came more to the fore in the nimble campaign in Afghanistan in 2001; and the Powell Doctrine was clearly represented in the huge use of land and air forces against Iraq in 2003 and since. Both of these primal constructs about the use of force arose during the Reagan years, and I observe in the course of my daily work that adherents of both views continue to pull and haul policy toward one or the other end of this strategic spectrum. My greatest concern is that the uniformed services—with the notable exception of the special operations community—strongly prefer the notion of using overwhelming force. This is troubling at a time when the greater flexibility of the Weinberger approach is likely to prove more useful in mastering the new challenges that have come our way and that will increasingly imperil us in the years ahead.[41]

Of all the ways in which Ronald Reagan affected the U.S. military during his time in office, the most important was his heartfelt approach to restoring the self-confidence of the services. He quickly put defeat in Vietnam in its proper context—by noting that it was a noble endeavor to try to prevent Communist expansion in Southeast Asia—and then proceeded to tackle the central strategic problems of the day. These problems went well beyond simply figuring out how to defend Western Europe; but solving that nettlesome problem would also go a long way toward widening the firebreak between conventional and nuclear war, Reagan's true strategic crusade. In this quest he was totally successful, crafting new forces and weapons that could stand off any conventional threat by conventional means. The great dividend of this revitalized military came in the wake of the Soviet Union's dissolution. For the precision weapons created to stem the tide of the Red Army turned out to be quite useful in other theaters—and gave the United States an edge that no regional opponents could ever hope to match.

Yet at the same time Reagan's unstinting support for the military had the unintended consequence of allowing all the services to forgo making painful choices about what we now call transformation. So the army continues to define itself principally in terms of heavy main battle tanks, the navy remains wedded to super aircraft carriers—after its brief, unsuccessful flirtation with "arsenal ships" (think of them as "super missile carriers")—and the air force is still searching for the elusive formula for successful strategic bombing. Thus the great cold war triumph, followed by the easy victory in our first war with Saddam Hussein, may have become a kind of trap that has kept the U.S. military far too traditional-looking for its own good.

At the organizational level, Reagan unleashed opposing forces that soon kindled renewed struggles for the soul of the American military. The rise of the Special Operations Command (SOCOM) gave voice to a strategic approach needed to manage the emergence of terror as a form of war. Yet the separate, servicelike nature of SOCOM placed our military elites in a most awkward position. Although under a new command, Green Berets and Rangers, along with SEALs and special tactics soldiers, remained members of the army, navy, and air force and depended heavily upon these senior services for career advancement as well as the material resources necessary for their daily operations. To borrow from St. Paul's notion of a good Christian, the special forces soldier found himself "in the (conventional military) world, but not of it."

So, naturally, the rise of SOCOM renewed tension between the regular and irregular elements in the U.S. military. This problem began before the dawn of the Republic, when Rogers' Rangers protected the frontier settlers in the mid-eighteenth century against terrorism by raiding Indian tribes in the pay of the French. George Washington deepened the divide, insisting on creating an army that would fight the British along conventional European lines, though the real American edge in the Revolution came from irregular forces like those led by Francis Marion, the "Swamp Fox." The tension has surfaced again and again throughout our history, culminating in catastrophe in Vietnam, when those in favor of fighting with "big units" prevailed over the unconventional warriors. In our current conflict the same tension has been evident. The initial special forces campaign in Afghanistan, which was highly successful, gave way to a much larger and more conventional occupying force that oversaw a return of parts of the country to the control of warlords and in some areas to resurgent Taliban fighters. This necessitated the redeployment of more of our special operations forces there, a move that quickly restored the equilibrium on the ground. Yet a similar pattern of falling back on conventional operations emerged in the Iraq campaign as well, with the innovations and breakthroughs of 2003 fading in the face of a traditional-looking— and much less effective—military occupation.

This renewed tension between special forces and conventional operators in the military was foreshadowed by Reagan having unleashed a set of dueling concepts during his time as commander-in-chief: the Weinberger and Powell doctrines. Reagan's secretary of defense sought a nuanced way to think about American uses of force in the future, including how to employ it precisely and proportionately. But the army general who rose to prominence during the Reagan years, and who later became a powerful new kind of chairman of the Joint Chiefs, saw

matters differently. For Colin Powell, America's cold war triumph—
and the fading of the risk of global nuclear holocaust—had created
new room to think in terms of the use of overwhelming force. In the
main, the Weinberger Doctrine has been bested by Powell's perspective over the past two decades. But, as will be discussed in the next
chapter, American ability to use force at all has increasingly become a
function of how the rest of the world perceives American purpose and
reacts to this perception. In an era when the battle of the story is every
bit as important as the battle on the ground, we are likely to find that
the notion of relying on overwhelming force will immediately cripple
us as we pursue our various national aims.

Reagan's openness of mind to competing concepts proved beneficial overall in the realm of military affairs. But his willingness to accommodate traditionalists just as much as innovators resulted in the
persistence of practices that have made the military less well prepared
for the kinds of conflicts it must now conduct, and has created new
impediments to efforts to tell and sell our story to the world. The area
of public diplomacy was particularly important to Reagan; and he
would no doubt have been deeply concerned to ensure that any use of
force in the future should be completely harmonized with what he
liked to call our information strategy. For he seemed to understand
implicitly that we could win every firefight and still lose the battle of
the story. A serious problem during his time, it is now a critical one.

6

The Nuances of Information Strategy

With just a few exceptions, American presidents have abstained from directly exercising their constitutionally mandated command over the military when in office. As president, George Washington formed and led an army to suppress the Whiskey Rebellion but spent most of his time keeping his own troops in line. James Madison took the field in battle—at Bladensburg in 1814, wearing his treasury secretary's dueling pistols strapped on his hips—and did poorly. Half a century later, Abraham Lincoln did better but limited himself to sacking generals—both good and bad—and checking at the telegraph office each day for war news. A hundred years or so after Lincoln, Lyndon Johnson was bent over the map table, selecting targets for the aerial bombardment of North Vietnam. His results were by far the worst. But if presidents should not immerse themselves in military strategy, the same cannot be said of what Ronald Reagan came to call information strategy, the use of communications techniques to shape others' perceptions and persuade them to accept our views.[1] Almost all presidents have been deeply involved in using information, including conveying it to other governments—sometimes even directly communicating with foreign mass publics—in the hope of advancing American causes, policies, and interests.

Of the Founding Fathers who rose to the presidency, Thomas Jefferson seemed most attuned to the potential benefits of telling our story to the world. He served as minister to France after independence and oversaw the opening of an information center there, the distant ancestor of what would become the United States Information Agency. During his two terms as president, he was a consistent practitioner of the persuasive arts, successfully steering a neutralist course during the Napoleonic Wars. In the wake of "Mr. Madison's War" (1812–1815), waged by Jefferson's immediate successor against the British, the president who had done so indifferently in the field at Bladensburg was also suffering mightily in the European press. So Jefferson, observing these troubles from retirement at Monticello, developed a recommendation that dealt with the problem of the moment but that has also characterized American information strategy at its best ever since:

> I hope that to preserve this weather gauge of public opinion, and to counteract the slanders and falsehoods disseminated by the British papers, the government will make it a standing instruction to their ministers at foreign courts to keep Europe truly informed of occurrences here, by publishing in their papers the naked truth always, whether favorable or unfavorable. For they will believe the good, if we tell them the bad also.[2]

This process of reaching out directly to foreign citizens rather than going strictly through official government contacts is called public diplomacy; and while Jefferson was focused most closely on the importance of the content to be conveyed, the evolving conduits of information have also been extremely important. When information traveled the world at the limited pace of the fastest oceangoing ship, ambassadors of necessity had to be the principal information strategists, advancing ideas and countering criticisms, more often than not on their own authority. With the coming of transatlantic telegraph connections, just after the Civil War in 1866, information could now move worldwide at previously unimaginable speed—down from months to minutes. In many respects, the change wrought by the telegraph, in a comparative sense, was far greater than that which accompanied the rise of the Internet.[3] This advance in telecommunications allowed for greater centralization and coordination of public diplomatic themes and content, though the press remained the principal means of reaching foreign mass publics for another sixty years, until the discovery in the 1920s that shortwave radio signals could be used to broadcast around the world.[4] For the next sixty years (1920s–1980s)—until the rise of cost-efficient direct broadcast satellite television—radio and its various refinements placed the masses ever more within direct reach of those who wanted to communicate with them.

American public diplomacy thus truly came into its own during the cold war. President Eisenhower, a great proponent of information strategy, founded the USIA (United States Information Agency) during his first year in office (1953) and had its director attend National Security Council meetings on a regular basis. USIA's Voice of America programs told oppressed peoples about life in the democratic United States, at their best keeping people "truly informed of occurrences here," to use Jefferson's phrase. Radio Liberty and Radio Free Europe featured programming that concentrated more on providing needed local news to those living in countries where information was controlled and heavily filtered. For their part of this cold war battle of the story, the Soviets and their satraps became expert at jamming radio signals to defend against the American information offensive. The matter of counterattacking with their own content was easy for the Communists, as they did not have to worry about opening up closed conduits. Their target audiences for the most part lived in free societies. This situation led them to focus heavily on content, though with much less attention given to the Jeffersonian injunction to stick to the truth. This information-based dimension of the cold war struggle played itself out for a quarter-century from the inception of the USIA and was a cut-and-thrust affair in which neither side could gain a decisive edge.

Then along came Ronald Reagan. In terms of what was needed to guide a successful information strategy, Reagan had all the right stuff. He was himself a trained professional communicator with a long, successful track record, and his experiences spanned both the radio and television eras. Further, he had honed his skills in attacking communism during his time with the Screen Actors Guild. When he entered the Oval Office he immediately sought ways to use the USIA more effectively, quickly seizing upon the need to shift its technological emphasis from radio to television. Although he upgraded radio broadcast capabilities, Reagan focused more closely on giving USIA a top-flight video arm. The visual medium would not only have more impact on the audience than radio, it was also much harder to jam, given the wide dispersion of the direct broadcast satellite (DBS) signal. Reagan understood all this and charted the new course even though DBS television was still in its relative infancy. As his appointed director of television and film for the USIA, Alvin Snyder, said, "Until Ronald Reagan became president and TV satellites were beaming images behind the Iron Curtain, the propaganda war of words was fought primarily via shortwave radio."[5]

Reagan also understood that a good information strategy required more than just effective conduits; it needed attractive content. You could only win the battle of the story with a great story of your own, he believed. And he soon began to participate in the crafting of a narrative that would portray the cold war in increasingly Manichaean terms—as "a struggle between right and wrong, good and evil," as Reagan encapsulated it in a March 1982 speech. Some of his own advisers opposed stating the terms of the struggle in this fashion.[6] And the press excoriated the president for speaking so bluntly, using criticism of the speech as a way to remind their readers that Reagan was "a simple-minded ideologue" and a "reckless cowboy."[7] Undeterred, Reagan pressed ahead and took the offensive, and in the coming years demonstrated what playwright and Czech president Vaclav Havel called "the power of words to change history."[8] Among the oppressed in totalitarian states, Reagan's words formed a rallying cry that guided their own opposition activities. His message got through even to the gulags, as Soviet dissident Natan Scharansky, for example, met as secretly as possible with his fellow prisoners for sessions composed of what they called their "Reaganite readings."[9]

Whatever the reservations expressed by critics and professional observers in the United States, Reagan believed he was on the right track. He continued with single-minded purpose to develop and unfold his information strategy. In the end this message-oriented aspect of his many-faceted plan for ending the cold war and reducing the threat of nuclear holocaust proved to be the most successful. Certainly his "cost-imposing strategy"—fueling anti-Communist insurgencies and building up our own military—put strains on the Soviet system. But something more than economic or military pressure drove Gorbachev to seek openness in his own society, the path that led ineluctably to the dissolution of the USSR. This something more was Reagan's simply stated, direct challenge to the legitimacy of everything that the Soviet Union stood for—a challenge to which Gorbachev, a true believer in his own political culture, felt compelled to respond. In the end he could not master the challenge, and he would learn firsthand about the ability of ideas to move millions from tyranny to freedom.

The reasons for reexamining Reagan's information strategy go beyond his signal success over the Soviets or the simple fact that he was a masterful communicator worthy of emulation. For his waging of what he called the war of ideas featured many complexities—in some respects, almost as many as accompany actual warfare. For example, he and his administration had to think through questions about the many varied implications of technological change for their policies. They had to consider the extent to which they should continue to invest in "old media" (especially radio broadcasting) as opposed to the "new media" possibilities afforded by the rise of direct broadcast satellite systems. The Reagan administration's skillful support of the former and careful nurturing of the latter may provide useful lessons today as we think about how television (now the "new" old medium), the Internet, and the World Wide Web can be thoughtfully integrated for maximum effect.

Another reason to look closely at information strategy in the 1980s is that we were up against a determined, skillful opponent. Although Soviet information operations are generally denigrated and most closely associated with the "big lie" concept, the Russians were often capable of nimbleness and nuance. Today our war on terror pits us against skillful adversaries who use the media, both old and new, very adroitly. And the war on terror, like the cold war, is hard to win militarily—raising the importance of the war of ideas. So it may prove useful to return to this earlier example of the application of information strategy against a tough, resourceful opponent.

The information war between the United States and the Soviet Union, in its scope and tempo of operations, can usefully be compared to real warfare. There were reasonably fixed lines of battle with constant skirmishing and sniping. These took the form of the daily rhetorical criticisms each side engaged in, which played out through discussion and debate about ongoing world events. This kind of attritional struggle could be clearly seen in the duel to portray events in Central America. The United States depicted the situation there as one of creeping communism, with Cuba engineering coups in places like Grenada and supporting the Sandinistas in Nicaragua. El Salvador was their next target, to be followed, it was thought, by Honduras, Guatemala, and, finally, the grand prize: Mexico.

For their part, the Soviets tried to show that the Americans were acting against the interests of the common people of Central America. Instead of the Nicaraguan contras being Reagan's freedom fighters, the Russians portrayed them as brutal thugs who sought to bring back the bad old authoritarian days. Government forces in El Salvador were riddled with illegal death squads, they claimed—and in this case the evidence suggests they were not far off. In the event, the Soviets held their own in Central America and in other theaters of the cold war. And wherever and whenever they could, they took advantage of freedom of the press and of the common citizens of the West to support groups of Americans and others outside their bloc who would willingly engage in loud public protests against U.S. policy.

Aside from this never-ending attritional struggle, there were identifiable major offensives that grew out of specific events and saw the employment of huge concentrations of resources in support of a particular objective. Perhaps the best case of this kind of specific information campaign arose in the wake of the Soviet shoot-down on August 30, 1983, of Korean Air Lines' Flight 007. A total of 269 people were killed in the incident, including a U.S. congressman and dozens of other Americans, as the flight strayed into Soviet airspace on its way to Seoul and was, after some hours, attacked by an SU-15 jet fighter aircraft. U.S. decision-makers quickly concluded that this event should be the catalyst for a depiction of the Soviets as having committed an act of deliberate mass murder. Further, it showed how dangerous and inefficient the Russian military was, shoring up both notions of the need for arms reductions *and* for modernization of U.S. strategic forces. A full-court press ensued, with Reagan himself taking to the broadcast airwaves and cutting a figure in this informational battle far better than Madison had during the firefight at Bladensburg. The president was joined by other high-level administration figures, with his United Nations ambassador Jeane Kirkpatrick playing a particularly compelling role. It was, in effect, an information-driven blitzkrieg of the first order.[10]

For their part, the Russians did poorly. From the outset they were reluctant even to admit the shoot-down had occurred. Then, under pressure of emerging evidence and the vehemence of the American attack, they slowly gave ground. Piece by piece they doled out information, admitting they had shot down the Korean airliner—where, when, and eventually why. The truth was that they had not committed an act of deliberate mass murder but rather had shadowed KAL 007 for hours, trying to make contact at first, then firing warning shots and trying to bring the plane to a forced landing. It turned out that the Soviet pilot could not talk on the same frequency with the unknown aircraft, which had strayed into sensitive military airspace over Sakhalin and the Sea of Okhotsk. In Russian eyes the "bogey" might have been an American spy plane, several of which had been shot down over the years.

The Soviets told the truth, but not fast enough. They dribbled out the relevant details one at a time but were overwhelmed by the vast amounts of information the Americans had already churned out. The lesson here, which would also resonate among the political advisers to candidates for high office, was that first impressions were crucially important. It was one thing to work on the psyches of the undecided, quite another to reshape the thinking of those whose minds were already set. In psychological terms, once a person has committed to a particular belief, he will work hard to ensure that new information is consistent with his original formulation—and will tend to discount discrepant information. Perhaps this is why decisions were taken to massage the facts of this case as the USIA prepared to go on the offensive. For example, U.S. intercepts made it clear that the Soviet pilot had attempted to identify and communicate with the pilot of the intruding aircraft—but these intercepts were withheld from the USIA, and its official line continued to be that this was an act of deliberate mass murder. And the audiotape that the American ambassador played at the United Nations during this crisis had a five-minute gap that cut out key material that was largely exculpatory of the Russians. Five days later the Department of State felt impelled to issue a public admission that warning shots had been fired. Too late. The "mass murder" label stuck.[11]

This problem of the enduring power of first impressions seems to be one that American political leaders have known about from very early on. At the outset of our Revolution, for example, an account of the initial battles with the British at Lexington and Concord was quickly written and sent on a fast schooner to Ireland, whence it was hand carried to the Lord Mayor of London, whose sympathies lay with the colonists. The report, which cast the Crown in a very bad light, caused an immediate sensation that only grew, as the official army report of the fighting did not arrive for another two weeks. By then the European press had also picked up the story. This coup of disseminating their side of the story first truly turned the exploits of the Minutemen who engaged the Redcoats into "shots heard round the world." When official rebuttals to the American story finally appeared, more than a month had elapsed, and there was simply no way to reshape the strong first impression that had been made and already consolidated.[12]

That the Reagan administration understood the power of striking first and hardest in an information battle meant, in practice, that Jefferson's injunction to stick to the truth was sometimes ignored. Besides selectively editing intercepts of Soviet radio transmissions during the Korean airliner incident, information strategists also bent the truth in another important situation. This one had to do with rigging the results of the early strategic missile defense experiments. Alvin Snyder tells the story of the intricate deception in this way:

> The Pentagon planned to put bombs aboard the missiles that were to be hit by incoming Star Wars projectiles, so that the explosion would prove the test firings were "successful," thereby conning the Soviets into thinking that American missile technology was more developed than was actually the case. . . . Bombs were duly placed aboard the target missiles in the first three tests, but the interceptor missed the target by such a great distance that detonating the bombs would have been ludicrous. For the fourth test, which took place over the Pacific, an incoming Minuteman missile was artificially heated and special heat-seeking sensors were placed aboard the interceptor, so it could more easily find its target. A radar beacon was also placed on the target, which was turned sideways to make a broader bull's-eye for the interceptor. . . . And, indeed, with the help of the many "enhancements," the fourth and final test firing was right on target.[13]

The deception worked in that the Russians took Star Wars extremely seriously, seeing in it a potentially mortal threat to the viability of their strategic deterrent forces. This led to much acrimony between the powers, probably delaying the implementation of the arms reductions that both Reagan and Gorbachev wanted. Indeed, the Russians' only response was to build more missiles—to try to swamp U.S. defenses—leading to enormous increases in the numbers of nuclear warheads and launchers on both sides during the Reagan years.[14]

The quickened pace of the arms race in the wake of the embellishment of Star Wars test results shows that sometimes, even if the deception works, the adversary's response is more troubling than the initial problem. During World War II, for example, the German *Luftwaffe* fell victim to this sort of difficulty. In the years before the war,

Nazi propaganda had helped enable Hitler's territorial grabs in central Europe by greatly overstating German air strength. This seemingly heightened threat of strategic bombing deterred France and Britain from standing in Germany's way as it annexed Austria and eventually all of Czechoslovakia.[15] But the deception backfired in the sense that it was so believable that it prompted the British to build a robust air defense system—just in time—that saved them during the 1940 Blitz.[16] All deceptions may have unintended consequences of this sort, which must be thought through. But deceptions should not be rejected simply because such risks exist.

Despite the Korean airliner incident and other skillful American ploys, the Russians had their innings too. If they suffered in the world's eyes in the wake of KAL 007 and had been duped by cooked-up data about missile defense, their predicament was no worse than that of the United States after the Russians finished vilifying the very notion of creating a neutron bomb. This weapon was intended to kill invading Soviet troops with radiation while sparing most infrastructure and buildings in the combat zone, due to its much lower blast effects. The Russians attacked this concept immediately and ferociously, on all fronts and with all sorts of official and unofficial (i.e., "front") organizations. In this case they did not make the same error of responding in piecemeal fashion that they had during the airliner incident. And the results were telling. Even though the United States went to great lengths to rebut the Soviet charges—at one point even acquiring a statement of support from the pope, who said the neutron bomb was an "ethically-minded" weapon—nothing could be done to change the first impression that had been planted by the Soviets. The neutron bomb had imprinted itself on the consciousness of global civil society as an ugly instrument of mass destruction. Score this one for the Soviets.[17]

So it went throughout the last decade of the cold war. My point is not so much that Reagan was better at this type of thing than the Russians—though, at the margin, he surely was better than Andropov and Chernenko, Gorbachev's immediate predecessors. Rather, he was good at information strategy in an absolute sense. He could be counted on to understand the dynamics and nuances of the battle of the story. And he weighed in forcefully and almost always in a timely manner. Ronald Reagan did not win every engagement in the war of ideas; but he was a formidable information strategist who almost always acquitted himself well.

Reagan's biggest stumble was no doubt the occasion when the arms-for-hostages deal—that linked Iran, the Nicaraguan contras, and Americans being held by terrorists—blew wide open. It became clear that the strong president who declared that there would be no deals with terrorists was indeed trying to make a deal. Further, financial proceeds from the said deal were apparently being passed to insurgents whom Congress had ordered be cut off from further U.S. support.[18] In spite of all this, Reagan suffered little in the eyes of the world, as it seemed he had acted out of deep concern for the hostages, in particular the suffering of CIA agent William Buckley, a captive of the terrorists who was being brutally tortured. If Reagan enjoyed a protective "Teflon coating" throughout this imbroglio, it is no doubt because people could understand and sympathize with his motivations.

Reagan's war of ideas, as I have portrayed it, was in many ways much like a more traditional war of attrition on the battlefield. Both sides had their tactical successes, yet neither seemed able to land a decisive blow. The United States got the "information edge" in the KAL 007 incident, but the fallout from it generated few strategic gains. Similarly the Russians' skillful public diplomacy stopped development and deployment of the neutron bomb; but this in no way damaged NATO forces' ability to cope with the threat of an invasion of Western Europe by the Warsaw Pact. And this was the pattern that repeated itself, in region after region, from Central America to southern Africa and throughout much of Asia. Thrust and parry, thrust and parry. The war of words was always sharp, the exchanges protracted, but the results were usually minimal. Yet one place did turn out to be the decisive point in the information campaign: Poland. It became the focus of information strategists on both sides, and the long struggle over its future became something of a "Verdun" in the Soviet-American information war.

When Poland came free at the end of the fight, the effects of this victory—much more than the muted strategic consequences of Verdun in World War I—quickly rippled through the rest of the Russian empire, fracturing it irretrievably. In this respect Poland once again played a pivotal historical role in an East-West struggle. In the thirteenth century, Poles formed the core of the forces that barred the Mongols' path to the conquest of Europe. Even in defeat at Liegnitz, their hard fighting convinced the Mongols that European resistance would prove too great to overcome. Four centuries later, in 1683, a Polish army thwarted the Ottoman Turkish invasion of Central Europe, once again protecting the West. And Poles had even dealt with the Russian threat to Europe in the wake of World War I, when the Red Army invaded—partly in response to Polish military adventurism on now-Soviet territory—and tried to impose communism in 1920 on a war-ravaged continent. Against all odds the Poles—whose country had just been put back on the map by the terms of the Treaty of Versailles, a century and a half after being "partitioned" out of existence—somehow won.[19] So, having initially contained the nascent Soviet threat nearly seventy years earlier, the Poles would now lead a different sort of charge to end it for good.

As in the origins of Reagan-era military spending increases and force modernization plans, President Carter also played an important catalyzing role in the realm of information strategy. On coming into office he quickly grasped the importance of Poland and decided to make his first foreign trip there. Perhaps Poland had been more on his mind because it had arisen as an important topic in a presidential debate with Gerald Ford—who in a famous gaffe that may have cost him the election prematurely declared Poland to be "free of Soviet control." Or perhaps Carter's Polish-born national security adviser, Zbigniew Brzezinski, raised his consciousness on this point. Brzezinski believed that Poland would play an important role in determining the outcome of the cold war. He therefore felt that a presidential visit to Poland would be of great value as it would "encourage the processes of liberalization that were gaining momentum there."[20] And even though the State Department recommended against the visit because it would be seen as "too provocative," President Carter decided to go anyway, for Poland was, in his words, "clearly the most important country in Eastern Europe."[21]

Carter's visit to Poland was the opening maneuver in the extended U.S. information campaign aimed at freeing that country. It featured two of the key elements that would support all U.S. public diplomatic efforts there: tapping into the deep Roman Catholic religious roots of the Polish people, and stoking their fanatical devotion to individual and national freedom. The overture to the Catholic church was made by Brzezinski and Rosalynn Carter, who went together to pay an unannounced visit to Cardinal Wyszynski, a Polish national hero who had openly resisted and survived Stalin-era intimidation. The State Department had strenuously objected to a presidential meeting with the cardinal, so instead Carter wrote a simple note that was hand-delivered to the prelate:

To Cardinal Wyszynski:

You have my best wishes and my prayers. I share your faith, I admire what you represent, I seek the same goals.

Jimmy Carter[22]

Carter also struck a nationalist chord on this same trip when he visited and laid a wreath at the monument to the Polish Home Army, which in 1944 had heroically risen up against the Nazi occupiers. Further, in his official meetings during the trip he spoke in favor of Polish independence.[23] Thus was the way paved for the Reagan-era initiatives that supported the Polish Solidarity movement's resistance to continued Soviet control.

For their part, the Russians also sensed that Poland was becoming the decisive theater in the information war. They had long understood the strategic importance of Poland, and had, since the end of World War II, been conducting a protracted psychological operations campaign to keep the Poles quiescent. It included three principal elements.

First, the USSR was portrayed primarily as Poland's liberator from Nazi oppression. Next, the Polish "People's Army"—Soviet formed and controlled—was given credit for much of the initial resistance to and later the climactic uprising against the Germans. Finally, the Soviets sought to instill in the Poles the sense that Soviet influence was economically beneficial in that it encouraged equality in a society historically riven by class conflicts and huge disparities in the distribution of wealth.[24]

In the main, the Soviet scheme worked reasonably well. Although the vast majority of Poles never saw their historic "enemy from the east" as a liberator, the People's Army enjoyed great esteem—despite the fact that it was falsely honored for having done the work of the Home Army. As to the Home Army itself, there were few veterans left who could speak out forcefully in rebuttal. For the Russians had secretly massacred those who had survived the fighting with the Germans, at Katyn Wood and other places.[25] So the Soviet deception—in which the heroism of the Home Army was ascribed to the puppets of the People's Army—worked. With regard to social beliefs about economic equality, the Soviets also seem to have made real and enduring gains, as the continuing electoral successes of the Socialists in post–cold war Poland today suggest.

By the time the Solidarity movement arose and began to exert ever-increasing pressure for liberation, the Soviets felt they had sown the seeds of an effective information strategy that would enable them to maintain control over Poland.[26] They believed this approach could be successfully employed in lieu of launching a military invasion, as they had done in dealing with unrest in 1956 in Hungary and in 1968 in Czechoslovakia. In the main the Soviet assessment was correct. For when the civil disobedience fomented by Solidarity leader Lech Walesa reached a fever pitch, the Soviets gave ground by having the Polish military, under the stewardship of Moscow-friendly General Wojciech Jaruzelski, declare a state of martial law. The Polish people acquiesced peacefully, as they still trusted their "own" military. And so order was kept.

But the fight over Poland proved to be intellectually exhausting for the Kremlin leadership, and after Gorbachev came to power in

1985 the controls on Poland and the other Eastern European countries behind the Iron Curtain were loosened. In Poland, for example, television satellite dishes went from being illegal to simply requiring a license, and thousands quickly sprouted throughout the country. The practice spread to other countries and, bit by bit, their peoples began to believe they were capable of freeing themselves—some acting as if they already were free because of their access to unfiltered information. At this point Mikhail Gorbachev could have chosen to reimpose rule by military means, but the costs and risks would have been high, both operationally and in terms of the consequences for his ambitious plan to restructure Soviet society. He chose to let the Eastern European countries go free, in return, he thought, for having a greater chance of success in maintaining the Soviet Union.

As events turned out, it appears that Gorbachev made a fatal misjudgment when it came to estimating his ability to maintain the unity of the USSR. And though U.S. information strategy did put pressure on the Soviets, their own defensive information operations worked pretty well too. Seen in this light, information strategy was one of a number of factors operating together to bring about an epochal change—but it was probably the single most important factor of them all. And the long cold war struggle between American and Soviet information strategists, it turns out, proved to be the overture to a new era in which the battle of the story has now risen to equal importance with the waging of real conflict itself. Sometimes the information war can be lost even after the battle on the ground has been won.

Ronald Reagan's immediate successor, George H. W. Bush, understood the power of story and ultimately proved to be a skilled information strategist. In some respects, though, this was unexpected, as he possessed an awkward oratorical style that was comprised in large part of mangled grammar and sometimes startling, herky-jerky arm movements. He was also a cautious "establishment" figure, one most unlikely to question or overturn recommendations that were the product of a bureaucratic consensus from below. So when Saddam Hussein began threatening Kuwait in July 1990, over issues of debt relief and allegedly illegal Kuwaiti "slant drilling" for oil across its border with Iraq, Bush went along with the State Department recommendation that a subtle, nuanced message be conveyed by Ambassador April Glaspie. The gist of the démarche was that the United States was not interested in Iraq-Kuwait border disputes but that they should be resolved without resort to the use of force.[27] What was needed at the time, however, was a simple, clear statement that any aggression against Kuwait would not be tolerated.

President Bush did not find his voice on this issue until after Kuwait was invaded. At this point he came into his own, taking the moral high ground in support of state sovereignty, declaring that "this aggression will not stand." He rode this story about the need to roll back the Iraqis all the way to receiving overwhelming support from the United Nations and to the cobbling together of more than thirty nations in a military coalition. The solid appeal of this liberation story gave him the running room he needed to whack Iraq. Yet Bush's careful appreciation of the basis of the global consensus he had built also led him to stop well short of sending U.S. forces to Baghdad in the immediate aftermath of the liberation of Kuwait. This decision was sensitive to and driven by the need to be consistent with the story about our intervention. But it left tens of thousands of Kurdish and Shiite rebels—who had been openly encouraged by the United States to rise up against Saddam in the spring of 1991—to be slaughtered by remaining Iraqi forces who finally found opponents whom they could defeat.

Bush's careful, limited policy toward Iraq also prompted sharp internal divisions within his administration. A key faction led intellectually by then-Undersecretary of Defense Paul Wolfowitz was soon calling for the long-term occupation of southern Iraq, a concept that eventually grew to include demands for the overthrow of Saddam Hussein and a complete reshaping of Iraqi society. Wolfowitz and company kept this hope alive throughout the 1990s, when they were out of office and Bill Clinton chose to deal with Iraq using sanctions and limited applications of air power. When they regained power in 2001, they resumed planning in earnest for an invasion. Al Qaeda's attacks on America proved to be the useful pretext needed to break through on the policy front, and Iraq was finally invaded and occupied in 2003—and quickly became a costly, bloody quagmire.

Aside from Iraq, the first Bush administration also devoted a great deal of attention to the endgame with the Soviet Union. Here the record on information strategy seems much more mixed. As it became apparent that the Soviet Union itself might be breaking up, Secretary of State James Baker actually gave a speech in the Ukraine—known ever after as the "Chicken Kiev" speech—which supported the notion of keeping the Soviet Union together. The calculation in this case was that dissolution would bring dangerous new disorder; but the idea of encouraging an adversary—at the moment of defeat—to buck up seemed wrongheaded. And it was, a point that was soon appreciated by the president, who shortly after shifted to a much more neutral tone.

Perhaps it was the emphasis on "order" that led to such cautious American public diplomacy during the first Bush administration, which also included a go-slow approach to German unification that Chancellor Helmut Kohl simply overrode. In terms of information strategy, this focus on order led to the greatest gaffe of the time, the insistence that the end of the cold war and the defeat of Iraqi aggression signaled the rise of an American-led "new world order." This was a policy only one word removed from the horrific Nazi concept of building a "new order" in Europe. The formulation almost surely guaranteed to stir up resentment among the Russians and others around the world who would be naturally inclined to resist being led. Without question the United States had amassed some impressive triumphs in the early 1990s; but from the perspective of information strategy there was little reason to trumpet them. The right tack would have been to take Reagan's humbler notion of the United States as an exemplar, in his words "a shining city on a hill," which sounded much less threatening.[28]

George H. W. Bush's successor, Bill Clinton, seemed to appreciate this point: little was heard about a "new world order" during his eight years in office. He seems to have come closer than his predecessor to

Reagan's preferred approach to statecraft, with its emphasis on encouraging the spread of "free peoples and free markets." In Clinton's words, this became a national strategy of seeking "democratic enlargement"—the continued spread of representative democracy. In the economic realm he also appears to have behaved as a Reagan heir, with the North American Free Trade Agreement of 1994 and the creation of the World Trade Organization during his second term serving as evidence of his fealty to the notion of free markets. Clinton also maintained good relations with the Russians, with virtually no signs of a resurgence of the old rhetorical battles of the cold war—despite sometimes sharp differences with Moscow on such issues as Serbian aggressiveness in the Balkans or Russian sharing of nuclear technology with the Iranians. As his deputy secretary of state, Strobe Talbott, observed of Cinton's style:

> Altercation and remonstration were forms of discourse that did not come naturally to him. His preference was to conciliate in other people's squabbles and to boost leaders whom he liked. A signature of his political technique was to begin his reply to almost any proposition by saying, "I agree with that," even when he didn't. This default to agreeableness was not just a reflection of his desire to be liked—it was also a means, both calculated and intuitive, of disarming those he was trying to persuade, of pretending to begin a conversation on common ground in order to get there before it was over.[29]

Ironically, it may have been Bill Clinton's own great skill at personal and public diplomacy that contributed to the decision in 1998 to disband the United States Information Agency—his greatest error as an information strategist. For new media—particularly the World Wide Web, the Internet, cellular phones that were virtual personal computers, and instant text messaging—were coming into their own at just this moment. Much as Ronald Reagan nurtured radio but focused on bringing the USIA into the satellite television age, Bill Clinton needed to keep television going while investing heavily in computer-based communications technologies. At the very time the USIA was closing up shop, its remnants merged into the State Department, civic activists of the *Otpor* movement were using the new media to help depose the dictator Slobodan Milosevic in Serbia. A similar mass movement soon arose to help remove President Estrada in the Philippines. All around the world, new media was on the cutting edge of the empowerment of civil society actors, putting increasing pressure on authoritarian regimes. Yet at this very moment the United States was signaling that the new media would not play a leading role in American public diplomacy. As late as 1996 the funding for radio broadcasts was seventeen times that for satellite television—and the budget for Web- and Net-based programs was but a tiny fraction of that for TV.[30] Further, Clinton's inattention in this area emboldened the Pentagon to take an ever more aggressive approach to controlling what it now called information operations. This looming estrangement of State from information strategy would soon have baleful effects.

Clinton's curious strategic errors were not corrected by his successor, George W. Bush, who came into office emphasizing his preference for improving American national security by means of pushing ahead with a national missile defense rather than with a skillful information strategy. The second Bush simply seemed much less interested in engaging the world with a lively new form of public diplomacy. He even declared that the United States would take a much less active role in the Israeli-Palestinian peace process, which had devoured so much of Clinton's energy over the years. Bush intended to wait for these parties to craft a peace together that Americans could perhaps then help implement. He cemented his Jacksonian standing by making it clear he had little interest in nation-building.

The younger Bush's passive inclinations toward information strategy were left abruptly by the wayside in the wake of al Qaeda's attacks on America. He was quickly galvanized by the notion that a new kind of war had been thrust upon us, this time waged by rising terror networks rather than rogue nation-states. And so he reached out first to the international community, to enlist its support in a war on terror, and then engaged the enemy directly in what has become a latter-day version of Reagan's war of ideas, which is still being waged today. While successful in gaining worldwide support for the ongoing struggle against terrorism—which was quite substantial for the invasion of al Qaeda's haven in Afghanistan and the ending of the Taliban's harsh rule there—Bush soon encountered difficulties in maintaining and expanding the international consensus on this issue.

The greatest problem was the extent of opposition to his notion of invading Iraq as the next step in the war on terror. Many across the international community and even in the United States—not to mention the overwhelming majority of the world's Muslims—disagreed with the idea that the overthrow of Saddam Hussein was the best way to conduct the war against al Qaeda and its affiliates. Support for the United States faltered when it became clear that the United Nations would not sanction a war on Iraq. Existing divisions only deepened and then boomeranged on Bush when his stated reason for attacking, the threat from Iraqi weapons of mass destruction, turned out to be illusory. International support waned further when the U.S. and its coalition of the willing continued to conduct an occasionally brutal occupation of Iraq that looked to the world ever less like liberation. Thus the precious global consensus in favor of defeating terrorism was undermined by an invasion that seemed on balance to have little to do with the actual opponent—al Qaeda and its associated terror networks.

Beyond the major problem caused by the decision to invade Iraq rather than concentrate first on tracking down the al Qaeda network's various cells and nodes, there were other serious problems with American information strategy. In the main it suffered from an attempt to treat the war of ideas with bin Laden as a kind of mudslinging political campaign. This was an exceptionally poor strategy, one accompanied by questionable tactics. For example, mass-produced psychological operations leaflets depicted Osama bin Laden in a doctored photograph as a clean-shaven coward in a polyester suit, with a caption saying he had abandoned his comrades, taken the money, and run away. Such initiatives—and there were many of them like this, some even worse—only alienated those throughout the Muslim world whom we needed to win over, and fed the bin Laden legend. And these clumsy smears were decisively rebutted by the release from time to time of videotapes showing bin Laden walking in the mountains with his fighters and speaking quietly and humbly about his continued dedication to the global jihad he had inspired.

As to attempts to reach out to the billion-plus Muslim masses, America displayed a similar ham-handedness, creating glossy infomercials showing happy Muslim families living in the United States. These totally missed the point that the issue in the war was not our treatment of Muslims in America but rather our policies toward the Muslim world in general. In poll after opinion poll across a swath of Islamic lands, from Morocco to Mindanao, the results were quite consistent. Muslims held positive views of the American people—and even of American culture—but by large majorities they sharply disagreed with our foreign policy as it affected them or their coreligionists.[31] Yet we did little to engage the policy debate, focusing instead on the hard sell and on traditional propaganda techniques.[32]

At the same time American information strategy was faltering, al Qaeda was showing its own brand of media-savvy aptitude for distributing its story to the world audience. Its greatest weapons were Osama bin Laden's own haunting videotapes which, by their very existence, proved he was capable of eluding—perhaps for years—the superpower-led manhunt for him. Their content was also powerful, reaffirming his goal of reducing the shadow cast by American power over the Muslim world. Bin Laden's continued labeling of Americans as "crusaders" was an important allusion to Islam's first series of clashes with the West nearly a thousand years earlier, when brave Muslims had ultimately defeated the Christian invaders.[33]

The effectiveness of al Qaeda's information strategy was greatly enhanced in the spring of 2004 when irrefutable evidence of American abuse of Iraqis at Abu Ghraib Prison—and of other detainees held elsewhere—was finally made public by Seymour Hersh, the same reporter who had broken the story of the My Lai Massacre during the Vietnam War.[34] The damage done by these revelations resonated not only throughout Muslim countries but in the rest of the world as well. The overall effect was to give rise to the perception that, though the war on terror was a just cause, the United States was not waging it in a just manner.

In the years ahead, the primary goal of American information strategy must be to restore the nation's tarnished reputation. Damage control must be done before we can go back on the offensive in the war of ideas. And in this case "offensive" simply means working actively to persuade others to support our cause. We can do this convincingly once the mudslinging approach is curtailed and we have made appropriate amends for our sometimes serious misconduct.

Beyond bin Laden, al Qaeda and its various affiliates have also made good use of the World Wide Web and the Internet to reach their target audiences. The profusion of pro-Qaeda websites and the huge numbers of hits they receive indicate that this twenty-first-century communications medium is heartily embraced by those whose mindsets are probably philosophically more attuned to the world of the fourteenth century. Yet they realize that cyberspace is the right place for fund-raising, recruitment, propaganda—and even for maintaining operational control over cells and nodes around the world. As the historian Arnold Toynbee once predicted might happen, some Muslims appear to have embraced Western technological advances in order to use them to defend against Western social influence and military incursions.[35] In this sense al Qaeda's information strategy may be seen as exceptionally modern in its orientation—and implies that the United States must develop its own cyberspace-based capability for waging the new war of ideas.

Al Qaeda has even done well in its use of psychological operations and deception. Ever since 9/11 the network has routinely issued new threats, both publicly and via seemingly secure communications routes that its various operatives know we monitor. So, at little cost or risk, staged al Qaeda chatter has been used to compel us to raise our alert levels and take costly precautions in anticipation of new attacks that may or may not be in the offing. There is only one instance, in my view, that can be categorized as a blunder by al Qaeda in this form of information warfare. Bin Laden missed an amazing opportunity in the months after 9/11, when an airliner coming out of New York City crashed shortly after takeoff. The world held its breath for a few days, then heaved a collective sigh of relief when the official explanation was given—a very involved theory about how the tail of the aircraft had simply sheared off. If al Qaeda had been on its toes, bin Laden or another recognizable leader of the network would have claimed credit for the crash. The effects would have been electric, with air travel being sharply curtailed and stocks falling further.

But just as every war sees its share of brilliant moves and blunders in the field, so too does the war of ideas. And if al Qaeda does not stand ten feet tall in its practice of information strategy, it has nevertheless acquitted itself well—better than the United States after the opening year of the war on terror. Now the challenge for American information strategists will be to stem their losses in the war of ideas and rekindle a winning story that they can tell—and sell—to people around the world. As next moves are pondered, American information strategists can hardly do better than return to the precepts that were nurtured and advanced by Ronald Reagan and his administration. What worked against the "evil empire" was, for the most part, a concerted, growing appeal to openness and decency.

Ronald Reagan, who first took the issue of information strategy seriously enough to discuss it explicitly in a national security decision directive, appreciated fully the complex interplay of ideas and actions. He understood that statecraft at the highest level required the skillful application of all of the different capabilities and resources of the country. Most important, he was open-minded enough to see that, in an emerging information age, perception and persuasion would matter at least as much as classical military power and coercion. On some occasions the various forms of "soft power" would trump hard power.[36] This was especially true of the struggle against the Soviets, which simply could not be won by force of arms. Thus Reagan was determined to see the United States practice information strategy wisely and effectively. For the most part, the story of his successes in ending the cold war and the nuclear arms race is largely a reflection of the power of persuasion.

The same can hardly be said of Reagan's successors. Each of them has, in one way or another, fallen back on conventional thinking, which is primarily driven by a belief in the superiority of hard coercive power. This has proven particularly unfortunate, given that the years since Reagan left office have seen the rise of adversaries with a keen appreciation of the power of ideas and images. This was true even before al Qaeda. In Somalia in 1993, for example, the tactical military triumph of Task Force Ranger turned into an informational debacle when the remains of some U.S. servicemen were dragged about the streets of Mogadishu. After these images were broadcast, American policy toward that sad land soon unraveled—just as the U.S. military triumph over Iraq ten years later came undone when the rationale for having waged the war in the first place failed to stand up to scrutiny. In a very real sense we live in what Christopher Hables Gray calls an era of "postmodern war," characterized by the rise of the information dimension and the receding of the purely military aspects of conflict.[37] Without a proper story about "why we fight," as filmmaker Frank Capra noted in his famous World War II–era documentary series, no amount of fighting can ever achieve enduring results.

Despite the clearly rising importance of story to the success of statecraft, American efforts to wage a war of ideas today have come largely under the control of the military. In my experience, the tendency of our field generals is simply to tell our information strategists what the military operation will be, then to order them to design and implement psychological operations and deceptions in support of a particular use of force. Their point of view is understandable but terribly wrongheaded. We live in an era when, unless military operations are initially crafted with their various informational consequences in mind, the effectiveness of both is likely to be sharply reduced. When the time came to bring down the Taliban, for example, the war plan called for aerial bombardment to the exclusion of other means.[38] By itself this form of attack was likely to do little to dislodge our opponents—like most bombing campaigns for the past century—and would alienate both Muslims and the rest of the world. Instead we should have developed a different sort of military strategy that would involve our small special forces teams in operations with indigenous anti-Taliban Muslims. Their presence on the ground would greatly enhance the effectiveness of the bombing and would also go a long way toward winning the battle of the story. We would no longer simply be raining down death from the sky; rather, our horseback-mounted troops would be fighting alongside other Afghans and bringing the country a new life. Although the uniformed services resisted this approach, Donald Rumsfeld himself ordered—after a month of ineffectual area bombing—that the campaign take on this new form. Two weeks later the Taliban were gone, on the run along with their al Qaeda allies. Today, several years after the toppling of the Taliban, only a small number of U.S. and allied forces remain in Afghanistan, a country that now holds regular elections. Problems persist, but skillful information strategy and nimble, networked military operations have scored a signal success here.

Our second war with Saddam Hussein offers a cautionary tale about the consequences of neglecting the information domain. Despite the lessons of the campaign in Afghanistan, senior Pentagon strategists called yet again for massive air raids that would engender, they thought, shock and awe among Iraqis—military action would create its own war-winning perceptual effects. A substantial minority of defense planners deeply opposed this approach, arguing that the war was being sold as a liberation of the Iraqi people who, even if they were shocked and awed, had little ability by themselves to force an end to the fighting. And every bit of damage that would be done to civilian infrastructure, and every innocent life lost, would only complicate reconstruction and kindle resentment of the occupation to follow. Instead of beginning with bombing, the dissenters argued for an "Afghanistan-plus"-sized operation that would feature special forces and small conventional detachments—closely networked with attack aircraft and using the swarm tactics that had worked so well against the Taliban. It was argued that this would suffice to defeat the Iraqi military and bring down Saddam with as little bloodshed as possible. In this case, proponents of the more traditional approach prevailed. But the conventional military triumph that followed nonetheless did so much unnecessary damage to those whom we said we were liberating that we swiftly lost the information campaign so essential to post-conflict security in Iraq.[39]

The need to integrate our military and information strategies can perhaps be best explained by considering how well or poorly we have done in each area during our various wars over the past century. Figure 11 provides some rough measures of our performance levels in these domains, from World War I to the present, and reflects some interesting patterns. For example, our decisive victories in the world wars eventually featured strong results in field operations, though we were never really tactically superior to our adversaries. But in both these wars our performance as information strategists was exceptional.[40] In a losing effort in Vietnam, we once again fought well in the field, but this time our information strategy was poor. Poor information strategy is the common thread in all our defeats. Our greatest success in combining military effectiveness with a strong story was achieved in a war that never got hot—Reagan's final campaign of the cold war against the Soviets.

It is ironic that, in our current war on terror, we have suffered such a disjunction between our military and information strategies. The irony arises because, instead of the long-standing tension between the State Department's emphasis on public diplomacy and the Pentagon's preference for field operations, both our military and information strategies have for some years been crafted mostly by the Department of Defense. Although the State Department actually has an undersecretary for public diplomacy (late in 2005 George W. Bush's trusted aide Karen Hughes took on this post), State has exerted very little influence on the overall direction of American information strategy. One might expect better results, given that interdepartmental pulling and hauling over "who owns information strategy" has, in practical terms, ended.

Figure 11. Wartime Performance of U.S. Military and Information Operations (1898–2003)

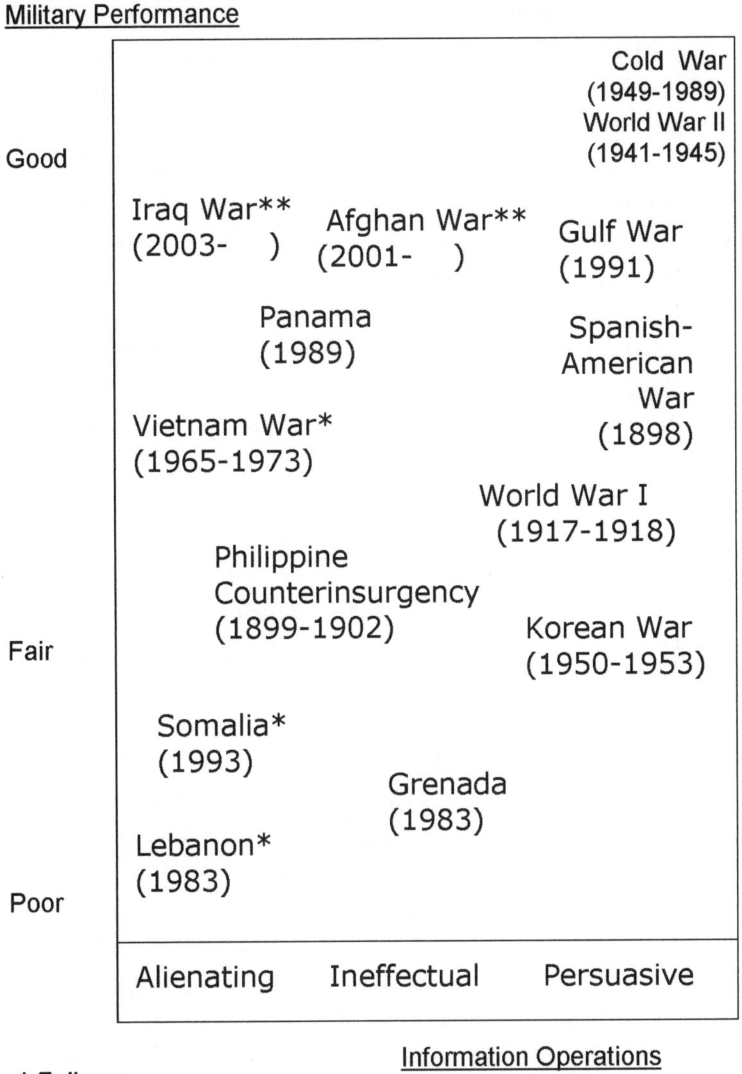

Military Performance

	Alienating	Ineffectual	Persuasive
Good			Cold War (1949-1989) World War II (1941-1945)
	Iraq War** (2003-)	Afghan War** (2001-)	Gulf War (1991)
		Panama (1989)	Spanish-American War (1898)
	Vietnam War* (1965-1973)		
			World War I (1917-1918)
Fair		Philippine Counterinsurgency (1899-1902)	Korean War (1950-1953)
	Somalia* (1993)		
		Grenada (1983)	
Poor	Lebanon* (1983)		

Information Operations

 * *Failures*
** *Conflict in Progress*

But consolidating too much power to develop national strategy in one department of government may have had a chilling effect on policy debates. The Pentagon has gone far astray in an area directly under its control. In the end, it seems that the military still does not understand that the battle of the story will increasingly trump traditional operations in the field.

Yet there is an even deeper irony here. Ronald Reagan left us with important lessons about the various uses of information strategy and gave us many examples of his skillful generalship in this realm during the cold war. But those who intone his name with the greatest reverence have nonetheless failed to appreciate the value of his insights and exemplary actions. The consequences of this problem will increasingly weigh down our chances of winning the ongoing war on terror which in many ways has emerged as the archetypal mode of conflict in the twenty-first century. We face skillful opponents who have relentlessly kept to their message that a clash of civilizations is under way. And the more we rely strictly on military force, the more their narrative will continue to resonate. For this is a conflict in which we can win every firefight and still lose the battle of the story.

This new kind of warfare demands that we rethink our basic approach to information strategy—just as it should also impel us to think innovatively about arms control and military transformation. There is much in Reagan's record to help us determine how all three of these factors might be knit together to meet our current needs. For it was Ronald Reagan who first understood that increasing our conventional forces would reduce our psychological dependence upon nuclear weapons, creating a way first to control and finally bring an end to the Soviet-American arms race. At the same time he clearly saw that the cold war was a conflict that could not be won militarily—it could only be lost by both sides. And so his greatest efforts, and truly his greatest successes, came with the development of an information strategy that persuaded a mortal enemy to lay down his arms willingly and negotiate a peace.

The great challenge now before us is to learn to lead with information strategy in the war on terror. Like the cold war, the struggle against al Qaeda and its affiliates is unlikely to be won militarily—though arms control to keep weapons of mass destruction out of terrorist hands is needed, along with skillful special operations in the field. But in the end, the people of the world will choose to join in eliminating terror only if they come to agree with the implicit American story that this is not a clash of civilizations but rather a fight for a future based on universally accepted liberal, human-rights-based values.

Perhaps the best thing for us to do now, as we ponder how to regain our lost momentum, is to mount a thorough, open-minded review of the lessons of Ronald Reagan's various information campaigns. For if we recall and rekindle what worked so well to end the cold war, we may be able to master or head off this emerging age of terror and replace it with the kind of global civil society whose eventual creation was Reagan's ultimate policy goal.

In terms of specific policy initiatives that would resonate loud and long in the informational war, it may be profitable to shift our focus away from only the war on terror. Other things might be done to redirect our own and the world community's energies in productive ways—measures that would require agreement on common moral imperatives and which could only be undertaken in a spirit of cooperation. Such issues as providing clean drinking water to the more than one-fifth of the world's people who do not have it should be a goal of global civil society. So should any number of transnational environmental issues. But both these problem areas suffer from a lack of binding international legal obligations and are bedeviled by ugly, self-interest-driven politics. In one area, though, international law already binds nations and compels them to take action: the 1948 Genocide Convention. If we select one major initiative with which to burnish our image anew, this should be it. For virtually all nations have spoken and sometimes even acted against those who wish to destroy a particular ethnic group simply because of racial or cultural differences.

The historical record shows that genocide has been very much with us over the past two centuries. The number of conflicts with serious genocidal dimensions has been rising over the past several

Figure 12.   The World's Deadliest Quarrels, 1830–1950

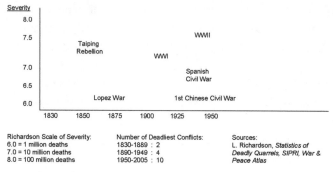

Richardson Scale of Severity:	Number of Deadliest Conflicts:	Sources:
6.0 = 1 million deaths	1830-1889 : 2	L. Richardson, *Statistics of*
7.0 = 10 million deaths	1890-1949 : 4	*Deadly Quarrels, SIPRI, War &*
8.0 = 100 million deaths	1950-2005 : 10	*Peace Atlas*

decades, as can be seen in Figure 12, which depicts the world's deadliest conflicts of the past 175 years.

In the first sixty-year period surveyed (1830–1890), the slaughters that occurred in both the Taiping Rebellion and in the Lopez War had genocidal elements. In the Lopez War, nearly 80 percent of adult male Paraguayans died, a mortality rate seldom seen in history. During the second sixty-year period (1890–1950), World War II certainly had a genocidal dimension, but the deadliest quarrels that were mostly about genocide came during the interwar period of the 1920s–1930s. In this period Stalin was engaging in horrific slaughters in the Ukraine and quite similar depredations were happening in China. But the real growth period for genocide has come in the years since 1950, when even small countries, torn by ethnic strife, easily surmounted the one-million-victim mark. The Ibo of Nigeria in the late 1960s and the Tutsi of Rwanda in 1994 are archetypal examples of this kind of genocide, which features the killing of very large percentages of the target populations. It is just this sort of crime against humanity that the United States should mobilize the world to fight. And, as noted above, it is already our *legal obligation* to do so.

Sadly, the U.S. government and many other governments of the world have stood by and simply watched most genocidal conflicts bloodily unfold. Given our raw power and preeminent position in the

Figure 12.   The World's Deadliest Quarrels, 1950–2005

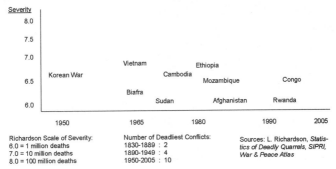

Richardson Scale of Severity:
6.0 = 1 million deaths
7.0 = 10 million deaths
8.0 = 100 million deaths

Number of Deadliest Conflicts:
1830-1889 : 2
1890-1949 : 4
1950-2005 : 10

Sources: L. Richardson, *Statistics of Deadly Quarrels, SIPRI, War & Peace Atlas*

world, though, it is shocking that we allowed the Ibo and the Tutsi to be decimated. In Nigeria the war went on for years, giving us plenty of time to act. In Rwanda there were only a few weeks' warning but still enough time to mobilize an international force of sufficient strength to deter murderers armed mostly with machetes. Reflecting on his failure to act in Rwanda, Bill Clinton viewed it as his "greatest regret."[41]

Another Rwanda-style catastrophe was averted in 2004 when the looming genocide in the Sudan prompted at least some reaction from the United States and the greater world community. This sort of positive development should be expanded upon, wherever and whenever ethnic-driven massacres threaten to erupt. At this writing the Darfur crisis in the Sudan still appears to be moving toward a resolution without mass ethnic killing—an important first step for the United States and for global civil society. The campaign against genocide is one that can be mounted even as we continue to wage the war on terror. Tamping down ethnic and religious hatred is probably the best way to preempt the rise of new terrorist threats.

The larger point here is that, in order to win the global "battle of the story" against terrorists, we need to do more than just portray them and their sponsors and affiliates as "evil." For we cannot hope to succeed simply by being against something. We must be *for* something as well. We must convince all peoples that our intentions are good, that we do not seek to rule the world but rather to improve the security and quality of life for all who live in it. And we can only do this by taking unequivocally lauded actions—such as stemming the tide of genocide in Darfur and providing aid for victims of the December 2004 Asian tsunami. Such actions will soften the memory of the fractious global debates that preceded our invasion of Iraq and salve the grave wound to the American public image that came with the abuses at Abu Ghraib and other places where we have held detainees.

If we choose to employ and are accurately perceived as using our great power for good, we shall likely find that our prospects in the war on terror will improve too. For it is in failed and failing states that terror cells thrive. As the dire problems of these countries are ameliorated, these reclaimed areas of the world will become far less attractive to terrorists. It is doubly in our interest to pursue policies that fulfill our international legal obligations while at the same time reminding the world community that Americans stand for the good of all. In this fashion we could undertake a most Reaganesque blending of military and information strategy, on a par with our finest moments during the last years of the cold war. But of course terror will not be fully tamed by thoughtfully crafted public diplomatic initiatives. Information strategy is an important element, but defeating terrorism also calls for the skillful application of much harder-edged policies.

7

The Protracted Struggle Against Terrorism

On Saturday, March 24, 1984—eight days after Muslim extremists kidnapped and began torturing the CIA's Beirut station chief, William Buckley—Secretary of State George Shultz convened a day-long meeting of terrorism experts in Washington. It was chaired by my colleague, Brian Jenkins, a tall, imposing former Green Beret with a sterling combat record in Vietnam and an equally impressive reputation as one of the RAND Corporation's top terrorism analysts. Along with Bruce Hoffman, Jenkins has for decades given RAND a voice in this issue area that has matched in importance the corporation's contributions to understanding nuclear strategy made by their intellectual forebears, Albert Wohlstetter and Bernard Brodie.[1] As Jenkins has described the basic intent of Shultz's meeting to me, it was "to take a no holds barred look at curtailing the growing terrorist threat." Secretary Shultz said, "I wanted to look at this issue with a fresh eye."[2]

Jenkins and the other attendees did just this, reaching a consensus about how terror was emerging as a new form of warfare for which the United States was poorly prepared. The Long Commission report—which had investigated the attack on the Marine barracks in Beirut the previous fall that killed 242 Americans—had reached a similar finding, but Shultz's Saturday seminar group went further than simply identifying the problem. They articulated just what an unconventional campaign against terror might look like and made a variety of clear-cut policy suggestions. Shultz was fully persuaded by the group's concrete recommendations and was soon arguing the case to President Reagan for waging a war on terror.

Apparently Shultz was successful, for ten days after the Saturday seminar Ronald Reagan signed National Security Decision Directive No. 138, still a highly classified document, only fragments of which have been made public. From these few available shards it is apparent that Reagan favored the idea of waging a war on terror, as NSDD 138 authorized the creation of

> secret FBI and CIA paramilitary squads and use of existing Pentagon military units—such as the Green Berets and the Navy SEALs—for conducting what amounted to guerrilla warfare against guerrillas . . . a *de facto* declaration of war. It authorized sabotage, killing . . . preemptive and retaliatory raids, deception and a significantly expanded [intelligence] collection program aimed at suspected radicals and people regarded as their sympathizers.[3]

The CIA, which had previously been opposed to launching such an all-out offensive against terror, seemed galvanized by the kidnapping of its agent, Buckley, and threw its full support to the president's new policy. The same was not true of some other departments of government, which were for the most part opposed. Vice President George H. W. Bush was initially cool to the idea as well, though he eventually warmed to it.

The sternest opposition to the new policy came from Secretary of Defense Caspar Weinberger, who never liked the idea of waging this kind of war against terror. So in response to NSDD 138 he articulated the series of six restrictive tests (see Chapter 5) that he argued must be passed before there could be any use of American force. Where Shultz was talking about fighting dispersed terror networks, Weinberger was still focusing on confronting other nations in a more classical form of conflict. He envisioned the use of force as a last resort, to be employed only after the final failure of diplomacy—and only after a period in which mass public opinion had been carefully cultivated. In spirit the Weinberger Doctrine was well harmonized with the ethical guidance contained in the traditional just war concepts of Augustine and Aquinas, which they articulated in the fifth and thirteenth centuries, respectively.[4] Weinberger was particularly attuned to the ethical principle of noncombatant immunity, and worried that Shultz's strategy, which he saw as an "unfocused . . . revenge approach," would result in injuries to and deaths of innocent civilians.[5]

What George Shultz was championing amounted to a new way of war. Instead of force being used on a massive scale and as a last resort, he intended to employ military and paramilitary capabilities on a small, surgical scale, often as a preemptive "first resort." As counterterror operations of this sort would be for the most part clandestine or covert in nature, there would be little or no public debate about taking such actions. Despite this fundamental fault line between the secretaries of defense and state, there was one area where the dueling ideas of Weinberger and Shultz arguably converged: the notion of economy of force. Weinberger's fourth principle enjoins us to use force in a manner proportionate to the need of the situation. The Shultz strategy was also inherently economical in nature, envisioning the use of small teams and surrogates to strike at distributed terror cells and nodes. But this is only a small area of possible agreement, one that I have had to tease out. Neither Shultz nor Weinberger ever made a point of this area being common ground between them, even though both had taken positions opposed, at least in practical terms, to what we now call the Powell Doctrine—the standard principle of resorting to the use of overwhelming force.

Instead of finding whatever areas of agreement they could, Weinberger and Shultz soon argued in a bitter bureaucratic struggle. Shultz remembers it this way:

> The argument turned into a battle royal between Cap Weinberger and me over the use of force. To Weinberger, as I heard him, our

forces were to be constantly built up but not used: everything in our defense structure seemed geared exclusively to deter World War III against the Soviets; diplomacy was to solve all the other problems we faced around the world; if the time ever came when force seemed to be required, how would prior "reasonable assurance" of support from the American people be obtained? By a congressional vote for action against a terrorist group or for a rescue operation for Americans in danger? Only if and when the population, by some open measure, agreed in advance would American armed forces be employed, and even then, only if we were assured of winning swiftly and at minimal cost. This was the Vietnam syndrome in spades, carried to an absurd level, and a complete abdication of the duties of leadership.[6]

Weinberger's rebuttal consisted of reiterating his concern about the harm to innocent civilians that could be done by the Shultz strategy. Reagan shared this concern but nonetheless wanted to be able to do something against terrorism. The right solution, as Weinberger saw it, was that

> we, the President and I, had agreed that we would make a "focused" response whenever we identified and located a terrorist; that is, a response appropriate to the terrorist action, and a response that had as its aim the discouragement of any country or any person using terrorism from ever doing it again.[7]

Despite Reagan's apparent preference for Weinberger's approach, Shultz and his adherents fought on for their vision of an effective way to defeat terror before it grew too dangerous. Yet the State-Defense rift over counterterrorism policy deepened, and inevitably their differences were aired and debated publicly. In a trenchant commentary in the *New York Times* of December 3, 1984, for example, William Safire depicted the whole matter as a "battle for President Reagan's strategic soul." As we have seen, the "soul" Safire referred to was a complex one, fully able to entertain *both* these intractably opposed views. And so, a generation ago, Ronald Reagan found what would today be called a "third way" approach that honored some of what each of his two great advisers had proposed.[8] Yes, there would occasionally be forceful responses to terrorist acts and threats; but they would almost never be preemptive and would generally take on the more conventional characteristics—both operational and diplomatic—of traditional conflicts. In practice this meant that, for the most part, Shultz's recommended secret war had been rejected and that a Reagan-administration-led war on terror would look quite a bit like traditional warfare, if and when uses of force were ever authorized.

The clearest evidence of Weinberger's policy triumph over Shultz can be found in the official overview of American foreign policy that was disseminated in March 1988 by the State Department. Four years after being awakened to the threat and lobbying Reagan to launch a covert war on terror, Shultz had nothing to say about the use of force against terrorists. Instead he noted only that the United States "must remain prepared to act directly and in conjunction with other nations—through diplomatic, legal, and economic means to stop the modern barbarity of terrorism."[9] There is no mention whatsoever of the use of force as a means of rooting out and ending this "modern barbarity."

The manner in which military force was used in response to terror during the Reagan years brings the practical aspects of Weinberger's strategy into clearer focus. For when Libya proved unwilling to give up its terrorist ways, and solid intelligence was available to prove what Qaddafi had been up to—in particular the bombing of a nightclub in Germany frequented by American soldiers—all in the Reagan administration agreed that something had to be done. But the action taken was limited to an air raid in 1986 that struck perilously close to the tent in which Qaddafi lived, killing one of his young children. The immediate effect was that, in the three months after the raid, terrorist attacks on U.S. targets increased. Qaddafi stayed in the terrorism business, with some of his people arranging the bombing of Pan American Flight 103, which was blown up over Lockerbie, Scotland, on December 21, 1988, killing all 259 people on board.[10]

If Qaddafi eventually became a reformed character, as he began saying in the mid-1990s, it was almost surely because his various odd economic and public works initiatives had all failed and had brought his country to the brink of financial ruin. One of the best-known fiascoes of this period had to do with his dream of engineering a new "greening" of the Sahara by bringing water to the desert via subterranean channels. In any event, Qaddafi's support for terror was hardly shaken by the small bit of bombing to which Reagan subjected him.

During the Reagan years the only significant exception to Weinberger's conventional approach to countering terrorism was the skillful manner in which the Abu Nidal Organization (ANO) was ripped apart. A decade before al Qaeda became known as the premier terror network in the world, Abu Nidal was in command of his own network. With about six hundred hard-core members capable of carrying out violent acts, the ANO operated on many continents, and its cells and nodes were fully habituated to independent action. Like al Qaeda, the ANO was well-heeled financially as it worked for hire for at least three nations during its heyday in the 1980s: Syria, Iraq, and Libya. In the course of spectacular attacks-for-hire, like its 1986 assault on a synagogue in Istanbul, the ANO amassed a net worth that Bruce Hoffman has estimated at about $400 million at its peak.[11] This organization needed to be taken down, but, being a network rather than a nation, it could not be defeated by carpet bombing or a conventional military invasion.

So different means were employed, including an operation whose details remain largely classified. What can be said, though, is that a deception was used to make Abu Nidal believe that many of his operatives—who in classic network fashion enjoyed considerable autonomy in the field—were stealing huge sums from the organization. The exact fashion in which the deception was employed remains secret, but it involved "turning" a network member whose job gave him an awareness of the ANO's funding flows. The information gleaned from him was used to make money appear in many network members' accounts in amounts that simply should not have been there. Bottom line: Abu Nidal believed that hundreds of his network members were cheating both him and the cause, so he rubbed them out.

The ANO never recovered from this marvelous covert operation. As one clipped, semi-official assessment of the group obliquely described it: "Financial problems and internal disorganization . . . reduced the group's activities."[12] Steve Coll, the journalist who chronicled terrorism from the Reagan era to 9/11 in his *Ghost Wars*, has noted that counterterrorism operatives at the CIA "helped accelerate [the ANO's] breakup through penetration and disinformation."[13] Both assessments are understated; after 1987 the ANO ceased attacking American targets and seldom struck anywhere else. This was a signal success for the Counterterrorism Center, which had been created in 1986, deliberately bringing together CIA field operators and analysts under the same roof. Washington had shown it could build a network of its own to fight the terror networks.

But the ANO takedown was just about the only point of light suggesting that George Shultz and those he had pulled together in March 1984 had known how to fight terrorism. For the most part, senior government officials and military commanders lined up behind the Weinberger Doctrine, thinking almost exclusively in terms of conventional uses of military force against terrorism—if force were to be used at all. Instead of striking at the terror nodes and cells themselves, the focus was on taking aim in our rare forceful actions at the various nations that we deemed to be "state sponsors of terror." The result of keeping the focus on state-level adversaries was that nonstate terrorist networks, which had only begun to grow during the 1980s—and to "Islamicize"—would continue to spread unimpeded.

Ronald Reagan is much to blame for having set a counterterror course in U.S. policy that proved far too conventional, and which was far too closely imitated by his successors in the dozen years between his departure from office and 9/11. Most galling about this development is that Reagan did perceive the problem clearly and strove to energize a covert campaign that, when used occasionally, succeeded spectacularly. He followed up his National Security Decision Directive No. 138—which authorized launching a secret war on terror—with yet another top secret directive, NSDD 207, which further amplified his thoughts on the subject. And, as Steve Coll reports, Reagan

consistently applied "intense pressure on the CIA to show more initiative in the fight against terror."[14] In response, an offensive against
terror was secretly planned; but Reagan, as noted earlier, was drawn
more to Weinberger's conventional approach.

In the wake of 9/11 much has been made of the various briefings
given to George W. Bush shortly before the attacks on America, and
of his failure to act more decisively in response to them. But the real
failure to handle this problem began in 1984, when the notion of
launching a covert war on terror was proposed to and then authorized
by Ronald Reagan but was soon crippled by bureaucratic infighting.
Clearly, as his later NSDD 207 and continued pressure on the CIA
showed, Reagan still wanted a war on terror. But he could not bring
himself to reject the idea that the capable conventional military could
do the job.

In fairness to Reagan, some might even say that our failure to prevent the rise of an age of terror began before he came to office. For
back in the 1970s, when a "Cabinet Committee to Combat Terrorism" was formed late in Richard Nixon's first term, it made recommendations that Shultz's working group would echo later on. Yet the
Cabinet Committee's official report, finally issued in 1977, failed to
win support for launching a campaign against terror during the
Carter years, foreshadowing the sorry fate of George Shultz's proposed counterterror strategy.[15]

Beyond members of Washington officialdom, a number of private
individuals wrote well and spoke articulately during the Reagan years
about the looming terrorist threat. Perhaps the most prescient private
observer was Gayle Rivers, a native New Zealander who had fought
alongside U.S. forces in Vietnam and later became something of a
prototype for what counterterrorist soldiers should look like. His operational career was recounted in 1985 in a best-selling memoir, *The
Specialist*, which features some actions of the type called for by NSDDs
138 and 207—far too few, though, from his point of view. Rivers wrote
another book, *The War Against the Terrorists*, that, seen twenty years
on, offers startling foresight about the evolving nature of the terrorist
threat. Rivers predicted the rise of terrorist networking as "a univer-

sal plague," warned of the insertion of "sleeper cells" into the United States, and even analyzed why New York City would become the prime target for terror.[16]

In terms of helping jump-start a war on terror, Rivers fared no better than Shultz. Perhaps this was because his recommendations for transforming the American military into the sort of force capable of fighting dispersed terror networks ran far too sharply counter to the conventional wisdom. For example, instead of massed incursions by heavy troops, Rivers asserted that the terrorists could be defeated with just a few hundred elite operatives working in small "squadrons" of twenty-five each. As he put it: "I am not talking about armies. . . . When it comes to counter-terrorist work, small *is* beautiful, because it has been proved to work. And large doesn't work."[17]

Such an approach was clearly a threat to the traditionalists in the U.S. military, which at the time was still fighting a rearguard action to forestall the creation of the Special Operations Command. Needless to say, Rivers's off-design approach was never authorized as U.S. core counterterror doctrine, though the kinds of squadrons he called for do exist in some of the top-secret domains of the Defense Department. They have simply never been unleashed as Shultz, Rivers, and others in the counterterrorism business would have liked.

As seen in Figure 13, the failure to launch a war on terror more than twenty years ago initially led to a slow rise in the number of serious terrorist incidents during the 1980s and on until 9/11.[18] A brief hiatus occurred as the cold war was ending, reflecting at least a statistical correlation with the notion that the Soviets had been the single most important sponsor fomenting terror. This idea was thoughtfully advanced by the late Claire Sterling in her book *The Terror Network*; but other experts pointed to the stunning Israeli victory in the Six Day War as the event that convinced most Muslims that the only way they could fight for their goals was by irregular means. There was simply no way for them to confront the modern mechanized armies of their adversaries with any hope of victory. From this point of view terrorism can be seen as having emerged as a matter of strategic choice and operational necessity, rather than from the wicked dreams of the KGB.

Figure 13.   Significant Acts of Terrorism, 1968–2004

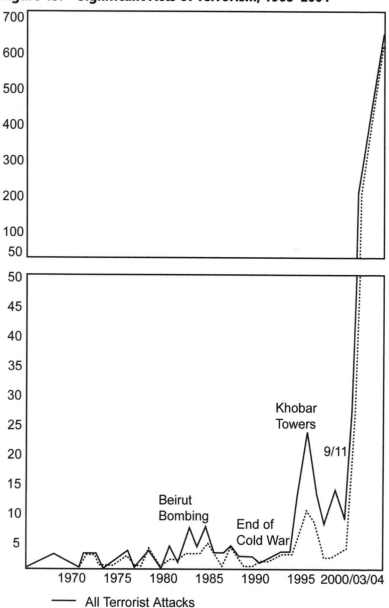

Although comprised of a great multitude of attacks too individually insignificant to make it into the State Department data-set reflected in the figure above, the Egyptian war of attrition against Israel in 1969 and 1970 seems an early indicator that terror was emerging as a form of war.[19] And Egypt's hard experience when it tried a conventional war one more time in 1973 may have reinforced this point further. The motivation to take up terrorism might also have been spurred by the emergence of the Israeli "Bloc of the Faithful" mass movement in 1974, among whose principal aims was the notion of expanding their settlements into areas that Muslims considered their territory. U.S. support for the anti-Soviet *mujahideen* in Afghanistan during the 1980s had the unintended consequence of energizing terror networks. But our proxy war in the Hindu Kush simply quickened a process that was already well under way, especially throughout the Muslim world.

Israeli, and later American, conventional military superiority was hardly likely to encourage reconciliation. As seen in Figure 13, the Muslim share of all significant acts of terrorism has continually grown since the end of the Yom Kippur War. And whatever the Soviet influence on the prevalence of terror during the cold war, the hiatus that accompanied the dissolution of the Soviet Union proved to be only a brief respite. Terror began to breathe again later in the 1990s and has been growing in scope and intensity ever since, especially in the wake of our invasion of Iraq, with more than 200 major attacks logged in 2003 and more than 650 in 2004. In mid-2005 the overwhelmed State Department ceased keeping count in its annual compendium of *Global Trends*, the new National Counterterrorism Center assuming the task. This new terrorism arose in the wake of the Soviet-American superpower rivalry in which mutual nuclear deterrence prevented open conventional conflict but encouraged terror and other forms of covert and irregular warfare.

These troubling developments were in the very early stages of unfolding during the Reagan years, a time when concerted effort against terrorism—along the lines recommended by Shultz—might well have mitigated the problem significantly. But Reagan, who saw the merits in both Shultz's and Weinberger's positions, preferred to navigate a compromise course. In this case he steered closer to Weinberger's more conventional views. Weinberger continued to think in traditional ways about conflict even after the cold war, as can be seen in his more recent (though still pre-9/11) book, *The Next War*. It is a catalog of possible conventional conflicts that he enjoins us to prepare for, though what endangers us now is the rise of the very sort of threat that Shultz had sought a way to counter.

The costs and consequences of Weinberger's victory in the debate over counterterrorism policy have been serious. Except for our success against the ANO, terrorists have largely been allowed to flourish, to root themselves deeply and broadly, to cast their shadows across the whole world, to become Rivers's "universal plague." For this Ronald Reagan bears much responsibility. In some ways the drift in counterterrorism policy during the Reagan years is analogous to wayward American policies in the 1930s toward the rising German and Japanese threats. To be sure, George H. W. Bush and Bill Clinton had their chances to deal with the specter of terror in the years after Reagan; and they failed too. As for George W. Bush, he warmed to the task only in the wake of the 9/11 attacks on America.

Ronald Reagan's failure to prevent or preempt terror when it would have been much easier to do so should not lead us to dismiss as irrelevant his various ideas about military and national security affairs in an age of terror. His grand strategy of making the world less nuclear, transforming the military, and crafting an effective information strategy—which did so much to win the cold war—may still offer the proper mix of ideas for countering the terrorist threat and winning the new "cool war" that has emerged.[20] The basic tenets of Reagan's strategy seem particularly timely today: they are perfectly suited to heading off the three ways in which terrorists might defeat us.

First, by focusing on making the world ever less nuclear we stand a good chance of thwarting terrorist efforts to obtain weapons of mass destruction. This war would take on something of the character of an extended, occasionally muscular arms-control campaign aimed at avoiding the nightmare world that would arise with terror networks in possession of even quite small arsenals. Clearly Ronald Reagan's over-arching vision of deep cuts in nuclear weapons—perhaps even to the extent of their abolition and the simultaneous development of robust defensive systems—remains especially relevant for coping with this challenge.

The second way we might lose the war on terror would be if we could not demonstrate the skills needed to rip networks apart cell by cell. If others—either hostile nations or nonstate actors—were to perceive that they could gain advantages by creating covert armies of this sort, the nightmare would be only marginally less frightening than the nuclear threat. Heading off this second threat depends on transforming the military along nimble, networked lines, giving us a chance to defeat existing terror networks and prevent them from fatally metastasizing. While Reagan's overall goal of transforming the military still makes sense, in practical terms the changes he encouraged during his time in office resulted in a continued focus on conventional war and have hamstrung almost all efforts to retool for this new kind of conflict.[21]

The third potential path to defeat lies in the informational domain. We could lose the battle of the story—the grand narrative we tell the world about why we must all work to overcome terrorism. If we do, we cannot hope to stem the tide of terrorist recruitment or forge a global coalition that will make the world a far less permissive place for terror. And if the good reputation of the United States as protector rather than imperator fails to be restored in the wake of divisiveness over the invasion of Iraq, Abu Ghraib, and other nettlesome controversies, new limits will soon be imposed on the American role in the world—on issues that go well beyond terrorism. The current counterterror strategy, which prominently features the goal of effecting democratic regime change—sometimes via use of Colin Powell's concept of overwhelming force—is one guaranteed to foster the kind of resentment we seek to minimize. In this area, Reagan's commitment to a thoughtful information strategy could provide the guidance needed for a change of course in counterterror policy. And it could greatly diminish the risk posed by this third path to defeat.

While U.S. ardor for arms control is slowly being rekindled, and a Reagan-like war of ideas is contemplated, when it comes to taking the kind of military actions needed to defeat the terrorists, Reagan's legacy has proven problematic. As Chapter 5 shows, the initiatives that Reagan pursued helped restore both the confidence and capabilities of the U.S. military and established a huge firebreak between conventional and nuclear war. But most of what Reagan wrought in the military realm also served to reinforce traditional views of warfare, by far outweighing the impact of his support for the creation of the Special Operations Command. Yet the fact that an increased capability for waging irregular warfare was nurtured at all twenty years ago made it possible for us to do as well as we have against terrorists and insurgents in recent years. The challenge now is to continue cultivating this more unconventional aspect of Reagan's military legacy.

In the wake of the September 2001 attacks on America, we needed to respond swiftly and decisively to this new mode of war that had burst upon us, much as Admiral Yamamoto's dive and torpedo bombers had done at Pearl Harbor sixty years earlier. But the real meaning of al Qaeda's attacks was that the cold war–era arms race had been supplemented by an organizational race. That is, the terrorists had been steadily developing their networks and the doctrines to guide their use for nearly two decades. During the same period the United States had taken some steps in this direction, for the most part only in the special operations community. Overall, though, it lagged far behind in the organizational race. Our military was still large and heavy, preferring and much more prepared to confront like-sized and like-thinking adversaries. Reagan had presided over an American military renaissance during his years in office; but the principal product of his efforts was largely made manifest in the restoration of a superb conventional force and in the shoring up of the staid, if not stodgy, leadership mind-sets that were intended to govern its employment in combat.

Figure 14.   War at a Glance

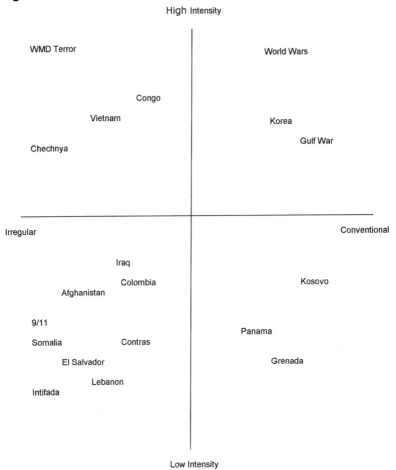

High Intensity

WMD Terror

World Wars

Congo

Vietnam

Korea

Gulf War

Chechnya

Irregular

Conventional

Iraq

Colombia

Kosovo

Afghanistan

9/11

Panama

Somalia

Contras

El Salvador

Grenada

Lebanon

Intifada

Low Intensity

Perhaps the best way to conceptualize the strategic dilemma that has emerged over the past few decades is to provide a graphic depiction of the overall landscape of conflict, showing where we are strong and where weak; where conflict has been, where it is now, and where it is going. Figure 14 uses two perpendicular lines to create four quadrants of conflict. Of the two axes created, the vertical one represents the spectrum of intensity from low to high, measured in terms of the numbers of people killed. The horizontal axis represents the type of war, with conventional conflicts on the right (think of the late George C. Scott in *Patton*, commanding a huge field army against a similarly armed foe). On the left, the conflicts are irregular, looking more like Oliver Stone's *Platoon*, with unseen enemies swarming out of the dark to mount bloody, suicidal assaults. Overall this intellectual space can help highlight our current problems.

Moving clockwise around the quadrants, the upper right fills in quickly with examples. The world wars and Korea come immediately to mind: big, bloody conventional conflicts with the horizontal axis forming a floor at, say, one million casualties. There are not many of these sorts of wars. Moving down to the lower right, the 1999 Kosovo War falls neatly into this quadrant. Our 1989 invasion of Panama belongs here too, as does the 1983 Reagan-era expedition to Grenada. This quadrant too is sparsely populated.

The lower left quadrant is where most of the action is. The U.S. military interventions in Lebanon (1983), Somalia (1993), and more recently in Iraq and Afghanistan belong here. So do the Palestinian intifada against the Israelis and al Qaeda's and/or its affiliates' attacks on America (2001), Bali (2002), Saudi Arabia (2003), and Spain (2004). Most of the world's other insurgencies fit in here as well: the "Lord's Resistance Army" in Uganda; the Tamils in Sri Lanka; the Moro Islamic Liberation Front in the Philippines; and the Colombian FARC. And on and on. This has probably been the most active quadrant since the rise of liberation movements against their old colonial masters in the wake of World War II. The pattern may hold even back to the nineteenth-century heyday of colonialism, the era of "small wars."[22]

While most irregular wars have remained at lower levels of intensity, at least in terms of lives lost, a few do rise higher. Vietnam is probably the best example of this, with well over a million deaths during the principal period of American involvement (1965–1975). Taken together the two Russo-Chechen Wars waged over the past decade probably belong here as well. The conflict in the Congo,

"Africa's World War," which has alternately raged and sputtered since 1998, fits in here too. Each of these wars features irregular operations by small units on at least one side, and heavy casualties. The Congo War, for example, may have caused as many as four million deaths.

But an irregular war at such levels of destruction is a comparatively rare occurrence, and most unconventional conflicts are likely to remain in that lower left quadrant—nasty, nettlesome, but hardly mortal threats to the world system. The one development that could overturn this logic and open the upper left quadrant to migration would be terrorist acquisition of even quite small arsenals of nuclear, biological, or chemical weapons. If such capabilities were to make their way from nations to networks, all that we know about strategy, security, and deterrence will be overturned. And the war on terror itself would probably be irretrievably lost. This is why Reagan's goal of making a "less nuclear" world principally by means of arms-control initiatives aimed at deep cuts—and eventually the total abolition of such weapons—remains the most useful guide to conducting a global campaign against terror.

To be sure, there will still be room for preventive or preemptive military action against rogue proliferators, and special operations must be planned in preparation for such contingencies as the fall of a friendly authoritarian ruler in nuclear-armed Pakistan and his replacement by rabidly anti-American forces. The use of preventive force to avert the threat of North Korea or Iran sending nuclear weapons "downstream" to terrorists is another possibility that must be considered. But our best hope of preventing terrorists from making their way to the far upper left quadrant of Figure 14 will depend heavily upon arms control. And how we articulate our attitude toward nuclear weapons will probably have a decisive effect on our ability to influence others. Among other things, we need to pledge that we will never use such weapons first, and that we will end new weapons development and testing (Reagan and all his successors have explicitly rejected a "no first-use" doctrine). If we do such things, the case can be made more convincingly to the world community—and to the rogues and pariahs out there—that it is truly in *all* our interests to build high, broad barriers between ourselves and even the possibility of warfare with nuclear weapons.[23] If we succeed in limiting conflict in such a way as to rule out the use of weapons of mass destruction—the central tenet of Reagan's security strategy—the remaining terrorist problem can be effectively addressed with our incomparable military working in conjunction with others. Still, ours is a military not yet well configured to the kind of fighting that looms ahead. And this is a clear result of policies put in place by Ronald Reagan.

To Reagan, military transformation meant refurbishing the armed services, making it possible for them to fight a protracted war without having to lean on the crutch of nuclear weapons to repel a Soviet invasion of Western Europe. He was wildly successful in crafting this new conventional war-fighting capability, which contained the seeds of what soon became a full-blown revolution in military affairs. But the vast resources he devoted to improving our sea, air, and land forces were spent, for the most part, with traditional conventional conflicts in mind. And little about military procurement and doctrinal development in the years after Reagan was changed by his successors in office. Big ships, heavy battle tanks, and the production of ever more remarkable high-performance aircraft accounted for 97 percent of defense spending. Only rounding-error-sized sums were left over in the defense budget to be sent to our special operations forces; and this has remained true during the several years since the onset of the war on terror.

Yet, as Figure 14 shows, most of the fighting in the world is taking place in the lower left quadrant. This is the realm of jihad and intifada, of irregular warfare. And while the military Reagan rebuilt was good for almost anything that might arise on the traditional-looking right side—at high or low levels of intensity—we have remained ill prepared for the war that has come upon us and for those like it that will follow. The problem of the lower left quadrant implies that each year we continue to misspend most of our defense budget. Still, it seems impossible to conceive of an American military machine that is not replete with heavy, industrial-policy weapons systems like its dozen aircraft carriers and thousands of main battle tanks. And the huge increases in the defense budget over the past four years appear simply to have allowed the military to forgo making hard choices about transforming its existing forces.

Beyond their habits of mind and institutional interests, those opposed to the idea that a transformed military means anything other than a bigger one do have at least one logical argument to advance. It is summed up neatly in the words a senior general officer used when I showed him my conflict spectrum figure: "If we build a leaner, lighter force to fight in the lower left quadrant, we won't be ready for the next big war in the upper right quadrant." My response to him was that the real meaning of the revolution in military affairs was that small combat groups had been greatly empowered by being networked to long-ranging, highly accurate weapons systems. In the future, nimble networked teams of quite small size would handily defeat old-fashioned heavy forces. We had seen the Chechens do this to the Russians in 1996, and al Qaeda had shown the power of a handful of their fighters on 9/11. Finally, we ourselves toppled the Taliban with just a few hundred special operations forces on the ground late in 2001 in Afghanistan.

The main point is that Ronald Reagan's call for military transformation is still valid, but the type of transformation needed now differs sharply from that of the 1980s. Instead of creating huge conventional capabilities, so as to tamp down the need to go nuclear in a crisis, the challenge is now to create a military that can strike swiftly and discriminately in an era of conflict characterized for the most part by a "hiders/finders" dynamic. If a large, old-style threat were to reemerge, such small, swift forces would rely on their mobility and the network of providers of supporting fire—attack aircraft, armed drones, and cruise missile-firing ships—to which they would be linked. This lean approach is not without risk; but the growing risk of continuing to try to fight against dispersed networks with our older, larger military formations already far surpasses it.

To date, few converts to the cause of building a nimbler, more networked military have appeared. Instead a bureaucratic compromise has been reached, one that calls for allowing the emergence of a new networked force *and* for keeping all our large military formations and their existing suite of heavy weapons. The result: huge defense spending and a continued desire to fight the terror war primarily by conventional means. Seen from this perspective, the large-scale invasion of Iraq in March 2003 may have had little to do with the irreducible preferences of high-level Bush advisers for war. Rather, it may have reflected the heartfelt desire of the military to try to solve the terror problem by the means it understood best—classic conventional war. Much evidence of this attitude was displayed during the year and a half between 9/11 and the U.S. invasion of Iraq, a time when yet another battle for our "strategic soul" erupted. Those in favor of using traditional approaches prevailed once again, much as Weinberger had carried the day against Shultz nearly twenty years earlier.[24] In terms of how the outcome of this strategic debate has affected the course of the war on terror, though, it seems clear that our shift in focus to conventional war-fighting approaches did little to cripple al Qaeda.

In 2003, for example, the State Department's official count reflected that 208 "significant" terrorist strikes were mounted around the world, almost five times 2002's total of 43 major attacks. And 2002 reflects a more than doubling from 2001's 19 serious incidents—itself a doubling of the year 2000 total (see Figure 13). Even these steady multiplications were dwarfed by the huge increase in 2004 to 651 significant attacks, according to the State Department—more than 3,000 per the newly formed National Counterterrorism Center.[25] And while al Qaeda was going back on the offensive in several countries around the world—not least in Tunisia, Turkey, Saudi Arabia, and Pakistan— our own conventional military approach was having little success in ending pesky ongoing insurgencies in Iraq and Afghanistan. Clearly terrorism has emerged as a mature form of war—something that George Shultz worried about two decades ago—and thinking about countering this scourge requires us to revisit the subject of military transformation.

The traditional approach to conflict simply does not work anymore. Our potential adversaries hardly seem likely to develop conventional capabilities with which to threaten us in the ways we would prefer to be threatened. And even if some rising rival did decide to spend several decades building an enormous, familiar-looking military, we would have ample time to respond in kind. Or we could simply rely on the lighter, nimbler, and more networked forces that have proven to be our most valuable assets in the fight against the terrorists. For we are in an information age, and, to paraphrase an old military saying, the state of play is now such that "your mass is grass." Small and swift will likely match up very well against big and balky.

But the legacy of large conventional forces that Ronald Reagan left us is proving exceptionally hard to overcome, even in the face of increasingly lethal terror networks. So it seems that this major aspect of his grand strategy will prove problematic in terms of meeting our changing national security needs in the twenty-first century—far more problematic than his arms-control strategy which, if revivified, would at least keep the terrorists from landing a knockout blow. But there is more to be done beyond relying on Reagan's approach to arms control and trying to emphasize special over conventional military forces in the war on terror. There must also be a clear-cut return to the informational element of Reagan's foreign policy strategy—what he liked to call, and we still call, the war of ideas.

The aspect of Ronald Reagan's grand strategy that is perhaps most applicable to our situation is the use of a skillful information campaign to accompany diplomatic initiatives and uses of force.

Currently we have a skillful opponent who has already enjoyed some success in portraying the war as a clash of civilizations—Harvard professor Samuel Huntington's phrase from a decade ago about the new kinds of conflicts that would be erupting.[26] Our task now is to refute Osama bin Laden sharply. Instead of confirming an endless clash of civilizations, the Reaganesque solution would be to emphasize that we are involved in a fight for the future based on universally accepted liberal ethics and values.[27]

In the months after 9/11, though, American information strategy came to be dominated by the tactics of hard-sell public relations and propaganda techniques. U.S. public diplomacy first came under the influence of Charlotte Beers, a marketing executive whose specialty in private life had been to purvey pet products throughout Latin America. She came and went quickly when it became clear that democracy could not be sold worldwide in the same manner as dog food. As to psychological operations and civil affairs in Afghanistan, the big innovation suggested by an outside public relations expert had been to ship thousands of small American flags to Kabul and distribute them to children who would be filmed waving them as our troops entered the city.

Needless to say, this proved to be an exercise in futility. The way in which our troops treated the Afghans every day had far more to do with how we were viewed. And once our first wave of special forces soldiers who had a deep understanding of the Afghan people were redeployed in preparation for the invasion of Iraq, their culturally ill-prepared replacements fared poorly. Resentment of the American presence grew in the wake of a number of incidents that saw innocent Afghans brutalized or killed—for example, a wedding party engaged in celebratory gunfire was bombed, leaving scores killed, a type of incident that would be repeated later in occupied Iraq. The problem deepened to the point that the Taliban, which had reverted to guerrilla warfare after its fall, began to regain support in the country. Indeed, by 2004 more than half of the twenty-two administrative districts in Afghanistan had fallen away from governmental control. A few areas have been reclaimed since, but clearly the Americans and their allies have worn out their welcome in Afghanistan. This point was reinforced in July 2005 when Russia, China, and a number of small central Asian countries jointly demanded the removal of all "international security assistance forces" (ISAF) from Afghanistan. Here was another indisputable sign that U.S. information strategy had faltered.

Beyond the simple problem that arose when those American troops who understood the local culture were replaced by newcomers who were unfamiliar with the theater, there was also evidence of the traditional Pentagon preference for conventional war. So the sprinkling of small detachments of special operations forces based around

Afghanistan gave way to much greater numbers of troops posted in just a few major garrisons. Little wonder that the government installed by the United States directly controlled only Kabul and its immediate environs. But this is hardly a catastrophic defeat for information strategy. The vast majority of Americans supported an attack on the al Qaeda haven in Afghanistan, as did much of the international community. The missed opportunity in this situation is that a much more skillful application of psychological operations, both before and during the invasion, might have splintered the Taliban internally and made the longer-term acceptance of regime change and occupation easier for the average Afghan to contemplate.[28]

This idea of reaching out to factions within the Taliban that may have been unfriendly to al Qaeda implies the possibility of developing a much broader negotiation strategy for the whole war on terror. The idea writ large would be to demonstrate to the Muslim world, to the rest of the international community, and to the average American that we stand for a just peace that would eliminate the scourge of terror around the world. And that we are committed not so much to leading the fight as to building a global network of our own to defeat terror networks and to end state sponsorship of them.

By 2005, attempts to reach out to insurgents in both Afghanistan and Iraq were finally getting under way—including offers of amnesty to members of the Taliban and Baathist cadres. These peace feelers were no doubt manifestations of the growing sense in the Pentagon that military-only solutions were unlikely to work—a point conceded openly to the press in June 2005 by senior general officers.[29] Much as Reagan had realized that the cold war could not be won by force of arms alone, so too it seems that the U.S. military leadership and their commander-in-chief George W. Bush have made the same discovery.

In this first global war between nations and networks, much inspiration can be derived from Ronald Reagan's ideas and diplomatic actions. As in our current conflict, he had to confront an intractable foe that could not be defeated militarily. Although he built up our military to keep deterrence strong, he also reached out to negotiate with those whose regime he had often described as the focus of evil in the modern world. In the end, Reagan's skillful blending of arms and ideas won a decisive victory with only a few scattered shots fired, the limited amount of actual fighting being undertaken mostly by proxy forces.

With regard to countering terrorism, we have seen how Reagan rejected George Shultz's call to mount a "war on terror." While this decision has had baleful effects in the decades since it was taken, it is important to note that Reagan also had something of an information strategy in mind when it came to dealing specifically with terrorism itself. The most important meaning of the Iran-Contra affair lies beyond its being simply a botched effort to secure the release of hostages or an attempt to circumvent the congressional will by funneling more funds and weapons to the Nicaraguan insurgents. The most significant aspect of the whole affair was the attempt to reduce the antipathy that had come between Iran—a leading state sponsor of terror—and the United States since the fall of the shah.

Reagan was simply trying to negotiate as part of his strategy for dealing with the terrorist threat, even back then. Michael Ledeen, a key administration figure in the Iran-Contra affair, has affirmed that some senior Iranian officials were "interested in pursuing a political dialogue with the United States and not in obtaining weapons for Iran."[30] It was not all business for the Iranians either. And much of the secret American and Iranian efforts to craft a peace were facilitated by the Israelis, who have themselves, for several decades, negotiated with those committing acts of terror against them, even while they have continued their own war on terror.[31] Yet at home Reagan was virtually alone in pursuing this negotiation strategy. State-Defense feuding was even tamped down, temporarily, so that both George Shultz and Caspar Weinberger could attack this policy. Shultz saw the initiative narrowly, as one in which "the U.S. government had violated its own policies on antiterrorism." Weinberger labeled it "the one serious mistake the Administration made."[32] Journalist Bill Moyers characterized the whole business in far darker terms, viewing the Iran-Contra matter as a grave threat to American democracy.[33] Nobody but Reagan seemed willing to consider the idea of opening negotiations with terrorists and their sponsors. Among his successors, only George W. Bush seems willing to consider moving in this direction—but only tentatively and quietly.

In the event, of course, the possibility of a warming of relations between Washington and Tehran fell afoul of the political scandal that soon broke. Neither Shultz nor Weinberger was able to mitigate its fallout. Soon after, the U.S. Navy and light Iranian coastal forces would be skirmishing in the Persian Gulf. And in July 1988 the *USS Vincennes,* an American warship, would shoot down Iran Air Flight 655, killing hundreds of innocent Iranians, deepening mutual antipathy rather than easing it. An important opportunity to stem the rising tide of terror had been lost. The fractiousness in Iranian-American relations has persisted now for decades, with fitful attempts to engage one of the Muslim world's most democratic countries interspersed with harsh American rhetoric charging Tehran with belonging to an "axis of evil." It would be good to remember that Reagan used the "e" word to describe the Russians as well—but it did not stop him from negotiating with them. There is a lesson in Reagan's dealings with the Russians, about finding a way to end the cold war, for our present information strategy in the war on terror.

In terms of learning from Reagan in such matters, it appears that his most apt pupil has been George W. Bush, who has used or sanctioned the use of some forms of negotiation on several occasions during the current conflict. Perhaps his showiest success was in efforts in 2004 to bring Moammar Qaddafi and his country back into the community of nations. In return for an end to U.S. military threats and economic sanctions, the Libyan dictator openly renounced terrorism and the secret nuclear weapons program that he had been pursuing. Similarly Bush has chosen negotiations in seeking an end to the proliferation threat from North Korea, yet another state sponsor of terrorism. On a smaller scale, as briefly mentioned above, Bush has made clear that most of the Taliban in Afghanistan and "reformed" Baathists in Iraq could become part of their societies again.

These examples notwithstanding, the quintessential tactical use of this more focused form of negotiations with those who had previously committed acts of terror took place in Fallujah, Iraq, after some weeks of fighting that had followed in the wake of the brutal murders and subsequent dismemberment of four Americans there. In April 2004, instead of continuing their assault on the city, the U.S. Marines redeployed their forces outside its limits, leaving soldiers of the former Baathist regime to keep the peace. In the main, they did; and Bush skillfully blended military operations—in the form of targeted raids or precision air strikes—and shows of force with a conciliatory information strategy, to great effect. Neither his father nor Bill Clinton ever mastered this type of operation.

Under pressure from his military advisers, however, Bush backtracked on this negotiation policy toward the Fallujah insurgents six months later and, in November 2004 the Marines returned with a crushing use of conventional force. The result: the city of Fallujah was flattened, but the overall military effect of this action on the insurgency was negligible, perhaps even counterproductive.[34] And the cost to the cause of U.S. public diplomacy across the Muslim world was huge. Many photos and videos of the destruction of Fallujah—taken by the insurgents during the battle—were soon spread across the broad swath of the Islamic world, with Muslims everywhere shocked and appalled by the event. It will be a long time before the United States recovers from this setback. This sort of city-busting operation has not been repeated in other parts of Iraq. So there appears to have been some sort of organizational learning at work.

Beyond Ronald Reagan and George W. Bush, though, the whole matter of mixing military threats and actions with quiet, often secret, diplomacy goes back a long way in American history. The best example of this occurred two hundred years ago when President Thomas Jefferson had to determine how to deal with the radical Muslim terrorist threat of his time: the Barbary pirates. They had preyed for years on American shipping in the Mediterranean and appear to have enjoyed some tacit support from Britain, which at the time was involved in a twenty-year-long conflict with the French Empire of Napoleon Bonaparte. Terrorist attacks on American and other neutral shipping tended to drive shippers to send their cargo with British carriers, a great economic boon to the British war effort.

At the time the United States had little ability to project much force as far away as the North African coast, but this did not stop Jefferson from sending an expedition to try to effect regime change by working with local rebels. A small naval squadron worked in tandem with the rebellion on the ground that he had authorized, but Jefferson also negotiated with the corsairs. The successes in the field of the small number of "special forces" he had sent there—under the joint leadership of the civilian William Eaton and Marine Corps Lieutenant Presley O'Bannon—made the pirate leaders most willing to negotiate. A peace treaty was soon signed, under whose terms the pirates released all hostages and pledged to cease their attacks on Americans.[35]

Perhaps a similar blending of military action and diplomacy can achieve similarly beneficial results in the current struggle with terrorists. Whatever the ultimate chances for successful negotiation, the early returns show that there are indeed ways to negotiate with networks, and that terrorists can occasionally be convinced to lay down their weapons. Some will not, of course, and these will have to be tracked down and eliminated. But the vast majority can probably be neutralized in this fashion, and a message can be sent to the billion-plus Muslims around the world that the United States stands for peace and prosperity for all, not terror and war. In the end, this will undoubtedly be the best way to reduce the recruiting appeal of those still trying to foment a global jihad.

In practical terms the logic of the idea of mixing in some negotiations with our military operations against terrorism is compelling; but no American political leader, of either major party, can risk the appearance of being "weak on terror." And so we find ourselves under the self-imposed constraint of pursuing a military strategy that aims at fighting other nations while the network that is our real enemy continues to elude us. We strive to democratize countries in the hope of creating new national environments less permissive of terror, when in fact the spread of more democratic institutions to places like Pakistan and Saudi Arabia will empower those Islamists most intractably opposed to us. In Pakistan it would give them control of nuclear weapons, in Saudi Arabia enormous leverage over the global economy. We should therefore be careful lest our wishes for these Muslim countries be granted.

Meanwhile our reluctance to consider deepening and broadening our diplomatic initiatives may doom us to continue a conflict that will rage on inconclusively for decades. Now, when the consequences of failing to end the current war could be disastrous, for ourselves and the world, what could possibly be the reason for failing to embrace the example set by Reagan of negotiating with one's enemies?

Many aspects of the problem of terrorism are the same today as they were during Reagan's time in office. To be sure, terrorism has grown more networked and has emerged as a form of warfare in its own right. But even these trends were already well under way in the 1980s when Abu Nidal built his own network and turned it into a roving band of latter-day Muslim mercenaries. Yet there is one new thing about terrorism in the early twenty-first century: it has entered the virtual world. As the electronic frontiers of the Internet and the World Wide Web have opened up to expansion and development, terrorists have moved in, right alongside virtual "homesteaders" and commercial enterprises. Terrorist organizations have their own websites that tell their story, engage in their version of public diplomacy, solicit donations—and coordinate the darker and more violent activities of their increasingly widely dispersed cells and nodes around the world.

Al Qaeda, of course, became the first terrorist group to master many aspects of life on the Web and the Net. But even this pioneering organization still has only a rudimentary ability to engage in acts of mass disruption that fall into the category of "cyberterror." Several years ago I led a team of military researchers in a classified undertaking whose goal was to assess whether any terrorist group could or would develop threatening cyber capabilities. Our findings then (1999) were that not even al Qaeda was within a decade of having a truly dangerous capacity for disruption. On the basis of detailed analyses of different group practices, we also judged that no terrorist organization would likely run the risk of recruiting a skilled Western hacker. This was because of the chance that he (almost all master hackers are male) might be a plant or could be under surveillance. All this was good news then. The bad news is that our study will soon be a decade old. And even if terrorists did not start growing their own hackers until 2000, there is only a short time until they can pose terribly costly, hard-to-counter threats to military and civilian information infrastructures.

A recent expert study suggests that al Qaeda has been actively developing such capabilities for several years, so our "grace period" is likely to expire at any moment.[36] Yet the rise of an era of cyberterror is impeded not only by the need to develop technical mastery of the subject. True master hacking requires skills that go many light-years beyond an ability to download viruses from websites; and it will be costly, risky, and time consuming for terrorists to invest in developing such capabilities. There is also the problem of the social chasm between terrorists and hackers. Traditional terrorists believe in the efficacy of and derive their emotional payoffs from breaking things and killing people. An act of mass disruption, most of the time, will simply impose economic costs. Even when these run into the billions of dollars, it is hard for most terrorists to see this as on par with blowing something or somebody up. A few terrorists may observe that acts of mass disruption can cause physical damage—for example, if the target is an air traffic control system in a key hub, at a busy time of day. Others will see that imposing economic costs with disruptive viruses confers upon them a kind of Robin Hood quality of stealing from the rich enemy. And this virtual means of "counting coup" can give them prestige without alienating their ethnic and religious core constituencies, who are on the whole likely to be squeamish about more traditionally bloody acts of terror.

On the counterterrorism side of the equation, the important point is that no global terror network can operate administratively—with even a modicum of security and efficiency—without using the Web and the Net. Therefore it behooves any who are involved in the struggle against terror to develop the skills needed to detect and track the enemy through cyberspace. A little of this is being done, but by far the lion's share of intelligence spending—estimated today at about $40 billion annually—still goes to cold war–vintage satellite systems designed to listen to phone conversations or to count tanks, planes, and ships from space. It is far past time to nurture intelligence gathering in the virtual realm, a technique that falls under a category called "clandestine technical collection."

In the years since the onset of the war on terror, we have not developed a sufficient amount of actionable intelligence to defeat our enemies. This is because they know how we gather information technically and because it is hard to insert human agents into terror networks. The clear implication for policy is to enhance our cyberspace-based intelligence-gathering capabilities. The huge spending increases for the military and intelligence communities that Reagan engineered so skillfully during his time in office have had the unintended consequence of reinforcing older bureaucratic preferences for existing costly collection systems. Just as true military transformation has been impeded by a bloated defense budget that aims at sustaining cold war–era "legacy systems," so intelligence transformation has been delayed by the fixation on maintaining a huge, capital-intensive spy satellite system. We find ourselves with the ability to watch the whole world—but having ever less ability to monitor the activities of those who pose the greatest threats to our security.

An interesting idea was pioneered during the Reagan years suggesting that we ought to begin engaging in "data mining" against our various enemies, and learn to manage the information already within our own systems more skillfully. The "product champion" for these ideas was Admiral John Poindexter, one of Reagan's national security advisers and a central player in the Iran-Contra affair, from which he emerged with a felony conviction but was later pardoned. Poindexter, who graduated from Annapolis at the head of his class, was among the first to understand the enormous potential that new advances in information technology would soon have for both intelligence gathering and for the overall management of national security and other governmental affairs. It was his creation of a White House "professional office system" (PROFS) that ironically proved to be his own undoing. PROFS was an early email network that linked everyone in the White House, the idea being that a well-informed staff would prove a boon to efficiency. Poindexter was right about this. What he may not have reckoned with was the fact that this made even sensitive data about secret initiatives with the Iranians susceptible to subpoena; and much of the information used to unravel the Iran-Contra scandal in fact came from the production of PROFS-derived documents.

This lesson was not lost on Poindexter, who became a leading proponent of transforming the intelligence-gathering process with advanced information technologies. In the wake of 9/11, George W. Bush tapped Poindexter to lead a "total information awareness" (TIA) initiative from his new office at the Defense Advanced Research Projects Agency (DARPA). Poindexter soon had his minions creating the kinds of data-mining capabilities that cyber punk novelist William Gibson so brilliantly imagined in his novels *Idoru* and *Pattern Recognition*. But TIA, which focused on searching for patterns in information already openly available, had a vaguely Orwellian feel, one that even changing the "T" from "Total" to the more politically correct "Terrorism" could not fix. So Congress officially shut down the initiative. Even so, this important concept lives on in less centralized fashion in each of the fifteen agencies that make up the national intelligence community today. And what activity there is in this sector has given us the best intelligence yet gleaned in the war on terror. There is much more progress to be made, but these ideas about the potential uses of information technology that were nurtured during the Reagan years will likely provide us with our best hope for tracking down terrorists today.

With the exception of the cyberterror phenomenon, which neither Reagan nor his advisers could likely have foretold, all the trends that today make terror a mortal threat to the United States—and to the civilized world—were well under way by the early 1980s. Terror networks were forming, and the terrorists themselves were developing strategies and doctrines that made it clear that this was to be their chosen mode of war. In reality, resorting to terror was their only viable strategic option, as they had neither the resources nor the skills to pose a more conventional threat to the United States. But our adversaries knew even then that it was becoming possible to use our advanced technology against us.

So the failure to deal with the rise of terror as a new form of war lands squarely on Ronald Reagan's shoulders. He had a trusted cabinet-level adviser urging him in 1984 to wage a war on terror. But he also had other highly valued advisers at that level urging him not to do any such thing. Reagan developed a hybrid approach, a compromise strategy that took a little bit from each camp of the contending bureaucracies. This approach proved to be almost wholly ineffectual, yet it was the one adopted and incrementally refined by each of his successors, until George W. Bush's epiphany after 9/11. Even since then, the huge conventional military and the costly suite of satellites that keeps it informed have been used for the most part in unimaginative ways against a wily, deadly adversary.

If we are to have any hope of averting terrorist acquisition of truly mass destructive weapons, such as "backpack nukes" or deadly biological toxins, we must revisit the strategy Reagan endorsed in NSDD 138. He was talked out of pursuing his own preferred policy then. Now it is time for us to pick up NSDD 138, dust it off, and run with it, for victory in the war on terror will go to the side that fields the better ideas. Two decades ago, Ronald Reagan and those who served him proposed all the concepts we need to win.

8

Ways of
Remembering Reagan

Perhaps the best way to measure Ronald
Reagan's impact on the international system is to think about what
the world would look like had he never risen to prominence. Had he
not been in a position to reach out to Mikhail Gorbachev, the cold war
would likely have continued—for some years, more likely for decades.
And if Saddam Hussein's 1990 invasion of Kuwait had come during
a period of continuing mutual antipathy between the United States
and the Soviet Union—as it well might have—it is hard to see how
American forces could have been used to drive the Iraqis out. The
risks of escalation to a larger, more general war would likely have been
seen as too great to risk a major campaign in the desert had Moscow
sided openly with Baghdad.

In the actual course of events, the fact that the Soviets lined up
with the United Nations against Iraq made it possible to form and deploy a multinational coalition force to roll back Saddam's aggression
in high style. Twelve years later, continued Russian quiescence allowed the United States to topple him from power. But the subsequent rise of a nettlesome insurgency in Iraq has prompted some to
think about the usefulness of having a counterweight to preponderant
American influence in the international system. Such a blocking

agent would serve to rein in the excesses that often come with what the theologian Reinhold Niebuhr once called America's "undue reliance on the obvious might which we possess."[1] Whatever else he achieved, for good or ill, Reagan brought an abrupt end to the longstanding stability of the cold war balance of power.

Had deadly terror networks arisen in a world still riven by cold war strife and nuclear arms racing, terrorists would face a less united international community and would surely also enjoy more secure havens. And the great powers, reluctant to fight each other in direct, face-to-face fashion, would probably emulate the example provided by easy-to-form, inexpensive teams of networked terrorists. Al Qaeda and its affiliates would have many colleagues and competitors, all capable of enormous disruption, especially if weapons of mass destruction were ultimately shipped downstream to them. In short, the world would be far more complicated and infinitely more dangerous had Ronald Reagan not risen to the presidency. But he did, making a favorable peace with the Russians just in time to give the United States the running room it needs to cope with a new era of complex problems and grave global challenges.

Reagan's successes in ending the nuclear arms race and sharply reducing Soviet-American antagonism were, as John Lewis Gaddis has said, "unexpected."[2] For Reagan was viewed throughout his political lifetime and until the past several years as a man capable of only limited spurts of introspection, even these constrained by his hard-set preconceptions.[3] Paul Nitze, the great diplomat and nuclear strategist who served presidents of both parties from Roosevelt's time, saw Reagan as "heir to the deeply conservative, isolationist tradition of the Republican right." Further, Nitze thought Reagan stood for "that streak in American politics of unrefined demagoguery."[4] Much was also made by others of Reagan's native distrust of diplomacy. The journalist Richard Burt noted at the outset of Reagan's presidency that he "has repeatedly said that the State Department has placed too much trust in arms control talks and that time after time naïve American diplomats have been outfoxed by Russians sitting across the negotiating table."[5]

What theories have informed these views of Reagan's character and policy predilections? The dominant one suggests that his ideas were largely the products of his religious faith and his career in the film industry. The evangelical Christianity with which he grew up, for example, is thought to account for his inherent distrust of Washington and his belief that the geographic insularity of America was a blessing from God and a mandate to build a new Zion as a beacon to the world. Where religion gave Reagan a set of general principles for viewing the world, the motion picture business, it has been argued, provided more specific guidelines for his thinking. His strong anti-Communist stance was thought to have grown out of the leadership role he played in attempts to purge Hollywood of Communists during the McCarthy era. Later on, his decade as a pitchman for General Electric on its long-running television show is thought to have solidified his pro-corporate and pro-defense thinking. As to Reagan's specific policy ideas, some scholars have advanced the argument that his positions came straight from movies in which he starred. The most famous example of this argument was the assertion by the late Dr. Michael Rogin, in his 1987 *"Ronald Reagan," The Movie*, that Reagan's Star Wars scheme for defending America against nuclear missiles had its origins in a 1940 Warner Brothers film, *Murder in the Air*. In this potboiler, Reagan starred as a confidential government agent whose duty was to protect an "inertia projector" that fired streams of electrons capable of bringing down enemy bombers, shielding the country from attack.[6]

These theories are interesting and no doubt have some merit. Yet they do not get us anywhere close enough to the "unexpected" Reagan and his ideas, as they leave off far too soon. For example, Reagan's evangelical religious experience, while influential in his adolescent and young adult years, was much tempered by his sometimes swinging Hollywood lifestyle and by several later decades of at best only intermittent attendance at church. Without question he was a deeply religious man, but his was a private practice of faith that he went out of his way to keep from entwining too closely with his public life. In this respect Reagan's religious persona stands in sharp contrast to the more public professions and affirmations of faith and its role in guiding policy that have been made by his successors Bill Clinton and George W. Bush.

As to the influence of the films in which he acted and in his role as a labor leader in the industry, these notions miss much as well. Theories based on his film industry experiences, for example, leave out the huge impact of the roughly twenty years between the effective end of his feature film career and his coming to the presidency. The 1960s and 1970s were the decades in which he generated and explicated the many insights derived during his extensive career as a radio commentator on public policy, especially his views on foreign policy and national security affairs. As one reads through his editorials, one can begin to glimpse the emergence of Reagan as a strategic thinker, not just an ideologue. Here lie the best clues to his later policies. For example, in a series of radio commentaries about the ideas of Professor Eugene Rostow that aired in October 1978, Reagan challenged much of the conventional wisdom about strategic affairs, especially popular notions of how massive retaliatory threats could somehow secure America. Reagan couched his critique in terms drawn closely from Rostow's own writings:

> Our leaders continue to tell us that if the Soviets cross certain lines we can kill millions of them without danger to ourselves. This was a plausible answer at the time of the Cuban Missile Crisis [but] it has long since lost even the appearance of conviction.[7]

Reagan was deeply drawn to the ideas of Rostow, a man whom he described on air as "an unquestioned liberal, a scholar who desires peace above all and who finally spoke out because he thinks we could be on the road to war."[8] This does not sound at all like a reflexive conservative whose views about national survival in a nuclear age were fueled by his roles in propaganda films more than thirty years earlier, or by some strand of Christian apocalyptic thought.

The same kind of nuance characterized the development of Reagan's thinking during his two terms as governor of California (1967–1975). His record of public utterances on foreign policy and security affairs during this time is not nearly as rich as during his radio heyday; but those close to him were well in tune with his thinking. On the matter of making the world less nuclear, for example, Reagan's close aide and confidant, Edwin L. Meese, told me that when Reagan first became governor in 1967 he learned in briefings exactly how destructive nuclear war would be—and how ineffective civil defenses were. The idea of holding civilians hostage to nuclear attack as a means of keeping the peace appalled Reagan, who found such a practice highly unethical. So, from his early days as governor, Reagan began thinking about finding a way out of the illogic of mutual assured destruction. He also took advantage of Meese's military background—the latter had risen to general officer rank in the reserves—to ask questions and try out his ideas for solving the security problems of the day. Meese continued to serve as a sounding board in private talks with Reagan through his presidential years.[9]

Here, then, lies the key to understanding Reagan's foreign policy and his approach to national security: he must be considered above all else as a strategic thinker. Yes, he was a Christian, an actor, and a radio commentator. Politically he was first a powerful union leader, later a governor, last a president. But what best explains why he was so often able to play against type is his preoccupation with strategy. For a strategist is someone able to challenge conventional wisdom, to act in seemingly paradoxical ways, to search always for the ideas that will give him an edge. A good strategist is idea-driven but cannot be an ideologue.

In the strategic realm Reagan finally came into his own, fielding one innovative idea after another, or taking existing ideas in almost wholly new directions. It is possible to see how, on the basis of his ideas, Reagan transformed American grand strategy. Beginning with his basic assumptions about the self-contradictions inherent in all dictatorial systems, the blindness of existing nuclear doctrine, and the too-defensive nature of the classic containment concept, Reagan blazed new paths for American policy. The many ideas he advanced can be summed up in five progressions from old to new foreign policy and security strategies:

1. From containment to rollback. By the time Reagan became president in 1981, the United States had been taking a reactive stance in the cold war for more than thirty years. Containment, as first conceptualized by George Kennan in his famous long telegram, was about stemming the tide of Communist expansion. It was about parrying Soviet thrusts wherever and whenever it became necessary to do so. It was about trying not to lose more ground. In addition to the inherent self-limiting scope of the containment strategy, Reagan entered office with all his principal advisers telling him that we had fallen dangerously behind the Soviet Union in the arms race, and that Communist forces were on the march in several areas of the world. Yet Reagan, considering all this, nevertheless decided to take the initiative away from the Soviets. Despite what appeared to be an unfavorable correlation of forces, Reagan believed the United States could not hope to win without becoming more proactive. And so he reversed course at the highest level, a strategic master stroke.

Reagan's imprint on presidential doctrine remains strong and clear. Where the reactive Truman Doctrine guided Eisenhower, Nixon, Ford, and even Carter—Kennedy was interested in being more pro-active but did not live long enough to do so—the Reagan Doctrine of taking the initiative in helping others free themselves has clearly driven the policies of his successors. To George H. W. Bush it meant pursuing a somewhat overexuberant vision of a "new world order" based on American leadership. To Bill Clinton it was about following a more circumspect but still explicitly Reaganesque concept that he called democratic enlargement. George W. Bush has taken matters much further, though, seeing his presidency as guided by a God-given mission to free the world of its terrors by any and all means. What we call the Bush Doctrine is actually a fusion of concepts: his father's new world order, and his predecessor Clinton's democratic enlargement. All three of Reagan's successors have thus articulated pro-active visions that stem directly from his historic turn away from simply practicing containment. Yet all three have, to varying degrees, deviated from Reagan's core idea of helping others help themselves, as all—but the younger Bush the most—increased the role of the U.S. military substantially.

2. *From deterrence to defense.* Along with being relegated to the generally passive role of containing Communist advances, cold war military thought was driven by the overarching concept of deterrence. This was based on the twin notions that the West could not hold out long against the modern armored hordes of the Soviets and that even a conventional war would inevitably escalate to see the use of nuclear weapons anyway. So war had to be avoided at all costs. Reagan the strategist turned this notion on its head, mounting a two-pronged counterattack. First he rejected the idea that all wars would end up going nuclear. His mantra that "a nuclear war cannot be won and must never be fought" was sincere; but in his view this realization meant that conventional war *was* possible and winnable with the right forces. Because nuclear war was so horrible, great powers would refrain from escalating a conventional war as long as they could fight ably with more traditional weapons. With this in mind, Reagan set about the business of revitalizing the American military in the wake of Vietnam, returning it to a usable instrument of statecraft. Then, to guard against the failure of deterrence, he shifted nuclear strategic thought away from the "assured destruction" idea to what he saw as the more ethical concept of ballistic missile defense.

As with his shift from containment to rollback, Reagan's rekindling of classical military concepts of war-fighting and defense have influenced each of his successors. George H. W. Bush would, in his single term in office, employ the U.S. military in two significant, victorious campaigns—in Panama in 1989 and in the Gulf War of 1991—that announced the full-bodied return of the use of force in American foreign policy. Bill Clinton would exercise military options even more frequently than his predecessor, though on a smaller scale, even in his major 1999 war against the Serbs over Kosovo. It would be left to George W. Bush to assert the right to use force preventively against terror—an apparent realization of Reagan's NSDD 138 but in fact a step beyond it, given Bush's broader emphasis on effecting regime change in rogue nations rather than on ripping apart terror networks.

3. From arms racing to arms reductions. Until Reagan came along, statesmen and strategists generally believed the superpowers were locked in an airtight, inescapable security dilemma. That is, actions that each side felt compelled to take for self-protection would always be perceived as threatening by the other, causing what Lewis Richardson, half a century ago, first termed "arms spirals."[10] These had no natural stopping point, save perhaps when they ended in major wars. The best that could be hoped for, it was thought, was to slow the pace of the arms race—the goal of the strategic arms limitations talks (SALT) undertaken by Nixon, Ford, and Carter. Reagan saw things differently. He believed that nuclear wars could not be won and must not be fought; therefore an end to arms racing had to be possible. In this view he came far closer to the ideas expressed by academics and civil society peace activists of his time than to the musings of military men and government officials. And he overruled all of officialdom in his quest for strategic arms reductions talks— the START process. The anti-nuclear activist Jonathan Schell has rightly called the Reagan years a "comparative golden age of arms control."

Reagan's imprint on arms reduction policies, though initially strong, has now begun to fade. Sharp reductions were made during the elder Bush's presidency, when the first START agreement was ratified. But the momentum for further reductions began to slow under Bill Clinton, and the second START agreement never took full effect because of the Russians' reluctance to ratify the treaty. Perhaps this was because, as Clinton's then deputy secretary of state Strobe Talbott noted, "the arsenal that Russia had inherited from the USSR . . . constituted one of the last vestiges of Russia's status as a superpower." Talbott continued, though, that the slowdown in arms reductions involved more than just Russian recalcitrance: "Clinton saw strategic arms control as old business: unfinished, worthwhile and necessary, to be sure, but nonetheless not high on his agenda."[11] For George W. Bush, the drive for arms reductions was further slowed by the distractions of an ongoing war on terror that dominated all but the first eight months of his presidency. Given the importance of keeping

WMD out of terrorist hands, though, it seems inevitable that Reagan's currently fading imprint in this realm will make a comeback.

4. From propaganda to public diplomacy. In the decades after he wrote the "long telegram" that convinced Harry Truman to contain Soviet expansion, George Kennan went out of his way to emphasize that he saw the cold war competition in ideational rather than primarily military terms. But there was little recognition of this point, with anti-Soviet strategy focusing on military considerations. In addition to Kennan, some voices in the academy tried to draw attention to the informational domain, most notably Reinhold Niebuhr, who spoke of the "channeling of aspirations" and believed that "force which coerces the body but does not persuade the will can have only negative significance."[12] But until Reagan came along, no one was willing to put ideas first in a systematic way. Ronald Reagan went far beyond the propaganda that had characterized the war of ideas before him, so far as to call for and create what he called an information strategy for winning the cold war.[13] His strategy consisted of steadily increasing pressure on our adversaries by communicating directly with those peoples they were oppressing.

This approach was startlingly successful and brought American public diplomacy finally into its own. Or perhaps it had just returned to the ideal that Thomas Jefferson first wrote about to James Madison.[14] Either way, information strategy won out in a long, perilous, nuclear-tipped conflict in which our military forces could not have hoped to achieve final victory in battle. And in this informational realm Reagan "the Great Communicator" left perhaps his most important legacy for the future of American statecraft. Yet the gains he made and the turn of institutional mind he cultivated in government were among the first assets to be dissipated by his inheritors. George H. W. Bush stumbled twice, first being slow to encourage the dissolution of the Soviet Union, later articulating a vision of U.S. global primacy that international mass publics, their governments, and even average Americans found troubling. Bill Clinton repaired some of this damage but inflicted some of his own by dissolving the United States Information Agency, stilling its distinct voice in our high councils of state. George W. Bush erred initially by relying unduly on military force to win the war on terror. By 2005, though, with even his own generals admitting the limits of military power, Bush proved more willing to accept the notion that a new war of ideas was upon us and that the outcome of the struggle against terror would depend heavily upon the success of U.S. information strategy.

5. *From coercion to constructive engagement.* When he thought the circumstances called for it—as in the case of replacing arms buildups with reductions and, for some types of weapons, elimination—Ronald Reagan completely reversed the course of American foreign policy. In other areas he adjusted course more subtly, as in the case of U.S. relations with tyrannical regimes. Reagan entered office early in the cold war's fourth decade, inheriting a diplomatic strategy that, in its emphasis on containment, had come to rely on cultivating friendly despots to help defend areas that might come under threat of Soviet influence or control. Thus the United States had many strange bedfellows; but the growing American emphasis on human rights, championed first by Gerald Ford and later by Jimmy Carter, was exposing the hypocrisy of our strategy and making it untenable. Reagan found a way out of the dilemma, drawing to some degree from the ideas of Jeane Kirkpatrick, a Democrat, who had articulated the view that some types of dictatorial regimes were less odious than others, and these could and should be dealt with. Reagan built his constructive engagement concept upon this idea and added his own flourish about all tyrannies of the mind being weak. Their inherent weakness made it possible for us to think in terms of engaging them diplomatically, for time was always on our side according to this point of view. And so Reagan opened up a huge playing field for the application of one of his other key concepts, information strategy, the goal being the attritional "wearing down" of authoritarian regimes around the world.

Both George H. W. Bush and Bill Clinton pursued policies recognizable as forms of constructive engagement, especially with regard to Russia, which had emerged from the haze of its Communist era as a shaky democracy with latent authoritarian tendencies. But the Reagan concept of constructive engagement is undergoing its most severe test in the current war on terror. In this conflict the United States must often count on the cooperation of dictatorial regimes to help root out nodes and cells of terror networks, though our declaratory strategy is that we are trying to win by transforming as many countries as possible into democracies. George W. Bush faces a different kind of evil empire than Reagan did—indeed, al Qaeda is something of an invisible empire—but the constructive engagement concept seems particularly appropriate now. Because undermining authoritarian rule in either Saudi Arabia or Pakistan, for example, could unleash huge, rabidly anti-American Islamist forces that would suddenly have global economic influence or access to nuclear weapons. Yet pushing both countries slowly in the direction of improved representational governance might, in the end, reduce the explosive pressure now building in each, allowing for eventual political transitions without an undue risk of radicalizing either one. The key caution for the younger Bush is to refrain from pressing for reform—in these countries and others—too quickly. The constructive part of Reagan's strategy involved effecting change without fomenting violent upheaval and without using the U.S. military as the agent of change. Reagan accomplished this time and again during his presidency. The challenge now is to rekindle this deftness.

The British philosopher Alfred North Whitehead once said, "We think in generalities; we live in details." This formulation is especially true of the interplay of ideas and policies during the Reagan years. Most of the overarching concepts that informed Ronald Reagan's worldview were of a highly general nature. For example, "the world can be made less nuclear." Or, "tyrants are weak, not strong." These are good enough for charting a strategic course; but they must be translated into specific policies. Reagan forged a strong bond between his ideas and policies, so much so that the strategic template he left behind has remained quite relevant to our needs. But making the transition from idea to policy is a tricky business, and Reagan did not get it right all the time. He fell short in three major areas, each of which bears critically upon our foreign policy and security strategy today.

The most serious misstep Reagan made was allowing Pakistan to continue to develop nuclear weapons. Although he reversed the course of the arms race with the Russians and took steps to keep nuclear weapons out of Latin America and to dissuade South Africa from acquiring weapons of mass destruction, the failure to forestall Pakistani proliferation has had grave consequences: the rise of the A. Q. Khan network—pieces of which are still operating today—and North Korean proliferation, as well as the possibility of nuclear arms ending up in the hands of terror networks. This failure occurred in part because of the perceived need to accommodate Pakistan at a time when it was supporting another element of Reagan's grand strategy: the cost-imposing campaign of the *mujahideen* in Afghanistan. Given that these fiery insurgents ended up as the hydra's teeth from which al Qaeda and its affiliates would rise, the unintended consequences of this generally useful strategy against the Soviets have turned out to be enormous.

Equally as important as Reagan's error is that the tenor of his policy toward Pakistan has continued to guide his successors. Even after the Soviets retreated from Afghanistan, the elder Bush did nothing to prevent the Pakistanis from developing nuclear weapons. Nor did Bill Clinton. Any of these three presidents—Reagan, the elder Bush, or Clinton—could have taken firm steps to prevent Pakistan from going nuclear, but none of them did. Perhaps the price would have been giving an American nuclear security guarantee to Pakistan against threats from others. That would have been a small price to pay, given the risks we now run. The principal peril that has grown from Reagan's miscue is that the government of Pakistan might be overthrown—by violence or votes, or perhaps both—with rabidly anti-American Islamists taking control of a nuclear-armed country. This core concern of George W. Bush has necessitated the development of plans anticipating the need to secure Pakistan's nuclear arsenal in the event of serious political upheaval in that country. This huge problem, as Senator John Glenn put it many years ago, far outweighs whatever gains we may have enjoyed from arming the *mujahideen* to fight the Russians during the 1980s.[15]

Reagan's second major mistake came when he and his advisers tried to turn the concept of waging a war on terror into practical policy initiatives. Recall that Secretary of State George Shultz became the point man in 1984 for those advocating an activist approach to countering terror. He was opposed by Secretary of Defense Caspar Weinberger, a man who agreed in general with the idea of fighting terror but wanted to do so in a conventional military manner rather than with covert special operations forces. In an effort to forge a bureaucratic peace, Reagan compromised by allowing the Shultz camp to undertake a few covert counterterror operations; but overall Reagan sided far more with Weinberger, who represented the views of the vast majority of the military. In this instance Reagan the strategist gave way to Reagan the politician. The consequences have been grave. Had Reagan's choice been to launch an irregular war on terror more than twenty years ago, the odds are that al Qaeda and other networks would not have become the potent threats they are today.

The formative power of Reagan's flawed approach to countering terror has been profound for each of the presidents who have followed him in office. Neither the elder Bush nor Bill Clinton took terror seriously enough to try to eliminate especially pernicious groups, despite mounting evidence that the threat they posed was rapidly metastasizing. Even George W. Bush failed to focus on terrorism before the attacks on America. Thus all three of Reagan's successors kept to the course he had set, engaging in some covert action but for the most part relying on conventional U.S. military power to protect America. To shift to a new course of action would have required expending a great deal of presidential political capital, as the 9/11 Commission suggested:

> If a president wanted to rally the American people to a warlike effort, he would need to publicize an assessment of the growing

al Qaeda danger. Our government could spark a full public discussion of who Usama bin Laden was, what kind of organization he led, what Bin Laden or al Qaeda intended, what past attacks they had sponsored or encouraged, and what capabilities they were bringing together for future assaults. We believe American and international opinion might have been different—and so might the range of opinion for a president—had they [the public] been informed of these details.[16]

Neither Reagan nor his first two successors chose to initiate such a discussion with the American public about the need for a war on terror. And George W. Bush did so only in the wake of attacks on America that seemed to make any debate moot. These shortcomings highlight the huge, continuing influence on policy of Ronald Reagan's choices a generation ago. The magnitude of his error has only become fully apparent in the years since 9/11. Today continuing difficulties in waging the kind of war first envisioned by George Shultz and his advisers in 1984 may be a symptom of the third problem area—military affairs—where it has proven hard for us to move efficiently from concepts to detailed policies.

In this third area of concern, unintended consequences have once again come to the fore. We have seen how Reagan relentlessly pursued the rebuilding of the American military, both in a material sense and in the restoration of its morale in the wake of the Vietnam debacle. This military renaissance allowed the United States to contemplate a reduction in nuclear arms—given its refreshed capacities for waging conventional war—and made it possible to become more pro-active in our overall approach to international security policy. But the revitalization of the military was undertaken by Reagan in such fashion as to allow the Pentagon's senior leadership virtually free rein in setting spending and force structuring priorities. Of this hands-off approach to transforming the military, Richard Burt noted (on the basis of many interviews with close friends of Reagan) that the president tended

to trust the judgment of military professionals, believing that many of the nation's most serious strategic mistakes, including Vietnam, stemmed from attempts by civilian "systems analysts" in the Pentagon and at private think tanks to usurp the rightful role of the military.[17]

The trust Reagan placed in senior military leaders resulted in a reaffirmation of the most traditional views of strategy and warfare at a time when the need to anticipate the rise of irregular adversaries was acute. The Special Operations Command was created on Reagan's watch, but only over the strong resistance of the services, and with only an embryonic capability for countering terror and confronting other emerging threats.

Hundreds of billions of dollars were spent by Reagan to prepare our military for a kind of warfare that was ever less likely to occur; and the pattern he set has governed all of his successors. George H. W. Bush waged two wars with lesser adversaries using the Reagan-made military. He won both times—in Panama and the Gulf—but the "force packages" were far larger than necessary and were used far less imaginatively than they should have been. Even so, the lopsided victories in each war seemed to affirm the validity of the Reagan military revival. Even when Bill Clinton came into office and tried to cash in on the peace dividend, he ended up ensuring the triumph of military traditionalism by concentrating almost all his reductions on manpower. He oversaw the reduction of about one-third of total U.S. forces during the 1990s, yet left procurement plans for almost all major weapons systems virtually intact. And he conducted the Kosovo War in the most traditional way possible—as a classical strategic bombing campaign—instead of setting loose special forces with Kosovar irregulars on the ground, a move that would have greatly enhanced the efficiency of NATO's air attacks on Serb forces.

Reagan's military legacy has had the most profound impact, though, on George W. Bush, whose presidency has been defined by a protracted war against a global network of terrorists. While the special operations capabilities cultivated during the 1980s have led to some tactical successes—most notably the toppling of the Taliban in Afghanistan by just a few hundred of our commandos—the war on terror has taken on an overarchingly traditional tint. The march up

Mesopotamia in 2003 and the subsequent occupation of Iraq were undertaken in a highly conventional manner, because U.S. forces are structured for and indoctrinated to wage war in this fashion. And Reagan's reach remains strong here as the military continues to clamor for more conventional capabilities. The younger Bush's response to this dilemma is redolent of Reagan as well, as his stated intent is to continue to spend heavily in support of the traditionalists *and* to allow the special operations forces to grow. Even if he can have it both ways, this approach is hugely inefficient; and the continued primacy of conventional thinkers—the ultimate outcome of Reagan's ideas about the military—ensures that identifying and adopting the correct strategy for waging the war on terror will remain a struggle. This we owe to Reagan's thinking and to the willingness of his successors to follow so closely in his wake.

Each of these three darker aspects of Reagan's legacy—the "reverse of the medal," if you will—has proven every bit as enduring as the more positive side of his contribution of ideas to American foreign policy and security strategy. In some ways his shortcomings in these three areas of horizontal proliferation, countering terror, and revitalization of the military have sticky consequences that are proving difficult to redress. Yet it is still possible to think in terms of quelling the crises in these three areas. For the proliferation of weapons of mass destruction can be stopped by rekindling a Reaganesque ardor for arms control. Terror networks can be defeated by the kind of strategy George Shultz identified and Ronald Reagan initially supported in 1984, and the U.S. armed forces have had in recent years both a commander-in-chief and a secretary of defense who have continually called for military transformation. In short, there is hope for improvement.

Moving from broad concepts to specific policies is unquestionably a complex business, yet it is not enough simply to observe and classify the various migratory paths that lead from one to the other. To delve into the factors that guide high-level decision-making processes requires that one consider the character of the decision-maker. Sometimes this can be done in a way that yields rich results. For example, the many studies undertaken of Adolf Hitler's character have provided remarkable insights over the years, both into his early diplomatic and military triumphs as well as his later series of catastrophic blunders. Ronald Reagan, however, lies at the other end of the spectrum of difficulty. His is one of the most elusive characters of a major world leader. Virtually all the personal memoirs of those who served directly under him resonate with the sense of being in the presence of an affable, cool, yet ultimately unknowable personality. Michael Deaver, who worked closely with Reagan for thirty years, may have put it best:

> As for his well-documented remoteness, the part of his personality that drives his biographers crazy, a lot of theories get bandied about as to what shaped Reagan's personality. He couldn't see very well as a child until his nearsightedness finally and belatedly led to him getting glasses. Is that why he was so disconnected from people? His father's drunkenness is often cited as having had a profound impact on his behavior. Perhaps this is the reason he learned to keep his distance from people, or why he invented a world of "make-believe" where America was always a beacon of hope on a shining hill. Far be it from me to analyze him. After all our years together, I could never completely understand what made him tick.[18]

So it is with much humility that I venture onto the dangerous ground of character interpretation. It is so perilous that I simply lay aside all the psycho-biographical speculation that still swirls around Reagan. Instead of trying to interpret him on this level, I want to consider instead the key character traits that seem to me to have made his many triumphs possible—and that can also account for his occasional errors. Aristotle once defined character as "the sum of a person's habits." At the most abstract level, then, it seems that the habits of mind that best accounted for Reagan's behavior were his flexibility, civility, and creativity.

Considering the first trait, flexibility, it quickly becomes apparent that this was why Reagan was able to negotiate a peace with the

Russians and end the mortally threatening nuclear arms race. Although he considered the Soviet Union to be "the focus of evil in the modern world," he was willing to leaven the military competition with a serious diplomatic effort to resolve our cold war differences by peaceful means. He launched his diplomatic initiatives despite the fact that they ran counter to his own rhetoric, which he had honed over a lifetime of anti-Communist activities. And in the process of negotiating with the Russians he enraged the very conservative intellectuals whose support had put him in office.

Reagan's flexibility was also an important factor in setting the overall mix of policies he pursued. Like a great hitter in baseball, he could go with the pitch as circumstances required, and his presidential record reflects this ability to consider and craft a wide range of policy options. He occasionally resorted to the use of force, but he did not overrely on military action. He was one of the least bellicose of presidents since World War II. Nor was his diplomacy coercive if there was any reasonable chance that a more persuasive approach might work.

As Figure 15 reflects, the range of Reagan's policies falls within a space defined by two axes. One runs vertically, with military or other "hard power" applications at the top, down to various "soft power" ideas and concepts below.[19] The horizontal axis extends from purely persuasive means on the left to total coercion on the right. Reagan's various policy initiatives cover all four of the quadrants created by these axes. This is the hallmark of the great strategist, the ability to conceptualize across the whole board and to use all of it as conditions permit.

If a similar exercise were undertaken to characterize Mikhail Gorbachev's strategy at the time, one would see sharp limits on the use of hard power policies, and a concentration on soft, persuasive initiatives instead. His unwillingness to act more forcefully in places such as Poland may actually have led to his undoing—a point perhaps understood by China's Communist leadership, which was not at all reluctant to employ military power against their own people in 1989 at Tiananmen Square. Coincidentally, Chinese leaders were cracking

Figure 15. Reagan's Policy Mix

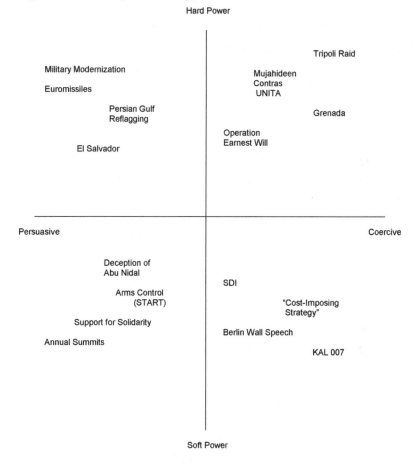

Hard Power

Tripoli Raid

Military Modernization

Mujahideen
Contras
UNITA

Euromissiles

Persian Gulf
Reflagging

Grenada

Operation
Earnest Will

El Salvador

Persuasive   Coercive

Deception of
Abu Nidal

SDI

Arms Control
(START)

"Cost-Imposing
Strategy"

Support for Solidarity

Berlin Wall Speech

Annual Summits

KAL 007

Soft Power

down on dissent almost concurrently with the velvet revolutions among the Soviet satellite countries.

On the American side, Reagan's immediate successors have tried to be "spray hitters" like him. But the elder Bush counted too much on a preponderance of hard power in trying to build his elusive new world order, and Bill Clinton overrelied on the more coercive aspects of soft power. In particular, Clinton's regular resort to economic sanctions—he is by far the record holder in terms of using this form of soft coercion, imposing embargoes on about half the world's population at one point—suggests there was an imbalance. Clinton also stayed on the coercive side of the policy space by his sending troops to Haiti, his several uses of force in the Balkans during the 1990s, and in his ongoing back-and-forth sniping with Saddam Hussein.

George W. Bush relied more than he probably should have on hard military coercion during his first term in office. But his willingness to negotiate with Moammar Qaddafi, the penitent Libyan terrorist leader, and his patient handling of proliferation crises with North Korea and Iran suggest that he has come to understand that relying on force alone imposes undue limits on a president's strategies. He has even allowed negotiations to be pursued with insurgent elements in both Afghanistan and Iraq. At least in this respect it seems that Bush has begun to distance himself from the coercion-minded "Vulcans" among his advisers who have propounded the idea of waging a primarily military war on terror.

Reagan's exemplary mix of all types of policies is yet another reflection of the flexibility of mind that seems to go hand-in-hand with winning strategies.

Reagan's second prominent personal trait was his unfailing civility toward all. He could be critical of others without rudeness, stake out radically new policy positions in a quiet, measured way, and engage in all the rough-and-tumble of American politics with a smile and a quip. His persona played a huge role in his two landslide presidential victories and was essential to building the national consensus needed to craft a new strategy aimed at ending the cold war.

Even his adversaries acknowledged the power and attraction of Reagan's personal charm. Democratic congressman Tip O'Neill, Speaker of the House during much of the Reagan era, was often opposed to the president on policy grounds, but the two nevertheless forged a friendly working relationship that kept legislation moving and government on an even keel. A more dramatic affirmation of Reagan's personal appeal came as something of a surprise when Walter Mondale, the Democratic presidential nominee in 1984, simply said, early on in a televised debate, "I like President Reagan."

Reagan's great cold war counterpart, Mikhail Gorbachev, could not conceivably have tried negotiating an end to the long Soviet-American struggle if he had not trusted Reagan. In comments made at the end of their last summit meeting in 1988, Gorbachev made it clear that a large part of Reagan's appeal as a negotiating partner was his flexibility and fundamental decency, both of which helped make him such a good strategist as well. On this point it is worth noting what Gorbachev had to say to the world press at the time:

> Yesterday, when the President conversed with our people, with me present, somebody asked him, and I think this got into the press, whether he still regarded the Soviet Union as an "evil empire." No, he replied. Moreover, he said this at a press conference near the Czar Cannon, in the Kremlin, in the center of the "evil empire." We take note of this and it means, as the ancient Greeks used to say, "everything flows and everything changes." This confirms my thought that the President has a sense of realism and that this is a very important quality for a politician.[20]

Sad to say, civility especially but also flexibility have suffered since Ronald Reagan left public life. George H. W. Bush took one of the first big steps toward churlishness in 1988 with his famous "Willie Horton" television advertisement—a spot used to paint his rival Michael Dukakis as weak on crime. By the 1992 presidential election campaign Bush had become habituated to derisiveness, openly referring to Bill Clinton's running mate Al Gore as "Ozone Man." The tone was set for the rest of the 1990s, when what came to be called "the politics of personal destruction" rose to prominence on the wings of scandals that brought down or imperiled leading politicians from both parties—and included the impeachment of Bill Clinton. Bitter divisiveness flared yet again at the turn of the millennium, as a disputed election result brought out the worst on both sides, the presidential election of 2000 decided in the end by a 5 to 4 vote of the Supreme Court.

After a brief period of unity in the immediate wake of the 9/11 terrorist attacks, the leaders and people of the United States fell back into their old pattern of fractiousness—particularly in March 2003 during the run-up to the invasion of Iraq. To my mind, though, the culminating moment came in June 2004 when Vice President Dick Cheney responded to critical comments from Senator Patrick Leahy by publicly telling him to "Go fuck yourself." Afterward there was no apology forthcoming. Instead Cheney told all who were interested that he "felt good" about what he had said. This incident ended the few weeks' period of comity that had followed Reagan's death earlier that month and hearkened to Edward Gibbon's observation that the loss of civility was the first important sign of Rome's irreversible, fatal decline.

As much as we may admire and value Reagan's civility toward friend and rival alike, it is necessary to note that his amiability was designed in part to reduce discord. Reagan disliked open contentiousness and always sought ways to reduce friction, though he wanted diverse viewpoints to be considered. An example of this was his view of how to cope with the enduring friction that he saw between the Defense and State departments:

> Conflicts between the Pentagon and Foggy Bottom were inevitable no matter who ran them, and they didn't start with my administration. I think it is important for presidents to have advisors who offer them different points of view and express disagreement instead of always expressing unanimity. I always encouraged the members of my cabinet to disagree not only with me but with each other.[21]

Most of the time this openness to diversity was a very good thing. For example, when it came to arms control, Reagan dealt with peace activists in an unfailingly polite fashion, participating in an ongoing public debate that helped drive policy in the right direction— toward first halting and then reversing the arms race. As Reagan said, in response to the growing public outcry against the arms race: "To those who protest against nuclear war, I can only say 'I am with you.'"[22]

As much as Reagan's civility was a key factor when it came to unifying the American arms control effort, his kindly nature was actually an impediment to making good counterterrorism policy in the 1980s. In this instance, he carried civility a bit too far. He failed to rule decisively or fully in favor of either George Shultz's or Caspar Weinberger's recommendations. Reagan came to take a policy line somewhat closer to Weinberger's preferences, the result being the emergence of a strategy that took too little action to prevent the rise of a new age of terror networks.

On the whole, though, Reagan's traits of flexibility of mind and civility in discourse led to good results. And the combination of these two traits made it possible for Reagan's third important attribute to come to the fore: his creativity. Reagan's willingness to move in new directions and his measured approach to policy deliberations ensured that innovative ideas—either his own or others' concepts—would almost always get a fair hearing. This environment generated a remarkable intellectual and decision-making ferment that resulted in the formulation of some of the most unusual—and by far the most effective—national security policies devised over the past century and beyond.

When it came to ending the arms race, for example, Reagan instinctively shied away from following the well-worn path of trying to slow the rate of growth of the American and Soviet nuclear arsenals. Instead he championed the process of making actual reductions, even going so far as to recommend zeroing out whole classes of nuclear weaponry. During his famous summit with Gorbachev at Reykjavik, the idea of nuclear abolition was seriously discussed. At the same time, however, Reagan was overseeing the building of intermediate- and short-range "theater" nuclear weapons in an attempt to show the Russians that any invasion of Europe they might contemplate could be handled, if necessary, with nuclear weapons located *in* Europe. Reagan's most innovative initiative in this realm, though, has to be his idea of developing real defenses against ballistic missile attack. Given the enormous scientific hurdles that would have to be overcome to achieve defensive capability, this was clearly not the thinking of someone driven or even much influenced by the existing wisdom on the subject.

In more conventional military terms, Reagan's openness to creative solutions was best expressed in new doctrines that aimed at ending our decades-long reliance on the policy of threatening nuclear escalation in response to conventional attacks. By shattering a paradigm that had stifled strategic thought since the 1950s, Reagan soon oversaw the creation of the American military's AirLand Battle doctrine. To carry out this concept of conventional war-fighting, U.S. armed forces were completely retooled so that they could fight without having to rely on a nuclear deus ex machina to bail them out of seemingly inevitable tight spots. At sea, AirLand Battle was complemented by a maritime strategy, which sought to use American naval mastery to wage amphibious campaigns against Russian allies overseas as well as to mount raids on the periphery of the Soviet Union itself. In one sense these doctrines were blasts from the past, as our new armored doctrine looked a bit like German maneuver warfare concepts from the 1930s, and the maritime strategy resembled the war plan developed by William Pitt against the French in the mid-eighteenth century. But even if this was old wine in new bottles, it was very good wine. And these were surprising, creative solutions to seemingly intractable strategic dilemmas.

The Reagan Doctrine, which held that the United States would help others free themselves, is yet another remarkably creative approach to modern statecraft. First, it straightforwardly rejected the notion that U.S. cold war strategy had to be confined to the defensive, simply to containing Soviet aggression when and where it arose. Instead we could now think of going on the offensive to roll back Soviet rule. When undertaken via the use of force, the Reagan Doctrine called for arming others whenever feasible so that they could fight for their own liberation. Where guerrilla warfare was not a preferred or even a possible option, Reagan spearheaded the development of an information strategy designed to place increasing pressure on totalitarian rule—his signal success in this realm resulting from his decision to help the Solidarity movement stay alive in Poland.

Reagan's creative notions did not produce unalloyed success. There are limits to the effectiveness of all innovations, and Reagan was no exception to this rule. The arms race did go on for a bit longer than needed, probably because of Reagan's belief that U.S. strategic forces should be modernized, though the ultimate goal was to dismantle as many nuclear weapons as prudence allowed. And his beloved Star Wars missile defense system did not actually work and may even have spurred the Soviets to continue the arms race. The army's AirLand Battle and the navy's maritime strategy doctrines were both implemented at the operational level in ways that discouraged tactical or organizational innovation. This tendency to pour new technologies and concepts into old divisional structures on land and battle fleets at sea posed a problem then that still impedes us from undertaking the necessary military transformation. Finally, even the military insurgencies supported by Reagan did not actually fare all that well in the field. Jonas Savimbi failed in Angola. The contras never defeated the Sandinistas, though the insurgents put enough pressure on the Communist regime in Nicaragua to force it to hold free and fair elections. And the *mujahideen* in Afghanistan, though they did eventually wear down Russian resolve, soon became the warriors of the global jihad that has sprung up against the United States.

Not all innovations are winners. But if you keep innovating and become habituated to thinking creatively, you are likely to do far more good than harm overall. This is the bottom-line assessment of Reagan's various policy innovations: far from perfect, but on balance quite good. Their cumulative effect was to change the world significantly for the better. It seems Henry Kissinger got it backward when he assessed Reagan's impact as being "more in the nature of a brilliant sunset than of the dawn of a new era."[23]

We should remember Ronald Reagan as a man of ideas who left a lasting imprint on America and the world. And as a leader whose style can still provide a useful model for others. With regard to those ideas he embraced and advanced, it is essential to note that they were almost completely divorced from ideology. If he did nothing else, Reagan proved the preeminence of ideas over and against any set of cohesive but often constraining beliefs. He was caricatured by all as a simple ideologue driven by "convictions and assumptions," yet he gave us living proof that ideas can trump ideology. He believed in strong defense but championed arms control. He saw the Soviets as "evil" but negotiated with them. He tried to reach out to the Iranians as well, even though during the 1980s they were among the world's leading state sponsors of terrorism.

In short, Reagan must be remembered above all as a strategist. For strategy lies in a pure ideational realm, and the great strategists have been renowned for their ability to rise above the conventional wisdom and innovate. This Reagan did, again and again, leaving in his wake a horde of disappointed conservatives—but also a general public very pleasantly surprised by his intellectual suppleness. Frances FitzGerald noted that

> by 1988 conservative spokesmen in Washington were complaining that the man they had thought a true conservative had turned out to be a man without substance or principles, particularly when it came to his dealings with the Soviet Union. These spokesmen, however, represented only a small fraction of the public. Most Americans did not want a continuing state of conflict with the Soviet Union . . .[24]

Much as Fabius Maximus Cunctator ("the Delayer") was once castigated by the ancient Roman Senate for his strategy of wearing down Hannibal by avoiding major pitched battles, so too was Reagan pilloried by many among the policy elite for a primarily conciliatory stance in his dealings with Mikhail Gorbachev. Like Fabius, Reagan was not averse to keeping smaller-scale attritional struggles going in some places, and both supported maintaining and revitalizing a large military. Both also knew that something quite unusual would be necessary in order to outlast and overcome a skillful and wily adversary. Both had a capacity for strategic surprise, and both contributed mightily to the triumph of their respective peoples over the sternest challenges the two republics had ever faced. Yet Plutarch observes that only

Fabius's first successors kept to his strategy while later consuls deviated from it.

A similar pattern has been unfolding since the Reagan years. While the elder Bush mostly continued to follow the strategic path set by his predecessor, both Bill Clinton and George W. Bush began to stray from it. The former lost whatever momentum for arms reductions still remained, while the latter has shown a risky thirst for direct battle—much as Fabius's successors did. The results: the world risks becoming more nuclear once again; and the attempt to defeat terrorism on a single, decisive central front—in Iraq—has gone largely awry at near ruinous cost. But just as Rome returned to and won with a Fabian strategy in the Second Punic War, U.S. foreign policy and military operations in the struggle against terrorism must reconfigure along Reaganesque lines if we are to hope for ultimate victory.

This is the most important reason for us to continue to reflect on Reagan's ideas and to remember and appreciate the various qualities of leadership that enlivened and empowered his presidency. For we live in a time of protracted warfare, and our goals must be victory and a just peace. Before these, political and ideological correctness must bow. And there can be no better example of how to put ideas before ideology than the life and work of Ronald Reagan. May we have the wit to gain a new appreciation of his approach to statecraft and the courage to emulate it.

Notes

Chapter 1. How to Think About Ronald Reagan

1. See Joseph J. Ellis, *American Sphinx: The Character of Thomas Jefferson* (New York, 1997).

2. Reagan served two terms as governor of California (1967–1975) and two as president (1981–1989).

3. Henry Kissinger, *Diplomacy* (New York, 1994), p. 766. Among their many contacts, Kissinger often briefed Reagan on national security affairs. Overall Kissinger notes of Reagan (also p. 766) that "he had an unusually pleasant and genuinely affable personality. Though he savaged me during his failed bid for the presidential nomination in 1976, I found it impossible to hold a lasting resentment."

4. Edmund Morris, *Dutch: A Memoir of Ronald Reagan* (New York, 1999), pp. 393–394.

5. See her chapter on Reagan in Robert A. Wilson, ed., *Character Above All* (New York, 1996). For her views on Reagan's remarkable mix of kindness and courage, see Peggy Noonan, *When Character Was King: A Story of Ronald Reagan* (New York, 2001).

6. Larry Speakes, with Robert Pack, *Speaking Out: Inside the Reagan White House* (New York, 1988), p. 92.

7. The first quote is from Charles Krauthammer, "The Week Washington Lost Its Head," *New Republic*, January 4, 1988, p. 19. The second is from George Will, "How Reagan Changed America," *Newsweek*, January 9, 1989. Dinesh D'Souza, *Ronald Reagan: How an Ordinary Man Became an Extraordinary Leader* (New York, 1997), p. 185, details other conservative critiques of Reagan—most of them quite ad hominem.

8. James David Barber, *The Presidential Character: Predicting Performance in the White House*, 4th ed. (Englewood Cliffs, N.J., 1992).

9. *Ibid.*, pp. 230–231.

10. Richard E. Neustadt, *Presidential Power and the Modern Presidents: The Politics of Leadership from Roosevelt to Reagan*, 4th ed. (New York, 1990).

11. *Ibid.*, p. 270. Neustadt is referring to the elder Bush here.

12. Samuel Kernell, *Going Public* (Washington, D.C., 1993).

13. Neustadt, *Presidential Power*, p. 276.

14. *Ibid.*, pp. 269, 290.

15. Sidney Warren, *The President as World Leader* (Philadelphia, 1964).

16. Walter Russell Mead, *Special Providence: American Foreign Policy and How It Changed the World* (New York, 2001).

17. Mead's formulation should be seen as building on Henry Kissinger's notion of three fundamental "styles" in American foreign policy. Kissinger refers explicitly to Wilsonian, Hamiltonian, and Jacksonian models quite like Mead's. Mead, however, has also advanced the fourth, or Jeffersonian, "voice" in the development of American foreign policy. See Henry Kissinger, *Does America Need a Foreign Policy?* (New York, 2001), especially p. 250.

18. Mead, *Special Providence*, pp. 199–204. On this point, see also Ernest R. May, *The Making of the Monroe Doctrine* (Cambridge, Mass., 1975).

19. Mead, *Special Providence*, p. 227.

20. Carter's growing awareness of the need for "muscle" to go with his moralistic approach to statecraft is nicely chronicled in Zbigniew Brzezinski, *Power and Principle: Memoirs of the National Security Adviser, 1977–1981* (New York, 1983).

21. Although a Democrat, Kirkpatrick would become Reagan's ambassador to the United Nations and would often provide the intellectual rigor needed to defend his administration's occasional dalliances with dictators. See her seminal article on this theme, "Dictatorships and Double Standards," *Commentary* (November 1979).

22. For more on this viewpoint, see George H. W. Bush and Brent Scowcroft, et al., *A World Transformed* (New York, 1998).

23. Clinton was inspired by Michael Doyle's theory about what has come to be called the "democratic peace," which advances the more qualified proposition that democracies tend not to fight *one another*. See his "Liberalism and World Politics," *American Political Science Review* 80, no. 4 (December 1986), pp. 1151–1169.

24. Thoughtful analysis of George W. Bush's foreign policy style can be found in Ivo H. Daalder and James M. Lindsay, "Bush's Foreign Policy Revolution," in Fred I. Greenstein, ed., *The George W. Bush Presidency* (Baltimore, 2003).

25. On this topic, see Miroslav Nincic, *Democracy and Foreign Policy* (New York, 1992).

26. The matter of Truman becoming disillusioned with Stalin is most closely examined in Deborah Welch Larson, *Origins of Containment: A Psychological Approach* (Princeton, N.J., 1985), and is also addressed in David McCullough, *Truman* (New York, 1993), and Lynn Etheridge Davis, *The Cold War Begins: Soviet-American Conflict over Eastern Europe* (Princeton, N.J., 1974).

27. See John Lewis Gaddis, *Strategies of Containment: A Critical Appraisal of Postwar American National Security Policy* (Oxford, England, 1982), p. 170.

28. *Ibid.*, p. 149.

29. What we call "flexible response" was first known as "symmetrical defense," a concept introduced by General Maxwell Taylor in his *The Uncertain Trumpet* (New York, 1959).

30. Robert Dallek, *The American Style of Foreign Policy* (Oxford, England, 1983), p. 224, describes Kennedy's break with preceding presidential doctrine: "If the Eisenhower approach to world affairs was 'stodgy, unimaginative, and illiberal,' Kennedy's seemed fresh and thoughtful. . . . America was once more to stand for freedom and the inalienable right to rebel against tyranny." Kennedy may thus be seen as foreshadowing Reagan's approach two decades later.

31. Kissinger, *Diplomacy,* p. 742.

32. This came to be known as the Schlesinger Doctrine, after his secretary of defense.

33. Peter Robinson, *How Ronald Reagan Changed My Life* (New York, 2003), pp. 70–71 in particular.

34. Caspar Weinberger, *Fighting for Peace: Seven Critical Years in the Pentagon* (New York, 1990), p. 12.

35. The clearest public exposition of this plan for primacy was an article at the time by Patrick F. Tyler, "Pentagon Imagines New Enemies to Fight in Post–Cold War Era," *New York Times,* January 17, 1992, pp. A1, 5. James Mann, *Rise of the Vulcans: The History of Bush's War Cabinet* (New York, 2004), p. 209, points out that Zalmay Khalilzad, who worked under Wolfowitz, actually wrote much of the guidance. During those years I was in occasional contact with Khalilzad—who later became George W. Bush's envoy to Afghanistan and in 2005 was named ambassador to Iraq. From our conversations at the time I inferred that he had indeed written much of the guidance, though his boss Wolfowitz gave it his imprimatur.

36. See Bush and Scowcroft, *A World Transformed.* On the early uncertainty among policymakers about how to react to the possible breakup of the Soviet Union, see James A. Baker, T. M. Defrank, and James A. Baker III, *The Politics of Diplomacy: Revolution, War and Peace 1989–1992* (New York, 1995).

37. I say "failed attempt" in describing the Tripoli raid because, after a short hiatus, Libya resumed its terrorist activities, culminating in its 1988 involvement in the destruction of a Pan Am jumbo jet over Lockerbie, Scotland. Qaddafi kept his hand in mischief for a long time, only in 2004 admitting to and renouncing his quest for weapons of mass destruction.

38. This is, of course, one of the key themes of Mann's magisterial *Rise of the Vulcans.*

39. The numbers of historians and biographers have varied from Schlesinger's original fifty-five to the Federalist Society's seventy-eight. Siena College in New York has polled as many as 132 presidential scholars.

40. Most presidential ranking systems exclude William Henry Harrison, who suffered a fatal illness just several weeks into his presidency, and James Garfield, who was assassinated six months into his term.

41. His ranking in the Siena College survey. Beyond the community of presidential scholars, the more journalistic studies of Reagan appearing in the first seven years after his term in office also tended toward the critical. A good example of this was Haynes Johnson's *Sleepwalking Through History: America in the Reagan Years* (New York, 1991).

42. In the Federalist Society/*Wall Street Journal* ranking. By this time the tone of more general assessments of Reagan had changed, the most exemplary book typifying this "second wave" of Reagan studies being D'Souza's *Ronald Reagan*.

Chapter 2. The Turn of the Tide in the Cold War

1. Cited in Adam Ulam, *The Communists* (New York, 1992), p. 450.

2. Some have speculated that, before the 1980 election, the Reagan team brokered a secret deal with the Iranians aimed at maximizing Jimmy Carter's discomfiture on the hostage issue by continuing to hold them until Reagan entered office. On this point see Gary Sick, *October Surprise: America's Hostages in Iran and the Election of Ronald Reagan* (New York, 1991). The theory aimed primarily at George H. W. Bush's alleged role in the affair and prompted a congressional investigation whose nearly thousand-page report refuted Sick's charges in extensive detail.

3. Will Durant, *Our Oriental Heritage* (New York, 1954), p. 283.

4. In his memoirs Zumwalt details the long conversation he had with Kissinger while they were traveling to and attending an Army-Navy football game. See Zumwalt's *On Watch* (New York, 1976), pp. 319–321. Patrick Parker, at the time a deputy assistant secretary of defense for intelligence and a good friend of Zumwalt's, has told me that the admiral shared with him the gist of—and his disagreement with—Kissinger's "prophecy of decline."

5. Cited in Gaddis, *Strategies of Containment*, p. 321.

6. RAND is an acronym, standing for "research and development." The corporation was founded just after World War II, and its analysts spent the next several decades interpreting the strategic implications of the nuclear age. Today RAND is trying to shift gears to begin understanding the meaning of the information age, for both society and security.

7. The classic study of these strategic debates—and the Brodie-Wohlstetter rivalry—remains Fred Kaplan's *The Wizards of Armageddon* (New York, 1984).

8. George Kennan, *The Cloud of Danger: Current Realities of American Foreign Policy* (Boston, 1977), p. 187.

9. *Ibid.*, p. 185. Here Kennan notes that "in this century national feelings have shown themselves to be more powerful as a political-economic force than ones related, as is the Marxist ideology, to class rather than to nation."

10. From a speech delivered at Westminster Palace, June 8, 1982.

11. The de facto new "autobiography" that has come together from his correspondence is the result of painstaking editorial work by Kiron Skinner and Annelise and Martin Anderson whose efforts to date have resulted in *Reagan in His Own Hand* and *Reagan: A Life in Letters* (New York, 2001, 2003).

12. Of course these were not the only points made in Reagan's national security strategy, which also called for a substantial military buildup.

13. A few years after Kennan penned his famous "long telegram," Nitze authored "NSC 68," a top secret, seventy-page National Security Council document that served as a guidepost to U.S. strategy throughout the cold war. Nitze, a conservative Democrat who had worked his way into Reagan's favor during the 1980 presidential campaign, felt just as Kissinger did about the United States having fallen be-

hind the Russians. His views are detailed in David Callahan, *Dangerous Capabilities: Paul Nitze and the Cold War* (New York, 1990).

14. Rowen's own epiphany came at the end of a trip behind the Iron Curtain. He recalls getting off a train just over the Austrian border and, having just observed all the privations suffered in the Soviet bloc, finding himself sitting in a *Platz*, drinking fresh coffee and enjoying wonderful pastry. From that moment on, he could never believe that the Soviets were somehow getting ahead of the West economically.

15. See John Keep, *Last of the Empires: A History of the Soviet Union, 1945–1991* (Oxford, England, 1995), pp. 223–224. A good English translation and analysis of a leading Soviet-era economist's assessment of the situation can be found in M. Harrison, "Soviet Economic Growth Since 1928: The Alternative Statistics of G. I. Khanin," *Europe-Asia Studies* 45 (Spring 1993), pp. 141–167.

16. In reality, the pressures imposed by huge budget deficits impelled Reagan to reduce the rate of defense spending as a percentage of gross domestic product during his second term. This reduction was still more than enough to outpace the Russians.

17. I have known Marshall for many years and have worked for and with him on a number of matters. In casual discussions as well as in more focused interviews he has elaborated ever more clearly what I am labeling an economic "cost-imposing strategy." Beyond what is described in this book, Marshall championed other initiatives, which remain classified, that compelled the Soviets to incur huge costs to counter the perceived new threats posed by our military to theirs.

18. The still-classified National Security Decision Directive No. 66, "Protracted Economic Warfare Against the USSR" (November 12, 1982), spelled out the campaign plan in some detail.

19. Adam Ulam, *Expansion and Coexistence: Soviet Foreign Policy 1917–73* (New York, 1974), p. 729.

20. While Marshall did not recall specific discussion of the Soviets having had a "cost advantage" in Vietnam, he remembered clearly that Afghanistan was thought of as a potential "Soviet Vietnam" where we could greatly discomfit them at low cost. From an interview with Andrew Marshall, November 6, 2003.

21. Marshall remembered personally briefing the president, that Reagan was "very taken" with the idea of the cost-imposing strategy, and that the policy requirement to adhere to it came down soon after his group met with the president. *Ibid.*, Marshall interview.

22. Malcolm Gladwell, *The Tipping Point: How Little Things Can Make a Big Difference* (Boston, 2000).

23. Mikhail S. Gorbachev, *Memoirs* (New York, 1995), p. 194.

24. In 1970, the average price for a barrel of oil was $2.50. By 1980 the average was more than $40.

25. Eric Hobsbawm, *The Age of Extremes: A History of the World, 1914–1991* (New York, 1994), p. 474.

26. East Germany, Poland, Czechoslovakia, Hungary, Romania, and Bulgaria.

27. The Reagan administration's efforts to roll back oil prices are related in Peter Schweizer, *Victory: The Reagan Administration's Secret Strategy That Hastened the Collapse of the Soviet Union* (New York, 1994).

28. The most thorough exposition of this argument is found in Steve Coll, *Ghost Wars: The Secret History of the CIA, Afghanistan, and Bin Laden, From the Soviet Invasion to September 10, 2001* (New York, 2004).

29. Brzezinski was candid about all this in an interview granted to *Le Nouvel Observateur*, January 15–21, 1998, p. 76, which ran under the title "How Jimmy Carter and I Started the Mujahideen." An English translation is at http://www.counterpunch.org/brzezinski.html.

30. For a thorough, albeit sympathetic, account of this imbroglio, see Michael Ledeen, *Perilous Statecraft: An Insider's Account of the Iran-Contra Affair* (New York, 1988).

31. Details of this strategic deception remain almost entirely classified.

32. Noel E. Firth and James H. Noren, *Soviet Defense Spending: A History of CIA Estimates, 1950–1990* (Austin, Tex., 1998), p. 112. They point out that strategic weapons spending never amounted to more than 8 percent of the Soviet military budget. And the growth rate in overall Soviet defense spending during the period 1975–1985 was only 1.3 percent. The rate of increase grew to 4.3 percent from 1985 to 1987, but strategic weapons still saw only a 1.4 percent rise.

33. Since the late 1960s overall megatonnage—the total amount of explosive power in both arsenals—had been declining. This decline was the result of the increasing accuracy of guidance systems, since the closer a missile could be counted on to land to its target, the less destructive power was needed to achieve a "kill."

34. Jonathan Schell, "The Second Age of Nuclear Danger," *Washington Post*, October 1, 1999.

35. D'Souza, *Ronald Reagan*, p. 194.

36. The Polish case is discussed in detail in Chapter 6.

37. Libya still refers to itself as a "socialist republic" and might be considered a sixth country living under Marxist concepts of governance. But the erratic rule of longtime dictator Moammar Qaddafi hardly fits the classic Communist mold. As for China, it continues to call itself Communist even as it adopts more and more of the trappings of free-market systems.

38. The phrase is Brzezinski's. See his *Power and Principle*. Gerald R. Ford should also be mentioned, for in his brief presidency he oversaw the enactment of the Helsinki Accords, a powerful affirmation of human rights.

39. Quotes from Gorbachev, *Memoirs*, pp. 481–482.

40. Anatol Lieven, *Chechnya: Tombstone of Russian Power* (New Haven, Conn., 1998).

41. See for example Richard Ned Lebow and Janice Gross Stein, *We All Lost the Cold War* (London, 1994).

42. From an interview with Monica Crowley given in January 1991, and cited in her *Nixon Off the Record* (New York, 1996), p. 24.

Chapter 3. The "Controlled Crash" of the Soviet Union

1. To this point the Soviet Union had been ruled by general secretaries and premiers who, to varying degrees, expressed the will of the small inner circle of Com-

munist party leaders who comprised the Politburo. A ceremonial presidency served as a "soft landing pad" for those such as the superannuated Andrei Gromyko, who was made president after losing his long-held position as foreign minister to Gorbachev's man, Eduard Shevardnadze.

2. Cited in Gail Sheehy, *The Man Who Changed the World: The Lives of Mikhail S. Gorbachev* (New York, 1990), p. 350.

3. An articulate exposition of this "economic warfare" argument can be found in Schweizer, *Victory*.

4. The Crimea paper in its entirety may be found in Mikhail Gorbachev, *The August Coup: The Truth and the Lessons* (New York, 1991), Appendix C, pp. 97–127. The passage cited may be found on p. 102.

5. *Ibid.*, p. 101.

6. Zbigniew Brzezinski, *The Grand Failure: The Birth and Death of Communism in the Twentieth Century* (New York, 1989), p. 18.

7. Sanford R. Lieberman, "Crisis Management in the USSR: The Wartime System of Administration and Control," in Susan J. Linz, ed., *The Impact of World War II on the Soviet Union* (Totowa, N.J.: 1985), p. 59.

8. Harrison Salisbury, *Russia* (New York, 1966), pp. 78–79.

9. Hobsbawm, *Age of Extremes*, p. 478.

10. I have summarized data compiled and thoughtfully analyzed by John Mearsheimer in *The Tragedy of Great Power Politics* (New York, 2001), pp. 74–75.

11. Lazar Pistrak, *The Grand Tactician: Khrushchev's Rise to Power* (New York, 1961), p. 247.

12. John B. Dunlop, *The Rise of Russia and the Fall of the Soviet Empire* (Princeton, N.J., 1993), p. 4.

13. Ulam, *The Communists*, p. 433.

14. Niccolò Machiavelli, *The Prince*, translated by W. K. Marriott (Chicago, 1952), p. 9.

15. See Marshall I. Goldman, *What Went Wrong with Perestroika* (New York, 1991), p. 192, which also discusses the Yarin matter and what I have referred to here as the "humane purge" process.

16. *Ibid.*, p. 173.

17. On this point, see Derek Leebaert and Timothy Dickinson, eds., *Soviet Strategy and New Military Thinking* (Cambridge, England, 1992).

18. Gorbachev, *August Coup*, pp. 33–34.

19. *Ibid.*, p. 34.

20. Lebed would rise to prominence in the wake of the failed coup, brokering a peace agreement to end the first Chechen conflict in 1996, serving as governor of the Krasnoyarsk region, and even standing in a presidential election (and losing to Yeltsin). He died in April 2002 when the Mi-8 helicopter in which he was traveling clipped some high-voltage power lines and crashed.

21. Boris Yeltsin, *The Struggle for Russia* (New York, 1994), p. 87.

22. See William E. Odom, *The Collapse of the Soviet Military* (New Haven, Conn., 1998), especially Chapter 14.

23. Goldman, *What Went Wrong*, p. 195.

24. See Dunlop, *Rise of Russia,* pp. 143–146.

25. David Pryce-Jones, *The Strange Death of the Soviet Empire* (New York, 1995).

26. Though crowned in 1682, when he was only ten years old, Peter spent seven hard years under the regency of Sophia, his ambitious half-sister whom he had to overthrow.

27. Bernard Pares, *A History of Russia,* 5th ed. (New York, 1948), pp. 206–207.

28. Allowing the prosecution of his son—which culminated in the tsarevich's death under still mysterious circumstances—demonstrated to Peter's opponents that he would let nothing stand in the way of fulfilling his vision for modernizing Russia. See Robert K. Massie, *Peter the Great: His Life and World* (New York, 1980), especially pp. 706–708.

29. Pares, *History of Russia,* p. 215.

30. One exception to this was the Russian navy, which had partially transitioned from solid shot to explosive shells, resulting in the destruction of nearly the entire Turkish fleet at Sinope early in the war.

31. On Russian diplomacy during the American Civil War, see Norman A. Graebner, "Northern Diplomacy and European Neutrality," in David Donald, ed., *Why the North Won the Civil War* (New York, 1962), especially pp. 57–58.

32. Pares, *History of Russia,* p. 327.

33. Sheehy, *Man Who Changed,* p. 200.

34. On Gorbachev's carefully crafted approach to dealing with the United States, see Thomas H. Naylor, *The Gorbachev Strategy: Opening the Closed Society* (Lexington, Mass., 1988), especially p. 176, where he notes that "Gorbachev has put together a first-rate foreign policy team that in a very short period of time has demonstrated that it is flexible, pragmatic, and nonideological."

35. Margaret Thatcher, *The Downing Street Years* (New York, 1993), p. 463.

36. D'Souza, *Ronald Reagan,* p. 197.

37. See Ralph K. White, *Fearful Warriors* (New York, 1984), p. 12.

38. George P. Shultz, *Turmoil and Triumph: My Years as Secretary of State* (New York, 1993), p. 888.

39. *Ibid.,* p. 889.

40. Seweryn Bialer and Michael Mandelbaum, *The Global Rivals* (New York, 1988), p. 173.

41. Theda Skocpol, *States and Social Revolutions* (New York, 1984).

42. Brzezinski, *Grand Failure,* p. 243.

43. D'Souza, *Ronald Reagan,* p. 132.

44. Ulam, *Communists,* pp. 412–413.

45. John Lewis Gaddis, *The United States and the End of the Cold War* (New York, 1992), p. 119.

46. Gorbachev, *Memoirs,* pp. 405, 408.

47. This is certainly the thrust of Jack Matlock's memoir of the interactions of these two leaders, *Reagan and Gorbachev: How the Cold War Ended* (New York, 2004). Matlock offers scintillating inside glimpses of their high-level courtship and the stunningly successful outcome Reagan and Gorbachev jointly crafted.

Chapter 4. Confronting the Perils of Proliferation

1. Today and for some years to come, "ultimate weapons" will continue really to mean nuclear explosives, which remain in a class by themselves. But within a few decades, if unchecked, biological weapons will become deadly enough to kill millions as well. Chemical weapons are unlikely ever to rise to this level.

2. On the intractable nature of mutual deterrence, see Bernard Brodie, *The Absolute Weapon* (New York, 1946), especially pp. 21–76. The counterargument appears in Albert Wohlstetter's "The Delicate Balance of Terror," *Foreign Affairs* 37, no. 1 (1959), pp. 211–234.

3. I wrote a short story on this theme, "The Great Cyberwar," in February 1998 in *Wired*. It featured crashing planes, an attack on the Pentagon, and a trail that led to Afghanistan and North Korea. But the real cause of the war was a rogue state that made it look like Russia and China were trying to wage a secret war against the United States. All of which fomented a near catastrophe.

4. Two of the best discussions of the failed attempts to articulate sustainable theories of nuclear war-fighting can be found in Solly Zuckerman, *Nuclear Illusion and Reality* (New York, 1982); and Robert Jervis, *The Illogic of American Nuclear Strategy* (Ithaca, N.Y., 1984).

5. Pakistan may have had a secretly held nuclear weapon earlier, but may not have completed its final assembly until some years after. A well-placed source has told me that the Pakistanis actually had a nuclear device assembled in 1984, but the source could not provide me with any documentary evidence of this. All this aside, in 1994 then Prime Minister Nawaz Sharif claimed publicly that Pakistan possessed nuclear weapons.

6. Seymour Hersh, *The Samson Option: Israel's Nuclear Arsenal and American Foreign Policy* (New York, 1991).

7. Leon V. Sigal, *Disarming Strangers: Nuclear Diplomacy with North Korea* (Princeton, N.J., 1998) makes the case that the United States came close to launching a preventive war against North Korea in 1994—a claim that former President Clinton has recently confirmed.

8. Years later some thought was also given to striking preventively at China.

9. Cited in David Alan Rosenberg, "U.S. Nuclear War Planning, 1945–60," in Desmond Ball and Jeffrey Richelson, eds., *Strategic Nuclear Targeting* (Ithaca, N.Y., 1986), p. 44.

10. *Ibid.*, p. 44.

11. Thomas Schelling, *Arms and Influence* (New Haven, Conn., 1966), p. 190.

12. On this Rube Goldbergesque theme, see Richard C. Thornton, *The Falklands Sting: Reagan, Thatcher, and Argentina's Bomb* (London, 1998).

13. United States Department of State, *Fundamentals of U.S. Foreign Policy* (Washington, D.C., 1988), p. 86.

14. In 2004, Dr. Khan publicly admitted this on television, after which Pakistani dictator General Pervez Musharraf—also in a televised address—immediately pardoned him. The United States made no effort to chastise or censure Pakistan publicly. For an excellent overview of the Pakistani proliferation problem in general and

the A. Q. Khan network in particular, see Leonard Weiss, "Pakistan: It's *Déjà Vu* All Over Again," *Bulletin of the Atomic Scientists*, May/June 2004, pp. 52–59.

15. Senator Glenn's remarks are cited in William E. Burrows and Robert Windrem, *Critical Mass: The Dangerous Race for Superweapons in a Fragmenting World* (New York, 1994), p. 77.

16. Caspar Weinberger, *Fighting for Peace: Seven Critical Years in the Pentagon* (New York, 1990), pp. 387–428, chronicles this campaign in detail.

17. Mikhail Gorbachev, *Reykjavik: Results and Lessons* (Madison, Conn., 1987), pp. 20–21.

18. Ronald Reagan, *An American Life* (New York, 1990), p. 685.

19. With the United States being the lone nuclear power only from 1945 to 1948.

20. For a discussion of both sides of the abolition issue, see General Andrew J. Goodpaster, "Nuclear Weapons: Time to Phase Them Out," and John Arquilla, "A Phase-out Increases Dangers," both in the *Christian Science Monitor*, December 18, 1996, p. 19.

21. Reagan, *American Life*, p. 294. Emphasis was Reagan's.

22. The various deployment schemes were all pretty outlandish. From Jimmy Carter's suggested rail-based "racetrack" to shuttle them around in a fixed area, to Reagan's "densepack"—which clustered them all close together, with the idea that attacking warheads would blow each other up—no satisfactory setup was ever identified. For an outstanding overview of the various dimensions of these and other debates about the nuclear arsenal, see Scott D. Sagan, *Moving Targets* (Princeton, N.J., 1989).

23. The exact numbers of "hardened, deeply-buried targets" (HDBTs) and their locations are, for the most part, highly classified items of information.

24. See the United States Government's 2003 "Nuclear Posture Review."

25. This is also a highly classified area of activity.

26. For a more complete discussion and analysis of the late 1960s missile defense problem, see Herbert F. York, *Race to Oblivion* (New York, 1970).

27. Reagan, *American Life*, p. 547.

28. Edward Teller was one of the most eloquent high-level supporters of what came to be called "Star Wars," but he was joined by a substantial group of other scientists and defense analysts. On the rise of this strategic defense "community," see B. Bruce-Briggs, *The Shield of Faith: Strategic Defense from Zeppelins to Star Wars* (New York, 1990). Also very interesting is General Daniel Graham, *High Frontier: A Strategy for National Survival* (New York, 1983). Finally, Reagan was receiving advice during his 1980 presidential campaign recommending that he "revive" the ABM concept and broaden it. This point was made in a confidential "strategic guidance" written by Richard V. Allen who for a short while was Reagan's first national security adviser.

29. Gorbachev, *Reykjavik*, p. 22. On Russian views of Star Wars as inherently offensive in nature, see Benjamin S. Lambeth, "Soviet Perspectives on the SDI," in Samuel F. Wells, Jr. and Robert S. Litwak, eds., *Strategic Defenses and Soviet-American Relations* (Cambridge, Mass., 1987).

30. Reagan, *American Life*, p. 631.

31. See Kai Bird and Martin J. Sherwin, *American Prometheus: The Triumph and Tragedy of J. Robert Oppenheimer* (New York, 2005), p. 349. Oppenheimer painted a grim picture in a colorful way, responding to a question about how to stop nuclear terror by saying one would need "a screwdriver to open every crate coming into the city." His testimony led to the commissioning of a study of the problem—aptly named the "Screwdriver Report"— that, more than half a century later, remains highly classified.

32. This story is recounted in Robert Cialdini, *Influence: The Psychology of Persuasion* (New York, 1993), p. 19.

33. See Bruce I. Gudmundsson, *Stormtroop Tactics: Innovation in the German Army, 1914–1918* (London, 1989), especially pp. 160–162.

34. The Japanese were the exception to this rule, as they did resort to such weapons, on a few rare occasions, during their campaign in China.

35. The best study of this phenomenon is Jared Diamond, *Guns, Germs, and Steel* (New York, 1997).

36. See Judith Miller, Stephen Engelberg, and William Broad, *Germs: Biological Weapons and America's Secret War* (New York, 2001).

37. See Zuckerman, *Nuclear Illusion and Reality*, particularly Chapter 4, "Fighting with Nuclear Weapons." Zuckerman was chief scientific adviser in the British ministry of defense from 1960 to 1966, and chief scientific adviser to the prime minister from 1967 to 1971, from which vantage points he carefully examined the issue of the first use of tactical nuclear weapons in the context of a new war in Europe.

38. Henry Kissinger, *The Necessity for Choice* (London, 1960). See the chapter entitled "Limited War: A Reappraisal."

39. The argument in favor of no first use was articulated by McGeorge Bundy, George F. Kennan, Robert S. McNamara, and Gerard Smith, "Nuclear Weapons and the Atlantic Alliance," *Foreign Affairs*, Spring 1982, pp. 753–768. They were opposed by Karl Kaiser, Georg Leber, Alois Mertes, and Franz-Josef Schulze, "Nuclear Weapons and the Preservation of Peace," *Foreign Affairs*, Summer 1982, pp. 1157–1171.

Chapter 5. Transforming the American Military

1. Kenneth N. Waltz, *Man, the State, and War* (New York, 1959), p. 236.

2. From his radio broadcast, "Strategy," May 4, 1977, the full text of which can be found in Skinner, et al., *In His Own Hand*, pp. 111–113.

3. James Fallows, *National Defense* (New York, 1981), p. 171.

4. On the durability of public support for continuing the war, see Eric Larson, *Casualties and Consensus: The Historical Role of Casualties in Public Support for U.S. Military Operations* (Santa Monica, Calif., 1996).

5. Cincinnatus, *Self-Destruction: The Disintegration and Decay of the United States Army During the Vietnam Era* (New York, 1981), pp. 9–10. For a view that dissents with such a harsh critique, see Lewis N. Sorley, *A Better War: The Unexamined Victories and the Final Tragedy of America's Last Years in Vietnam* (New York, 1999).

6. The best exposition of Russian strategic thought at this time remains Peter Vigor, *Soviet Blitzkrieg Theory* (New York, 1983). Vigor's work implies a deep Russian understanding of U.S. military doctrine. For an American assessment of Soviet military concepts, see Nathan Leites, *Soviet Style in War* (Washington, D.C., 1982).

7. For a balanced assessment—written at the time—of the potential of precision munitions, as well as of tele-operated and autonomous weapons systems, see Frank Barnaby's classic *The Automated Battlefield* (New York, 1986).

8. For an overview of Russian views, see Leebaert and Dickinson, *Soviet Strategy*.

9. The best account of the crafting of AirLand Battle as a distinct doctrine can be found in Alvin and Heidi Toffler, *War and Anti-War: Survival at the Dawn of the Twenty-first Century* (Boston, 1993).

10. See Richard R. Muller, "Close Air Support: The German, British, and American Experiences, 1918–1941," in Williamson Murray and Allan R. Millett, eds., *Military Innovation in the Interwar Period* (Cambridge, England, 1992).

11. George W. Ball, "The Cosmic Bluff," *New York Review of Books*, July 21, 1983, pp. 37–40.

12. The acronym stands for "sea-air-land."

13. A comprehensive analysis of this brief campaign can be found in Mark Adkin, *Urgent Fury: The Battle for Grenada* (New York, 1984).

14. On the various actions taken to keep Persian Gulf shipping lanes open, see David B. Crist, "Operations in Support of Earnest Will," *Joint Force Quarterly*, Autumn/Winter 2001–2002.

15. This can be said accurately despite the loss of eleven SEALs in Eastern Afghanistan in July 2005, as eight of the eleven were lost when an Army Chinook helicopter was shot down. This loss was more than offset by the serious damage done by the SEALs to the local insurgents.

16. Winston S. Churchill, *A History of the English Speaking Peoples*, vol. 3, *The Age of Revolution* (New York, 1957), p. 148. Americans call their part in this global conflict the "French and Indian War."

17. For a synoptic view of the Reagan-era "maritime strategy," see John F. Lehman, Jr., *Command of the Seas: Building the 600-Ship Navy* (New York, 1988).

18. *Ibid.*, p. 128.

19. A thoughtful discussion of these problems with the maritime strategy can be found in John Mearsheimer, "A Strategic Misstep: The Maritime Strategy and Deterrence in Europe," *International Security* 11, no. 2 (Fall 1986), pp. 3–57.

20. The Iraqis claimed that the attack was a case of "mistaken identification," and apologized and offered to pay compensation. The ship itself was nearly lost and thirty-seven American sailors died in the incident.

21. On this line of argument, see Jack Beatty, "In Harm's Way," *Atlantic Monthly*, May 1987.

22. See Sergei Gorshkov, *The Sea Power of the State* (New York, 1980).

23. John Keegan, *The Price of Admiralty: The Evolution of Naval Warfare* (New York, 1989), especially pp. 266–275.

24. On the chasm between ideas about strategic bombing and actual results of air campaigns, see Robert A. Pape, Jr., *Bombing to Win: Air Power and Coercion in War*

(Ithaca, N.Y., 1996); and Tami Davis Biddle, *Rhetoric and Reality in Air Warfare* (Princeton, N.J., 2002).

25. John Warden, *The Air Campaign: Planning for Combat* (London, 1989).

26. Richard P. Hallion, *Storm Over Iraq* (Washington, D.C., 1992), p. 188, notes that "approximately 9%—7,400 tons—of the tonnage expended by American forces was precision munitions."

27. Andrew L. Stigler, "A Clear Victory for Air Power: NATO's Empty Threat to Invade Kosovo," *International Security* 27, no. 3 (Winter 2003).

28. The most balanced analysis of the air campaign can be found in Benjamin S. Lambeth, *NATO's Air War for Kosovo: A Strategic and Operational Assessment* (Santa Monica, Calif., 2001). On the other reasons (beyond the bombing) why the Serbs ultimately retreated, see Ivo Daalder and Michael O'Hanlon, *Winning Ugly: NATO's War to Save Kosovo* (Washington, D.C., 2000).

29. One of my graduate students, who had led a special forces team during the campaign, told me that being on horseback reduced their chances of being attacked unwittingly by American aircraft. As he noted, "In the beginning, our attack aircraft shot at anything in a vehicle, so we kept to our horses."

30. See Harlan Ullman, James P. Wade, and L. A. Edney, *Shock and Awe: Achieving Rapid Dominance* (Washington, D.C., 1996), which profoundly influenced U.S. Air Force strategic planning before our second war with Saddam Hussein.

31. From his radio broadcast, "The B-1 Bomber," that aired on March 13, 1978. For the full text, see Skinner, et al., *In His Own Hand*, pp. 103–104.

32. Michael Ignatieff, *Virtual War: Kosovo and Beyond* (New York, 2000).

33. Walter J. Boyne, *Beyond the Wild Blue: A History of the United States Air Force, 1947–1997* (New York, 1997), p. 176.

34. Linda Robinson, *Masters of Chaos: The Secret History of the Special Forces* (New York, 2004), p. 18, notes the similarity in views between Kennedy and Reagan on the strategic utility of special operations forces. On Kennedy's zealous support of elite military forces, see Eliot Cohen, *Commandos and Politicians* (Cambridge, Mass., 1978), pp. 40–44.

35. The most detailed history of the long struggle to create the Special Operations Command is Susan Marquis, *Unconventional Warfare: Rebuilding U.S. Special Operations Forces* (Washington, D.C., 1997).

36. Two excellent accounts of the Iraq campaign are: Williamson Murray and Robert A. Scales, Jr., *The War in Iraq: A Military History* (Cambridge, Mass., 2003); and Anthony H. Cordesman, *The Iraq War: Strategy, Tactics, and Military Lessons* (New York, 2003).

37. Bill Owens and Ed Offley, *Lifting the Fog of War* (New York, 2000), p. 164. The quoted phrase earlier in the paragraph is from p. 163.

38. See Wesley Clark, *Waging Modern War: Bosnia, Kosovo, and the Future of Combat* (New York, 2001), especially pp. 342–343 for Clark's rejection of Shelton's special operations plan. During this war I was closely involved with a number of strategic matters and had recommended using small special forces teams, network-style, to enliven the air campaign. For analysis of what that campaign would have looked like—a foreshadowing of the Afghan campaign of 2001—see John Arquilla

and David Ronfeldt, "Need for Networked, High-Tech Cyberwar," *Los Angeles Times,* June 20, 1999.

39. Weinberger, *Fighting for Peace,* p. 402.

40. In addition to the formulations of Augustine and Aquinas, an important reappraisal of just war theory in light of the ethical dilemmas posed by modern weapons and tactics can be found in Michael Walzer, *Just and Unjust Wars* (New York, 1977).

41. This said, we shall see in Chapter 7 how the Weinberger Doctrine was initially used during the mid-1980s to oppose the launching of a covert war on terror.

Chapter 6. The Nuances of Information Strategy

1. The phrase "information strategy" first appears as an independent category of activity in a secret (now declassified) National Security Decision Directive No. 130 dated March 6, 1984.

2. See Paul Leicester Ford, ed., *The Writings of Thomas Jefferson* (New York, 1898).

3. On the profound societal impact of the telegraph, see Tom Standage, *The Victorian Internet: The Remarkable Story of the Telegraph and the Nineteenth Century's On-Line Pioneers* (New York, 1998).

4. Daniel R. Headrick, *The Invisible Weapon: Telecommunications and International Politics, 1851–1945* (New York, 1991), provides a comprehensive overview of how advances in information systems influenced world politics in peacetime, crisis, and conflict.

5. Alvin A. Snyder, *Warriors of Disinformation: American Propaganda, Soviet Lies, and the Winning of the Cold War* (New York, 1995), p. 25.

6. See D'Souza, *Ronald Reagan,* p. 134, for a description of Secretary of State Alexander Haig's eye-rolling response.

7. Mark Hertsgaard, *On Bended Knee: The Press and the Reagan Presidency* (New York, 1988), p. 134.

8. Cited in D'Souza, *Ronald Reagan,* p. 135.

9. Natan Scharansky, *Fear No Evil* (New York, 1988), p. 366.

10. See Snyder, *Warriors of Disinformation,* especially Chapter 4.

11. *Ibid.,* pp. 68–70.

12. The best account of this Revolutionary Era battle of the story can be found in David Hackett Fischer, *Paul Revere's Ride* (Oxford, England, 1994), pp. 273–276.

13. Snyder, *Warriors of Disinformation,* pp. 122–123. In the more clipped prose of Government Accountability Office Report No. 94-219, publicly disseminated in July 1994: "The plan was to set off an explosion if the interceptor flew by without hitting the target, which was to fool Soviet sensors expected to monitor the test. The target's explosion was to simulate the effect of a strike by the interceptor."

14. From 1980 to 1990 the Soviet strategic arsenal grew by about 50 percent, the American arsenal by about a third. See Figure 5.

15. On this point see George Quester, *Deterrence Before Hiroshima* (New York, 1966).

16. The most detailed analysis of the unintended consequence of the German information strategy can be found in Michael Mihalka, *German Strategic Deception in the 1930s* (Santa Monica, Calif., 1980), N-1557-NA.

17. On the types of Soviet "active measures" taken to discredit the idea of keeping the neutron bomb in the U.S. nuclear arsenal—which were also turned to attack Star Wars—see DeWitt S. Copp, "Soviet Active Measures," in Frank L. Goldstein, ed., *Psychological Operations: Principles and Case Studies* (Maxwell Air Force Base, 1996). Jimmy Carter first decided to forgo acquisition of a neutron bomb capability. Although Reagan was attracted to the weapon, even he could not overcome the skillful Soviet information campaign that had been mounted against it.

18. The most thorough public telling of these events is Ledeen's *Perilous Statecraft*.

19. O. Halecki, *A History of Poland* (New York, 1992 edition) is a good scholarly study of Polish history. Those who prefer a lively narrative to go along with the historical panorama should read James Michener's *Poland*. On the Russo-Polish conflict in the wake of World War I, see Norman Davies, *White Eagle, Red Star: The Polish-Soviet War, 1919–1920* (New York, 1972).

20. Brzezinski, *Power and Principle*, p. 297.

21. *Ibid.*, p. 297.

22. *Ibid.*, p. 298.

23. *Ibid.*, pp. 298–299.

24. See Teresa Rakowska-Harmstone, "Communist Regimes' Psychological Warfare Against Their Societies: The Case of Poland," in Janos Radvanyi, ed., *Psychological Operations and Political Warfare in Long-term Strategic Planning* (New York, 1990).

25. The Katyn Wood massacre took place in 1939, when the Soviets had joined the Nazis in attacking Poland. But many other smaller-scale atrocities of this sort occurred later in the war and in the early postwar years.

26. On the remarkable rise of this movement, see Roman Laba's magisterial *The Roots of Solidarity: A Political Sociology of Poland's Working Class Democratization* (Princeton, N.J., 1991).

27. Saddam Hussein taped his meeting with Ambassador Glaspie and later released transcripts that the United States has never disavowed. During this period I met on two occasions with Ambassador Glaspie to discuss her role in prewar diplomacy. I came away convinced that far more could and should have been allowed to be said to deter Saddam by being explicit with him about the consequences of any attack on Kuwait.

28. The Pilgrim governor of colonial Massachusetts in the seventeenth century, John Winthrop, first employed this "city on a hill" metaphor. He used it to make the case that the colonists should always behave well, for as a "city on a hill," all could see what they were doing.

29. Strobe Talbott, *The Russia Hand: A Memoir of Presidential Diplomacy* (New York, 2002), p. 185.

30. Snyder, *Warriors of Disinformation*, p. 271.

31. This finding emerged from all the major polls undertaken in the wake of the March 2003 American invasion of Iraq. Perhaps the most comprehensive of them were

the Zogby polls, conducted across a swath of fifteen Muslim countries in 2004, several of them Arab. The consistency in the results across all these countries is striking.

32. On classical propaganda techniques, see Jacques Ellul, *Propaganda: The Formation of Men's Attitudes* (New York, 1965), translated by Konrad Kellen and Jean Lerner.

33. Amin Maalouf, *The Crusades Through Arab Eyes* (New York, 1985). On bin Laden's use of the Crusader analogy, see Michael Scott Doran, "Somebody Else's Civil War," in James F. Hoge, Jr., and Gideon Rose, eds., *How Did This Happen? Terrorism and the New War* (New York, 2001), especially pp. 36–40. For an overview of how terrorists have employed information strategy in recent decades, see Brigitte Nacos, *Terrorism and the Media* (New York, 1994).

34. The story of detainee abuse, as well as official efforts to limit the public relations damage, can be found in Seymour Hersh, *Chain of Command: The Road from 9/11 to Abu Ghraib* (New York, 2004). On the high-level decision-making that led to misconduct toward prisoners, see Karen J. Greely and Joshua L. Dratel, eds., *The Torture Papers: The Road to Abu Ghraib* (Cambridge, England, 2005).

35. Arnold J. Toynbee, *The World and the West* (London, 1953), Chapter 2, "Islam and the West," especially p. 25.

36. The term is from Harvard's Joseph Nye, who refers to soft power in terms of the attractiveness of American ideals and values. See his *Soft Power: The Means to Success in World Politics* (New York, 2004).

37. Christopher Hables Gray, *Postmodern War: The New Politics of Conflict* (New York, 1997).

38. See the discussion of this in Bob Woodward, *Bush at War* (New York, 2002), especially p. 175, where he notes of the war planning for the campaign in Afghanistan: "The discussion was almost exclusively about aerial bombing."

39. For an account of the sulphurous Pentagon debates about the war on Iraq, see Nina Bernstein, "Strategists Fight a War About the War," *New York Times*, April 13, 2003.

40. On American information strategy during World War I, see James R. Mock and Cedric Larson, *Words That Won the War: The Story of the Committee on Public Information, 1917–1919* (Princeton, N.J., 1939). The role of information strategy in highlighting the ethical imperatives that galvanized the fight against fascism is nicely described in Richard Overy, *Why the Allies Won* (New York, 1995), see Chapter 9, "The Moral Contest."

41. Bill Clinton, *My Life* (New York, 2004), p. 593.

Chapter 7. The Protracted Struggle Against Terrorism

1. Brodie's and Wohlstetter's competing views on nuclear strategy are summarized in Chapter 4.

2. George P. Shultz, *Turmoil and Triumph: My Years as Secretary of State* (New York, 1993), p. 645.

3. Christopher Simpson, *National Security Directives of the Reagan and Bush Administrations: The Declassified History of U.S. Political and Military Policy, 1981–1991* (Oxford, England, 1995), pp. 365–366.

4. See Walzer, *Just and Unjust Wars*. See also Michael Howard, George J. Andreopoulos, and Mark R. Shulman, eds., *The Laws of War* (New Haven, Conn., 1994).

5. Weinberger, *Fighting for Peace*, p. 188.

6. Shultz, *Turmoil and Triumph*, p. 650.

7. Weinberger, *Fighting for Peace*, p. 188.

8. The late Anthony Giddens, an eminent British sociologist, introduced this concept of a third approach—a way to synthesize opposing views. In the 1990s Prime Minister Tony Blair adopted this approach to return his Labor party to power. Concurrently Bill Clinton was practicing a variant he called "triangulation."

9. Department of State, Bureau of Public Affairs, *Fundamentals of U.S. Foreign Policy* (Washington, D.C., 1988), p. 5.

10. Bruce Hoffman, *Inside Terrorism* (New York, 1998), p. 192, notes that the "U.S. air strike against Libya is frequently cited as proof of the effectiveness of [conventional] military retaliation; yet, rather than having deterred the Qaddafi regime from engaging in state-sponsored terrorism, it appears that it may have had precisely the opposite effect."

11. *Ibid.*, p. 187.

12. R. D. Howard and R. L. Sawyer, *Terrorism and Counterterrorism* (Guilford, Conn., 2003), p. 554.

13. Coll, *Ghost Wars*, p. 142.

14. *Ibid.*, p. 139.

15. Unclassified materials about the Cabinet Committee's activities and its report can be accessed at http://wid.ap.org/documents/nixonterror.html.

16. See Gayle Rivers, *The War Against the Terrorists: How to Win It* (New York, 1986), pp. 88, 120–134.

17. *Ibid.*, p. 246. Emphasis in the original.

18. The RAND Corporation and the University of Saint Andrews have maintained more complete databases of all terrorism-related incidents since the 1960s. Figure 13 confines itself to major acts of terror. For insight into some of the "counting problems" that have emerged in the effort to analyze the patterns of this form of conflict, see Corine Hegland, "Global Jihad," *National Journal*, May 8, 2004.

19. See Chaim Herzog, *The Arab-Israeli Wars* (New York, 1982), Part IV, "The War of Attrition," pp. 209–243.

20. Frederik Pohl used this phrase in his classic 1979 novel *The Cool War*, a story about covert warfare waged by terror networks in the service of many different countries.

21. The rise of the Special Operations Command in 1986 being the sole exception to the U.S. military's continuing conventional-mindedness.

22. The classic study of these conflicts is Charles Callwell, *Small Wars: Their Principles and Practice* (London, 1906). The British, who had the largest empire, necessarily had a great deal of experience in irregular warfare. For a study focused specifically on Britain's military involvements during this period, see Byron Farwell, *Queen Victoria's Little Wars* (New York, 1972).

23. For a recent analysis of these issues, see Graham Allison, *Nuclear Terrorism: The Ultimate Preventable Catastrophe* (New York, 2004).

24. See Bernstein, "Strategists Fight a War," which chronicles the fight between the traditional thinkers in the Pentagon and the leading advocates for change.

25. About half the State Department's 2004 total of significant terrorist attacks were accounted for by simmering Indo-Pakistani tensions over Kashmir. Of course these incidents still fall into the category of that portion of terror in which Muslims are involved. The Counterterrorism Center's new method of counting is to include all attacks that deliberately target noncombatants. This shift, which took place in the summer of 2005, began a new era in data collection on terrorism, and it has made comparative analysis with previous years problematic. Perhaps this new approach will briefly obscure the fact that, since the "war on terror" was launched in the fall of 2001, terror has continued, quite vigorously, to make war on us.

26. For a full exposition of this idea, see Samuel P. Huntington, *The Clash of Civilizations and the Remaking of World Order* (New York, 1997).

27. This approach to countering bin Laden's "story"—and a networked way to fight his adherents in the field—were the issues addressed in David Ronfeldt and John Arquilla, "Networks, Netwars, and the Fight for the Future," *First Monday*, October 2001. See also John Arquilla and David Ronfeldt, "How to Beat a Terror Network," *Wired*, December 2001.

28. See Hy Rothstein, *The Challenge of Unconventional Warfare* (Monterey, Calif., 2003), and Seymour Hersh, "The Other War," *New Yorker*, April 12, 2004.

29. Tom Lasseter, "Officers Say Arms Can't End Iraq War," *Knight Ridder Newspapers*, June 13, 2005.

30. Ledeen, *Perilous Statecraft*, p. 139.

31. On the Israeli role in opening up secret negotiations with Iran, see Samuel Segev, *The Iranian Triangle: The Untold Story of Israel's Role in the Iran-Contra Affair* (New York, 1988).

32. Shultz, *Turmoil and Triumph*, p. 811; Weinberger, *Fighting for Peace*, p. 353.

33. Bill Moyers, *The Secret Government: The Constitution in Crisis* (Washington, D.C., 1988).

34. It quickly grew clear that Marine Corps claims about this battle having "broken the back of the insurgency" were grossly mistaken. In part the ineffectiveness of the assault grew out of the humanitarian need to give advance warning to "innocent civilians" to leave the city in the weeks before the attack. Many insurgents seized this opportunity to escape.

35. An excellent account of this case can be found in A. B. C. Whipple, *To the Shores of Tripoli* (New York, 1991). On this and other instances of nineteenth-century American presidents engaging in secret wars and secret negotiations to end foreign policy crises, see William Knott, *Secret and Sanctioned: Covert Operations and the American Presidency* (Oxford, England, 1996).

36. See Dan Verton's exhaustively researched *Black Ice: The Invisible Threat of Cyberterrorism* (New York, 2003).

Chapter 8. Ways of Remembering Reagan

1. From Reinhold Niebuhr, *The World Crisis and American Responsibility* (New York, 1958), p. 116.

2. See the exposition of Gaddis's point of view in Chapter 1.

3. D'Souza, *Ronald Reagan*, is one of the first biographies to paint a sharply different portrait of Reagan's personality and intellectual capabilities. Although their tone was satirical, some credit should also be given to the writers of NBC's *Saturday Night Live* who, during Reagan's presidency, portrayed him in a skit as nodding through staff meetings, then coming to life as a dynamic, multilingual world leader once everybody else had gone to bed.

4. Both quotes are from Callahan, *Dangerous Capabilities*, p. 417. It is important to note that Nitze would eventually come to revise upward his low estimation of Reagan's intellectual capacities.

5. Richard Burt, "Arms and the Man," Staff of *New York Times*, eds., *Reagan, the Man, the President* (New York, 1980), p. 85.

6. For a thorough overview of theories about the origins of Reagan's beliefs and preferences, see Frances FitzGerald, *Way Out There in the Blue: Reagan, Star Wars and the End of the Cold War* (New York, 2000), especially pp. 19–31.

7. This broadcast aired October 10, 1978. Its full text can be found in Skinner, et al., *In His Own Hand*, pp. 98–99.

8. *Ibid.*, p. 99.

9. From an interview with Edwin L. Meese, April 23, 2004.

10. See Lewis Richardson, *Arms and Insecurity* (Chicago, 1960).

11. Both quotes are from Talbott, *Russia Hand*, p. 43.

12. Niebuhr, *World Crisis*, p. 121.

13. Reagan first used the phrase officially in the now declassified National Security Decision Directive No. 130, which he signed in March 1984.

14. See the discussion of Jefferson's concept of public diplomacy in Chapter 6.

15. See the citation from Senator Glenn's speech in Chapter 4.

16. *Final Report of the Commission on Terrorist Attacks Upon the United States* (New York, 2004), p. 341.

17. Burt, "Arms and the Man," p. 85.

18. Michael K. Deaver, *A Different Drummer: My Thirty Years with Ronald Reagan* (New York, 2001), p. 3.

19. By soft power I mean Harvard professor Joseph Nye's notion of the attractiveness of ideas and values. See his *Soft Power*. Between a military invasion on one end and pure public diplomacy on the other, I would locate something like economic sanctions, which are coercive but not violent, near the midpoint of the vertical axis.

20. From his "Statement at the Press Conference of June 1, 1988." Full text of his remarks can be found in Mikhail Gorbachev, *At the Summit: How the Two Superpowers Set the World on a Course for Peace* (New York, 1988), pp. 252–253.

21. Reagan, *American Life*, p. 512.

22. Cited in Lawrence Wittner, "The Power of Protest," *Bulletin of the Atomic Scientists* 60, no. 4 (July/August 2004), p. 24.

23. See Kissinger, *Diplomacy*, p. 802.

24. FitzGerald, *Way Out There*, p. 40. For some of the more vitriolic comments from conservative analysts like Charles Krauthammer and George Will, see Chapter 3.

Index

flexibility of, 227, 228, 230; failures of, x, xi, 222, 223, 226; foreign policy of, x, 220; influence of, xi, 28, 29, 109, 211, 212, 216, 217, 224; Gorbachev and, 79, 80, 81, 87, 96; as Great Communicator, 8, 219; information strategy of, x, 147, 149, 150, 151, 155, 156, 157, 169, 174, 175, 190, 199, 202, 219; intellect of, 7, 17; Iran-Contra scandal and, 8, 202, 203; Iranian arms-for-hostages deal and, 44, 157; Iranian hostage crisis and, 32; Iraq and, 95; as Jacksonian, 12; kindliness of, and counterterrorism policy, as impediment to, 233; kindness of, 4; legacy of, 26, 219; as loner, 4, 5; as man of ideas, 235, 236; maritime strategy of, 45; military interventions of, 114 (*fig.*), 115, 116; military legacy of, 225; motion picture industry, influence on, 213, 214; on mutual assured destruction (MAD), 101; National Security Decision Directive No. 130 and, 257n13; National Security Decision Directive No. 138 and, 180, 185, 210, 217; National Security Decision Directive No. 207 and, 185, 186; neutron bomb and, 99, 253n17; nuclear first use doctrine and, 106, 110, 111, 125, 195; nuclear war and, x, 22, 217; nuclear weapons and, 23, 80, 190, 191, 195, 196; nuclear weapons, abolition of, 96, 97, 98; Pakistan and, 95, 109, 222; paradox of, ix; persuasive skills of, 8; policies of, 229 (*fig.*); policy innovations, assessment of, 235; post-Vietnam malaise, impact on, 118; as private, 3, 4; proliferation, view of, 91; public approval rating of, 8; public persona of, 5, 8; ranking of, 26, 28,

241n41, 242n42; religion, influence on, 213; reputation of, 113; rollback and, 23; *Saturday Night Live*, skit on, 257n3; soft power, use of, 169; special operations forces, revitalization of, 138; Star Wars and, 213, 235; statecraft, approach to, 99; strategic bombing, supporter of, 135; strategic missile defense and, 96, 99; as strategic thinker, 214, 215, 228, 236; terrorists, negotiating with, 202; as "unexpected," 212, 213; U.S. Air Force and, 132; U.S. Navy and, 128, 129, 130, 131, 235; war of ideas and, 51, 56, 151, 157, 199, 219; war on terror, compromise approach to, 189–90, 210, 223; war on terror, conventional approach to, xi, 180, 182, 183, 185, 186, 190; war on terror, and information strategy, 202; weaknesses of, 4; zero option and, 100

Reaganomics, xii

realpolitik, 55, 81, 95; tests of war and, 142

Rebuilding Russia (Solzhenitsyn), 76

Red Army, 43, 45, 123, 144, 158

Red Navy, 130

Revolution in Military Affairs (RMA), 123

Richardson, Lewis, 218

Rickover, Hyman, 38

Rivers, Gayle, 186, 190; sleeper cells and, 187

Roberts, Michael, 123

Rogers' Rangers, 145

Rogin, Michael, 213

Romania, 53

Rome, 237; fall of, 32, 232

Rommel, Erwin, 124

Ronald Reagan (D'Souza), 242n42

"Ronald Reagan," The Movie (Rogin), 213

A NOTE ON THE AUTHOR

John Arquilla is professor of defense analysis at the United States Naval Postgraduate School in Monterey, California. Born in Oak Park, Illinois, he studied at Rosary College and received M.A. and Ph.D. degrees from Stanford University. As a policy analyst at the RAND Corporation, he consulted to General Norman Schwarzkopf during the first Gulf War, and to the deputy secretary of defense during the Kosovo War. His other books include *From Troy to Entebbe: Special Operations in Ancient and Modern Times*; *In Athena's Camp: Preparing for Conflict in the Information Age*; and *Networks and Netwars: The future of Terror, Crime, and Militancy*. He is married with two children and lives in Monterey, California.